T0289562

WITTGENSTEIN AND CRITICAL THEORY

WITTGENSTEIN
AND CRITICAL THEORY

*Beyond Postmodern Criticism
and Toward Descriptive Investigations*

Susan B. Brill

Ohio University Press
Athens

Ohio University Press, Athens, Ohio 45701
© 1995 by Susan B. Brill
Printed in the United States of America
All rights reserved

99 98 97 96 95   5 4 3 2

Ohio University Press books are printed on acid-free paper ∞

Library of Congress Cataloging-in-Publication Data

Brill, Susan B.
    Wittgenstein and critical theory : beyond postmodern criticism and
toward descriptive investigations / Susan B. Brill.
        p.   cm.
    Includes bibliographical references and index.
    ISBN 0-8214-1092-X (cloth). — ISBN 0-8214-1093-8 (pbk.)
    1. Criticism.   2. Wittgenstein, Ludwig 1889–1951—Contributions in
criticism.   3. Postmodernism.   I. Title.
PN98.P67B75   1995   94-31577
801′.95—dc20   CIP

To Professor Alexander B. Chambers

Contents

ACKNOWLEDGMENTS

Debts in writing a book are far more complex than any acknowledgments can begin to address. The initial impetus for the entire project arose out of my studies in Native American Indian literatures and Navajo language. This work continually forced me to question traditional Western ways (modern or postmodern) of approaching the world and literary texts. I particularly want to thank Roseann Willink, my Navajo language instructor, for bearing with my struggles to learn the language, and Luci Tapahonso, literature professor and poet, for helping me to understand that learning need not be linear and that the standard university paradigms for classroom education can take diverse forms, often with more meaningful and lasting results.

Preliminary stages of my work on Wittgenstein encompassed the final period of my graduate work at the University of New Mexico. I am grateful to all of my professors in the English Department, who encouraged my work in the idiosyncratic directions it has taken. Professors Michael Fischer, Russell Goodman, Minrose Gwin, and Hector Torres provided substantial input during this time. I am especially thankful to Russell Goodman, who helped me avoid any serious misunderstandings and misrepresentations of Wittgenstein. Any readings that diverge from standard philosophical interpretations of Wittgenstein (either erroneous or new) are mine.

Michael Fischer, my dissertation director, supported the project from its origins in New Mexico through its substantial evolution and additions thereafter. His comments, criticisms, and advice have always proven useful, and I shall always be indebted to him.

Much of the present volume was written during my first two years at Bradley University. My thanks to my students in the graduate classes in contemporary critical theory. In teaching these classes, the very real profundity of the current state of critical studies was continually brought home to me as we noted both the values and limits inherent in each critical method and theory studied.

Additional thanks goes to Bradley University's Office of Research and Teaching Excellence. Bradley University supported my work with a small grant for research at the Univesity of Illinois libraries and, more importantly, with a generous summer stipend in 1992 so that I could devote all my attention to this project. During that summer, the research and writing of Chapter 2 was accomplished. I also want to thank my brother, Robert M. Brill, who provided additional information on descriptive psychology and assisted my understanding of that field. Technical support throughout the project was provided by Tim Mullen, Bruce Jaffe, Roger Coe, Willie Heberer, and David Tyler.

I am grateful to the following for permission to quote from copyrighted material: Macmillan College Publishing Company, for permission to quote from *Philosophical Investigations;* the University of Chicago Press, for permission to quote from *Culture and Value;* and Basil Blackwell Ltd., for world rights to quote from *Philosophical Investigations* and *Culture and Value.*

Personal thanks go to friends and colleagues too numerous to mention completely, including Jim Sullivan, Bob Rosa (and the guys at the Central Illinois Weightlifting Gym who regularly provided needed reality checks for my work), Tracy Harris, Haifa Khoury, Donita Holloway, Kambiz Victory, Alice Ouwerkerk, and the Albuquerque and Peoria Bahá'í communities. This work would not have been possible without their loving support.

Most importantly, I give thanks to God. As a Bahá'í, I am profoundly aware of the essential interrelationship between work and worship. Whatever is of value in my work is of God; all errors and weaknesses are my own.

Finally, I thank Professor Alexander B. Chambers, my professor as an undergraduate at the University of Wisconsin-Madison. Little more than a month before his death, he went over my doctoral dissertation and provided substantial comments for its revision and eventual development into a publishable manuscript. It is to him that I dedicate this, my first book.

ABBREVIATIONS

Throughout the text, the works of Ludwig Wittgenstein have been cited using the following abbreviations. References are made according to page numbers, except in the cases of RC, TLP, Z, and section I of PI for which references are to Wittgenstein's textual numbering system.

BB   *The Blue and Brown Books* (Harper, 1965).

CV   *Culture and Value* (University of Chicago Press, 1984).

L&C   *Lectures and Conversations on Aesthetics, Psychology and Religious Belief* (University of California Press, 1967).

LWVC   *Ludwig Wittgenstein and the Vienna Circle: Conversations Recorded by Friedrich Waismann* (Basil Blackwell, 1979).

N   *Notebooks 1914–16* (Basil Blackwell, 1961).

OC   *On Certainty* (Harper, 1969).

PI   *Philosophical Investigations* (Macmillan, 1968). References to Part I use sections (e.g., PI, I, 43), and references to Part II use page numbers (e.g., PI, 212e).

RC   *Remarks on Color* (University of California Press, 1977).

RFGB   *Remarks on Frazer's "Golden Bough"* (Brynmill, 1979).

RPPI   *Remarks on the Philosophy of Psychology*, volume I (University of Chicago Press, 1988).

RPPII   *Remarks on the Philosophy of Psychology*, volume II (University of Chicago Press, 1988).

TLP   *Tractatus Logico-Philosophicus* (Routledge, 1988).

Z   *Zettel* (University of California Press, 1970).

INTRODUCTION

The past two decades of scholarly work have resulted in a tremendous proliferation of literary theories and critical methods available to literary scholars. No longer limited by one acceptable method, often determined by one's institutional affiliation (methods such as the New Criticism or the Chicago School of Criticism), critics and theorists may now choose from a wide range of critical paths (e.g., deconstruction, New Historicism, feminism, cultural criticism, semiotics, structuralism, etc.). This critical development has become problematic in several ways. The number of critical methods available alone is daunting; few are the practitioners capable of comprehending all of the contemporary criticisms. Furthermore, even were critics sufficiently well versed in multiple critical strategies, the actual usefulness of these approaches in regard to particular texts is rarely considered.

It is far from clear that each critical method or theory is a useful means of examining *every* text. In fact, it is more likely the case that certain approaches might be more (or less) useful in certain cases. Yet, as Thomas M. Kavanagh notes, instead of questioning the appropriate use of critical theories and methods in specific cases, "many critics have devoted themselves to elaborating and defending various critical theories by which, they argue, all analyses of literary works must justify themselves if they are to claim coherence and validity" (1). As we shall see in the course of this volume, such deliberations are misdirected and less useful to critical work than would be a redirected focus on the actual value of theoretical and critical determinations.

Much of the philosophy of Ludwig Wittgenstein can be brought to bear directly on such concerns. Wittgenstein writes: "We find certain things about seeing puzzling, because we do not find the whole business of seeing puzzling enough" (PI 212e). Relating this statement to critical theory, we might note that our debates regarding theory are due to our lack of investigating the essential foundations of the diverse language games involved in literary criticism. Such Wittgensteinian investigations can help us to clarify, and thereby remove, many of the confusions and puzzlements rife in our field. Instead of debating which theory is best, we need to describe when theories work—and when they do not.

Wittgenstein provides a descriptive and evaluative methodology which is fundamentally based on his heuristic of the language game. Like a language game whose constitutive parts include a structural center in its essential grammar (or rules) and a temporal and contingent diversity in its actual uses (or playing moves), Wittgensteinian philosophy as adapted herein for literary criticism points towards a strategy of descriptive investigations whose coherence and usefulness is demonstrated in its circumstantial adaptability and responsiveness to

1

diverse texts (literary, critical, and theoretical). As Wittgenstein says, "we now demonstrate a method, by examples. . . . There is not *a* philosophical method, though there are indeed methods, like different therapies" (PI, I, 133). Wittgenstein presents a method which is manifested variously for each given situation or context. The method is single in the sense that our strategy is always the same—that of generating a clear view of texts by means of a descriptive rather than explanatory criticism. However, our focus on the *use* ("Let the use *teach* you the meaning" [PI 212e]) of any text necessitates that our descriptive methodology be differentially adapted or modified for each textual analysis. As Wittgenstein emphasizes, specifically in relation to our understandings of various statements, what is important is that we ask ourselves "in what special circumstances this sentence is actually used. There it does make sense" (PI, I, 117).

One contemporary critic, Ellen Messer-Davidow, argues for a perspectivist type of feminist literary criticism, which "would restructure inquiry by institutionalizing a diversity grounded in cultural, personal, technical, and self-reflexive variables; by using viewpoints as a chief methodology" (88). There are obvious parallels between the sort of perspectivism Messer-Davidow advocates and Wittgenstein's descriptive investigations. While such perspectivism is an essential part of an informed and clear textual investigation, a reliance on Wittgensteinian philosophy adds a means of discriminating among divergent perspectives insofar as certain perspectives will be more or less appropriate or useful in opening up different texts. For Wittgenstein, every path to a text may be different, but that does not make all equally useful or efficacious in every case.

My own understanding of Wittgenstein's writings leads me to the realization that it is, in fact, possible to achieve a mediating stance between the divergent threads of contemporary theoretical debate. The major claim of this study is that by relying upon Wittgensteinian philosophy, literary critics will be enabled to escape the stultifying positions of absolutist critical discourses without being left bereft of any satisfactory means of evaluating and selecting among the variety of critical stances current today. This is not to advocate any devaluation of particular critical positions in and of themselves, but rather to note their limitations so that they can be put to better use.

If we desire meaningful and effective entry into texts, it is crucial that we shift our method from a preconceived critical textual entry—at times a ready entry, but all too often an entry that is forced—and, instead, move forward beyond the dialectical pulls of our contemporary modern/postmodern aporia toward a new critical method informed by Wittgenstein's philosophy that will aid critical scholars, students, and general readers in the conjoined activities of reading, interpreting, and evaluating texts. Such a method, introduced in this book, is that of descriptive criticism.

As will be clear to scholars of Wittgensteinian philosophy, this volume is far from a comprehensive presentation of the range of Wittgenstein's work. Some elements of his thought, useful to the critical process, have not been addressed herein (for example, his discussions of private language, sensations, and emotions). I have chosen to focus my deliberations more directly on the applicability of Wittgenstein for literary criticism. This book is targeted primarily to scholars of literature who, it is presumed, are not thoroughly familiar with Wittgenstein. I have therefore spent additional time clarifying those elements of his philosophy germane to the critical project. Accordingly, there is also some repetition of crucial points from one chapter to another—a strategy undertaken in light of this presumed lack of familiarity with Wittgenstein.

Chapter 1 investigates the possibilities of revamping literary critical endeavors in light of Wittgenstein's philosophical writings. Several elements of his philosophy are introduced as a means of delineating both the current conflicts in critical theory and the expected benefits resulting from a Wittgensteinian way of looking at literature. This chapter discusses Wittgenstein's heuristic of the language game, his rejection of theory, and his methodology of descriptive investigations. These three elements prove to be powerful tools by which literary critics can more effectively open texts on the various levels of the language games in which they participate. The boundaries of those language games help us to determine the efficaciousness of our different critical discourses towards particular texts. Specifically, Wittgensteinian concepts and terminologies help us to avoid the disadvantages of either side of the modern/postmodern critical dialectic.

Chapters 2 through 6 focus more directly on applications of Wittgenstein for literary criticism and theory. Chapter 2 turns to the concerns of psychoanalytic and semiotic critical orientations and introduces a Wittgensteinian-based psychological criticism that draws on the insights of contemporary descriptive psychology. The third, fourth, and concluding chapters specifically address literary concerns of inclusivity and exclusivity. In the third chapter, a Wittgensteinian literary methodology is demonstrated as particularly useful for feminist literary concerns. Chapter 4 turns to the production and preservation of literary canons (particularly in relation to the nascent canon of Native American literature) and delineates the implications of Wittgensteinian philosophy for such determinations of inclusion and exclusion. Chapter 4 also looks at the poetry of Nia Francisco, presenting the usefulness of Wittgenstein's philosophy in determinations of value and canonicity (literary and critical). The fifth chapter compares Wittgensteinian philosophy and the deconstructive project. While a few critics have come to the conclusion that Wittgenstein's work can be easily read to fit within the framework of deconstruction, the chapter clarifies the fundamental differences between the two philosophies, relying most heavily on Wittgenstein's *On Certainty*.

The sixth and concluding chapter points the way for future uses of Wittgenstein for literary criticism and theory. By relying upon the Wittgensteinian concern for a clear delineation of the limits surrounding literary and critical endeavors, I briefly inquire into the implications of Wittgensteinian philosophy for axiological determinations of literary and critical texts, future deliberations of canonicity, and the parallels with and divergences from the poststructural critical approaches of the New Historicism and cultural criticism. The conclusion ends with a short discussion of the importance of Wittgenstein for access to the works of many contemporary Language poets who have been ostensibly influenced by his philosophy.

As the book points out, literary critics and theorists need not feel constrained by the limitations inherent in the various forms of contemporary critical theory, nor need we feel that we must make an abstracted choice and affiliate ourselves with certain critical perspectives. While we cannot be completely conversant or comfortable with all criticisms and theories, Wittgenstein makes it clear that our approaches need to work with the texts rather than forcing them to fit into preconceived networks of criticism which might not be the most useful for entering those texts. The crucial point is that of fit: which critical methods prove most useful in opening up which texts?

Close investigations into the parameters of the language games of texts, critics, and methods will enable us to determine which paths to take towards more complete descriptive analyses and critiques. This critical focus shifts the role of critic out of a dialectical framework of recontextualization in which the critic as subject molds texts after the shape of particular preconceived theoretical constructs—a godlike role where the critic as creator recreates the literary text after his or her own image. A Wittgensteinian emphasis on method reorients literary criticism towards a conjoint responsibility to both reader and text as the literary critic assumes the more humble role of a guide who assists a reader's passage in/to diverse literary texts.

Wittgenstein's philosophical approach provides a means of avoiding many of the circular debates in our field. Rather than abstractly debating different types of criticisms or theories, we investigate them in use. This enables us to disengage from the critical practice of forcing texts into preconceived critical constructs which may not reflect what is actually going on in the texts themselves. As Wittgenstein writes: "It's possible to look intently without seeing anything, or to keep thinking you see something without being able to see clearly. Looking can tire you even when you don't see anything" (CV, 74e). Wittgensteinian critical investigations prove to be a methodology that empowers the critic via investigations into textual/contextual language games, rather than automatically imposing any prior critical dogma willy-nilly upon all texts. As Wittgenstein reminds us, "A man will be *imprisoned* in a room with a door that's unlocked and opens inwards; as long as it does not occur to him to *pull* rather than push it" (CV, 42e). Wittgenstein's philosophy provides a strong means of developing such a method for literary criticism—a method that points the way beyond postmodern criticisms toward a categorically new approach to literary texts—namely descriptive criticism.

1

Moving Beyond the Modern/Postmodern Dialectic: Wittgensteinian Directives for Literary Theory and Criticism

IN THIS AGE of postmodern skepticism and différance, literary criticism and critical theory are torn between the equally anxious efforts of scholars either to maintain the supposed stability of an earlier logocentric foundationalism or to subvert such absolutist discursive structures (and their larger contextual realities), which are seen as hegemonically oppressive. The philosophy of Ludwig Wittgenstein, translated and applied to literary theory and criticism, provides a timely mediation between these two opposing camps. Within the bounds of a Wittgensteinian orientation (as presented most fully in his later philosophical writings), we can safely navigate a course that includes both sites of the traditionalist/postmodern critical dialectic while refusing to be mired in a debate that inevitably ends up where it begins (namely, in the seemingly endless repetition of theses and antitheses—a self-serving process that continually reproduces itself within the bounds of the traditionalist/postmodern dialectic).

Wittgenstein explicitly discusses such a problematic of being caught within a particular theoretical or explanatory mode such that the only apparent alternatives seem to be either an acceptance of the set theoretic or a reactive overturning of that theoretic (a response that is just as dependent upon the original—rejected—orientation as is the initial stance). The problem here is one of forcing a static concept upon an ever-changing world. The concept proves to be inadequate, as the reactive responses of postmodern critiques correctly point out. As Wittgenstein writes, "Again and again a use of the word emerges that seems not to be compatible with the concept that other uses have led us to form. We say: but that *isn't* how it is!" (CV, 30e). However, rather than opting for an entirely different language game, we continue to battle back and forth between the opposing camps: "We say: but that *isn't* how it is!—it *is* like that though! and all we can do is keep repeating these

7

antitheses" (CV, 30e). Wittgenstein makes the inutility of such debates clear as he gives them the tone of an argument between two small children: "Es *ist* doch nicht es!—aber es *ist* doch so!" (no, it *isn't!*—yes, it *is!*)—and on and on. Neither side is capable of disengaging from the argument by virtue of being one *side* of the debate. Each side is dependent upon the other.

The Wittgensteinian response would not engage in the endless repetition of antitheses, but would avoid the problem altogether by choosing to play a different game. If, in fact, we are interested in a critical methodology that is not rooted, one way or the other, in the various logocentric discursive structures of an absolutist and anachronistic order, then it is clear that an utterly new and alternative critical methodology must be devised—and here we must emphasize that those postmodern theories and methods inextricably linked to earlier approaches in their reactive orientations are inadequate for such a purpose. The directions indicated for literary theory and criticism, by means of a number of Wittgensteinian signposts, point us away from the rigid limitations of an absolutist traditionalism that only provides one path (at times erroneous, always limited by its own preconceived critical boundaries, and often hegemonic in its effects). And yet we need not be left to wander in the postmodern skepticism of a wasteland fraught with multiplicitous paths that only *seem* to go somewhere. The directions of a Wittgensteinian map do provide a clear course that we might follow; however, this way is neither wholly fixed nor unbounded, but rather organically progressive. Perhaps the motto for our critical course might be "systemic unity with diversity": unity in the sense that there are better and worse paths such that we can discern correct courses to follow for any given case, and diversity in the sense that there are many different acceptable options—options that vary across time and place.[1] In fact, Austin E. Quigley notes Wittgenstein's "attempts to reconcile unity and variety" and points out the parallel of this concern with "attempts to mediate between foundationalism and skepticism" (219).

Whereas the modern period provided us with the metaphor of the melting pot to signify the dissolution of differences between groups melting down to one common denominator (usually hegemonically defined), the postmodern reaction is to offer the alternative metaphor of a stew or salad bowl—two new images both of which emphasize a heterogeneous pluralism. The obvious problem with all three of these images is that they do not provide any sense of positive development or growth. Rather than offering examples of life, we imagine processes of decaying, melting, stewing, or wilting. A more Wittgensteinian image might be that of a garden in which we can experience a living diversity that is unified within the bounds of the garden's limits. Such a Wittgensteinian perspective places us outside the traditionalist/postmodern dialectic. Rather than being post-anything (postmodern, poststructural, postcolonial, postpatriarchal), which carries the sense of not being where we have been, but not really being anywhere else yet (by virtue of being in a constant reverse frame of reference), we shall see that a clear reliance upon much of Wittgenstein's philosophy will help us to gain, if not a mooring, certainly our bearings.

In this chapter, several diverse threads of Wittgenstein's philosophy will be linked in a discussion of the usefulness of his work for literary theory and criticism. I will not be discussing Wittgenstein's philosophy as a whole but borrowing from it three elements particularly useful to literary theory: his heuristic of the language game, his rejection of theory, and his methodology of descriptive investigations. Each of these concepts are further considered in light of their implications for a critical methodology and theoretic which is organically progressive in a multiplicitous heterogeneity across both time and place. The result for literary criticism and theory is a procedure for establishing clear limits surrounding the various language games in which both literary texts and critical approaches participate—thereby providing a means of accessing and assessing diverse pathways in/to texts. As we weave within and between these several topics, we shall clearly see that the philosophy of Ludwig Wittgenstein offers a powerful means of navigating our way beyond the seemingly stagnant pool of traditionalist criticism and the directionless chasm of postmodern literary theory in which all interpretations of texts are considered equally valid.[2]

The Rejection of Theory

This methodology of descriptive investigations (discussed in greater detail later in this chapter) is a direct product or consequence of Wittgenstein's rejection of theory—a stance he consistently holds throughout much of his later work. "For me, a theory is without value. A theory gives me nothing" (LWVC, 117). What is particularly notable in these statements, insofar as our purposes are concerned, are the repeated first person references. Wittgenstein is not asserting that theory per se is valueless, rather that theory is useless ("without value") for *him*. Key here are two related concerns which will prove useful for much of our investigations—both regarding the specific issue of theory and the larger question of the applicability of Wittgensteinian philosophy for literary theory and criticism. The first is that of definition. We need to clarify what Wittgenstein means by theory in order to better ascertain why it is that he rejects it. The second concern, inextricably linked with the first, is that of the various contexts or domains in which theory might be applied.

Regarding the issue of definition, Wittgenstein makes it abundantly clear that he is rejecting one specific usage of the term "theory." By theory, he is referring to the term as it is generally used in science and mathematics—namely, a preconceived hypothesis (generally abstract and systemic) against which the world is measured, evaluated, and explained. Such theories are rejected for philosophical use by virtue of their being static and unresponsive to the actual contingent realities of our world. This is not to say that theory is without its use when applied within its appropriate domain. Wittgenstein understands the value of theoretical work in science; within the natural world, there is actual evidence that demonstrates the accuracy of particular scientific theories. However, this is not the case for philosophy (or for that matter, mathematics or aesthetics). Wittgenstein holds that these fields are more dependent upon human perception and, as such, are not conducive to the explanatory confirmations available in natural science.[3]

Insofar as theory is concerned in non-scientific endeavors, Wittgenstein makes two crucial assertions. First, he rejects its usefulness, seeing theory as a static imposition of a biased "preconceived idea to which reality *must* correspond" (PI, I, 131). The emphasis placed on the word "must" indicates Wittgenstein's view that theory, when misused (misplaced), "dogmatically forces" itself on the world. Such a misuse of "theory" (improperly used outside the bounds of natural science) leads to Wittgenstein's categoric rejection. Examples in the realm of literary criticism where theoretical doctrines have imposed their orientations upon various literary texts might be the allegorical work of Northrop Frye as expounded in *The Anatomy of Criticism* or the New Critical theories to which Frye was in part responding. Both of these critical approaches were, and still are, useful in their close readings of particular texts. However, to attempt to apply their larger theoretical frameworks willy-nilly to any text would lead to misreadings, with texts artificially forced into the bounds of the theory's reading. Wittgenstein stresses that to "*see* something according to an *interpretation* [is] as if something were being forced into a form it did not really fit" (PI, 200e). For Wittgenstein, interpretation is the process of theorizing: "It is easy to recognize cases in which we are *interpreting*. When we interpret we form hypotheses, which may prove false" (PI, 212e). By and large, critics have tended to be aware of the boundary problems regarding such interpretive schemas and have, accordingly, avoided the extreme case of a categorically meaningless criticism by choosing to approach those texts which are less resistant to particular critical theories. Northrop Frye's allegorical readings avoided most works by women writers, works which would have strongly resisted his critical orientation, and the New Critics shied away from works resistant to their approach, choosing to privilege the poetry of the early seventeenth century. Such discriminations are inevitable in the critical practice of imposing general theories upon literary texts.

The problem of clearly establishing which texts might be most suitably approached by certain interpretive theories raises the question of just what we mean when we, in literature departments, say that we are doing "theory." As we have seen, some of our work does fall under the rubric of theory—denigrated by Wittgenstein when applied in non-scientific fields. The work of Frye, R. S. Crane, and the New Critics can be included within the bounds of theory as defined by Murray Krieger: "The systematic construct that accounts for and makes consistent the individual critiques of works of literature" (3). Such demands for consistency are what both Wittgenstein and many postmodern critics reject as discursively limiting and hegemonically elitist. In the introduction to Paul de Man's *The Resistance to Theory*, Wlad Godzich clearly points out that the restrictive and absolutist nature of theory is problematic in literary criticism insofar as theory presents a "system of concepts that aims to give a global explanation to an area of knowledge" (xiii). However, the rejection of demands for consistency or global explanation does not necessarily indicate the need for categorically rejecting all that is named literary or critical theory.

Wittgenstein even notes that much of what is termed "theory" is less the establishment of global hypotheses and rather a sort of meta-discussion about the actual practice or work in particular fields. Wittgenstein observed the occurrence of such activity in mathematics. David Hilbert, an early twentieth-century mathematician, worked towards establishing a formalist approach to the foundations of mathematics—an endeavor analogous to the work of structural theorists like Roland Barthes. Friedrich Waismann explicitly asked Wittgenstein about such theoretical work, inquiring whether Hilbert's "meta-mathematics" should be considered a theory of mathematics. Wittgenstein's response is clear. He asserts that such meta-mathematics is not theory, but instead another mathematical discourse.[4] Just as algebra may portray mathematical calculations in a more general way than by using numbers, algebra (like Hilbert's formalism) is not the theory of mathematics, but just another expression of mathematics, another calculus. A number of literary analogies come to mind but be our examples structural literary theory, feminist literary theory, or even deconstructive literary theory, Wittgenstein would point out that each would be more appropriately termed meta-criticism than theory because none provides the global consistency one expects in scientific theory. Instead of establishing general hypotheses upon which literary texts can be explained, literary theory often ends up providing an alternative discourse which may help us approach various texts more effectively (just as algebra helps one to understand geometry—not by explaining geometry, but by offering a different language or approach with which to describe the same phenomena).

Wittgenstein's devaluation of theory is specifically concerned with not being attached to any set ways of interpreting the world (or, for our purposes, a text). The problem that he sees here is that the constraints imposed by any theoretical orientation may serve to impair our actual view, such that our understanding of the world is rather a misunderstanding.[5] In such a case, we end up "entangled in our own rules" (PI, I, 125). Wittgenstein explains that "the fundamental fact here is that we lay down rules, a technique, for a game, and that then when we follow the rules, things do not turn out as we had assumed" (PI, I, 125). And yet the rules that we have set down, the constraints which artificially limit our vision, are the problem. Playing the same game, only from a different or opposing angle, is insufficient, insofar as Wittgenstein is concerned. Such a shift is merely superficial. The problem must be solved "deep down" at the foundational level of the rules: "If it is grasped near the surface it simply remains the difficulty it was. It has to be pulled out by the roots; and that involves our beginning to think about these things in a new way. . . . Once the new way of thinking has been established, the old problems vanish; indeed they become hard to recapture" (CV, 48e). Key here is the crucial step taken when we opt for a language game that is not bound up with the prior thesis (as thesis or as antithesis). Wittgenstein insists that such a problematic can only be avoided by means of a dynamic methodology which is descriptively responsive to a changing world (or a text) instead of being reactively interpretive. Quigley remarks that "what [Wittgenstein] offers is a philosophical technique displayed in action" (218).

Wittgenstein's rejection of theory does not necessarily imply the need for a complete rejection of literary theory—the demise of which has been recently hailed by Stanley Fish.[6] While Wittgenstein also rejects the philosophy of his day, he nevertheless produces his own form of philosophy. The difference that he elucidates between the two types of philosophy is that of a descriptive methodology (his own) versus metaphysical explanation. He notes that philosophy never really explains the actual essence of the world but rather "traces round the frame through which we look at it" (PI, I, 114). Therefore, he advises us "to bring words back from their metaphysical to their everyday use" (PI, I, 116). The literary analogue here would be to situate a literary text within its everyday use (or actual larger discursive context) and provide a descriptive analysis that strives towards both a clarity and a comprehensive substantiality—which means avoiding, insofar as it is possible, the narrowing effect of our theoretical constructs.

Language Games

WITTGENSTEIN SUGGESTS that in place of a reliance on theoretical preconceptions we substitute a descriptive methodology that focuses our attention upon concrete examples rather than on abstract concepts. Such a method draws upon his discussion of the language game—his heuristic description of the actualized practices of the discursive structures of the world. Each language game (as is the case for any game, by Wittgenstein's definition) consists of those essential rules that serve to define each particular game and the various manifestations of those rules as they are actually applied in practice or play. While the moves of each game are manipulable within the context of the game and the rules are not so manipulable, the rules of a language game are seen by Wittgenstein to be discursive constructs that do change across time and place. The seeming paradox between necessary rules that cannot change and those rules that do change is resolved when we understand that, for Wittgenstein, such games are organic in nature and progressive in practice. Quigley also notes the organicism of Wittgenstein's language game metaphor: "The multiplicity of language is not the multiplicity of a fixed state but the multiplicity of an evolving organism" (217). However, once the rules change and the game thereby takes on another form, it becomes a different game as defined by its new set of rules. As Wittgenstein points out, "it is just *another* language-game; even though it is related to [the previous one]" (PI, I, 64).

The organicity of a language game is evident in Wittgenstein's many organic metaphors (of plants, human bodies, animals, human behavior). However, he emphasizes that only when language games are being played is life manifested. Words and other signs have life only when they are being used. "Every sign *by itself* seems dead. *What* gives it life?—In use it is *alive.* Is life breathed into it there?—Or is the *use* its life?" (PI, I, 432). Wittgenstein uses an example of a piece of wood made in the form of man to clarify that the outward sign or form is not sufficient to produce life: "The stupid block . . . hadn't even any similarity to a living being" (PI, I, 430). Any sign in and of itself is insufficient in the sense that outside its use it is not alive. Beyond the metaphor of a sign in use as alive, Wittgenstein explicitly refers to the organic unity of a work of art ("der Organismus des Kunstwerks" [CV, 4]) and refers to his own work as following in the Romantic tradition: "It derives from Schumann's time. It does at least strike me as continuing that ideal, though not in the way it was actually continued at the time. That is to say, the second half of the Nineteenth Century has been left out. This, I ought to say, has been a purely instinctive development and not the result of reflection" (CV, 2e).

And here we see the appropriateness of the organic metaphor which refers to Wittgenstein's Romanticism as an "instinctive (*instinktmassig*) development." Yuval Lurie specifically places Wittgenstein in the Romantic tradition because of his "outlook on human life which bridges the formerly perceived gap between culture and Nature" (380). It is therefore particularly fitting that his philosophy would be such that takes the very dynamic form of a descriptive method of analysis rather than the static absolutism of theory.

The significance of his language game concept for the literary critic or theorist is paramount, for it provides a means by which both similarities and dissimilarities between and within texts can be noted. Instead of attempting to discern the meaning of a text, we ascertain the language game(s) in which the text participates—a process that necessitates a familiarity with those games on the part of the critic. Peter Winch points out that distinctions "between truth and falsity can only be made at all to the extent that those who play the language-game in question manifest considerable 'agreement in judgments' as well as agreement in definitions'" (272). This is to say that in order to work within the framework of a particular language game, the language game of postcolonial literature, for example, the critic must acknowledge the defining parameters of such a body of literature in order to prevent a reductionist assimilation of such texts into a canon (or language game) that devalues such works for not fitting the rules of the dominant literary language game. Wittgenstein asserts that "the question is not one of explaining a language-game by means of our experiences, but of noting a language-game" (PI, I, 655). When we investigate the limits of a work of literature insofar as they are determined by its respective language games, we see more clearly the difference between the essential and inessential rules of the game. This differentiation between essential and inessential rules will help the critic interpret and evaluate various works of literature by more accurately grouping together actual cases and avoiding the problematic misconstruals of foundationalist approaches to literature.

The greater comprehensiveness of such groupings of texts could point to a radically new organizational structure for the way we look at literature. This would solve or prevent the problems that arise when works are artificially grouped together according to various preconceived notions regarding the proper divisions of literature. For example, the works of Jane Austen have often been neglected in period survey courses because they do not quite fit into either the Enlightenment or Romantic literary categories. An investigation into the rules of various literary-games could help prevent such problems by re-evaluating current categories and providing courses that more adequately address the nature of the works taught. Such an investigation might indicate that Jane Austen is not an aberrant turn-of-the-century writer who, unlike the Romantic poets, is silent regarding the more "significant" issues of the day. A Wittgensteinian approach would involve an investigation, not only into the literature of the period, but also into the critical boundaries and evaluations which have artificially divided English literature by events such as the French Revolution.

The parallels between such a Wittgensteinian approach and the revisioning of history as called for by feminists, New Historicists, and others concerned about the effects of narrow interpretations of history (and thereby of literature as well) are evident. In the specific case of Jane Austen's novels, a Wittgensteinian stance would acknowledge that traditional critical divisions such as "the eighteenth century" or "Romanticism" are the discursive constructs of literary critics who define, accept, and play the "eighteenth century literature" or the "Romantic literature" language games. This is not to say that these games are useless, just that they are limited by their own exclusionary boundaries. Within these games, there may very well be little room for Jane Austen's novels, but rather than destroying these games (which might provide some insights into their own respective works) or attempting to force Austen's works into problematic critical constructs, we discern which games *are* played by Austen's novels as a means of more properly situating her works within both critical and pedagogical frameworks.

Here we see the importance of contextual and circumstantial analyses to prevent avoidable misreadings and problematic canonical groupings. The problems that generally occur in our analyses arise due to our attempts to arrive at some sort of explanatory interpretation regarding works of literature. Wittgenstein makes it very clear that such problems can only be avoided by opting for the less dramatic, but more realistic, descriptive response. Misinterpretation is inevitable, especially when such interpretations cut across time and place: "One age misunderstands another; and a *petty* age misunderstands all the others in its own nasty way" (CV, 86e). A related concern for our postmodern times is whether or not an age without one set mooring might also misunderstand other ages, but in a variety of ways. The Wittgensteinian response here is clear and raises the question regarding the right game to play ("das rechte Spiel").

Even particular signs appearing in distinctly different contexts within the same work might imply entirely different meanings since even the rules within one work could vary throughout the work. And any text might participate in a multiplicity of games. For example, a sonnet of Shakespeare's might participate in the "sonnet" game (a familiarity with other sonnets being helpful here), the "Renaissance poetry" game (where one investigates other poems of the Renaissance), the "Shakespeare" game (which includes other types of writing by Shakespeare), the "homosexual writer" game (where the critic looks at works by other writers who had homosexual relationships), or the "mistress" game (involving writings addressed to the writer's mistress). Such a diversity of language-game structurings has led Richard Shusterman to conclude that a Wittgensteinian approach to literary criticism invariably leads to an acceptance of critical pluralism. He asserts that the "logical plurality of critical discourse [is] a second important Wittgensteinian theme which helped to change the field of aesthetics and generate a new account of critical reasoning" (1986c, 96). While it is true that Wittgenstein does acknowledge the diversity of approaches to (or perspectives on) the world, he still leaves us with a means of more accurately discerning more and less acceptable approaches in given circumstances. For example, a reading of Luci Tapahonso's poetry that ignores the nonphallocentrism of a Navajo worldview, and interprets her poems in terms of Western feminist critical strategies, would clearly be a misreading (insofar as a dialectics of gender is concerned). However, such a misreading might very well prove useful nevertheless. A feminist reading of Tapahonso's poetry, while forcing the poetry into a Western feminism that the text resists, might yield insights, albeit insights informed and limited by their interpretive boundaries. As Wittgenstein notes, "I can't be making a mistake,—but some day, rightly or wrongly, I may think I realize that I was not competent to judge" (OC, 645).[7] Clearly, for Wittgenstein, judgments may be more or less correct, and often the future is necessary to clarify earlier errors.

The distinctions and relationships within and between texts, as evidenced in our critical readings, are manifested in what Wittgenstein refers to as "aspects." In relation to a drawing, he notes that what we "perceive in the dawning of an aspect is not a property of the object, but an internal relation between it and other objects" (PI, 212e). As such, the aspects of a text are only apparent within the framework of the perceptual activity of a perceiver. Reed Way Dasenbrock sees this concept as an important means of providing us with "a more concrete account of change" (1987a, 1039), which is to say that our shifting perceptions of aspects offers a clear account for the divergent readings of texts. In such a fashion, we see the suitability of a Wittgensteinian approach towards literature in light of the critical instability of postmodernism. Lurie notes the Wittgensteinian view that when a society is bereft of culture (namely, that language game which serves to unite people), artists and writers "tend to fly off in all directions—relinquishing in the process all constraints of past tradition" (392). It is important to point out that Wittgenstein does not see such fragmentation or play as positive. He writes: "In an age without culture . . . forces become fragmented and the power of an individual man is used up in overcoming opposing forces and frictional resistances" (CV, 6e).

However this is not to say that Wittgenstein is advocating any sort of logocentric privileging. Lurie explains that, for Wittgenstein, the "emerging hegemony of European and American civilization" is implicated in the "disappearance of a culture" (378). The alternative offered is that of multiple language games. Where logocentric essentialist readings have been shown to be the discursive products of their own historicity, the language game offers a heuristic that posits the nonessentialist reality of a certainty that is contextually central and mutably organic. Shusterman emphasizes Wittgenstein's usefulness in the field of aesthetics for "providing the ammunition . . . for exploding all theories of art which aim at essentialist definitions" (1986c, 92) That which constitutes this nonessentialist certainty central to the language game is the set of rules which, in their totality, so define a particular game. A more specific discussion of the applicability of the language game for both literary theory and criticism will follow an explication of Wittgenstein's investigations into the subjects of theory and aesthetics—both of immediate concern for the fields of criticism and theory.

Literary or Critical Theory

THROUGHOUT MUCH OF Wittgenstein's writings, he clearly and strongly points out the limitations of theory while asserting the value of philosophical investigations. His arguments regarding the diversity and organicity of language games and, hence, the impossibility of arriving at any theory sufficient to encompass all evolving language games are persuasive. However, the usefulness of Wittgensteinian philosophy for literary theory need not be reduced to the meaningless oxymoron, Wittgensteinian theory. The primary reason that this is the case is due to the divergent domains of the fields of philosophy and English (literary criticism and critical theory). The domain of philosophy, according to Alan Montefiore, includes "the necessary structures and conditions of all meaningful thought in all their aspects and in all its different areas, . . . [as well as] the various contexts of breakdown or failure of meaningfulness" (62). This can be clearly differentiated from the domain of English (which consists of literature and other writings composed in the English language). The difference between these domains is significant in that it clarifies the limits by which Wittgenstein's work can be usefully applied in the arena of both literary criticism and theory. Whereas Wittgenstein categorically rejects the meaningfulness of theory for philosophical endeavors, we shall see that his concerns nevertheless lay the groundwork for delineating the boundaries within which literary theory proves most useful and beyond which it is either less useful or, in the extreme case, fundamentally meaningless.

While there are major shifts that occur between Wittgenstein's earlier and later writings, his concern with theory is apparent throughout. In the *Tractatus*, Wittgenstein acknowledges the importance of theory while delineating some of its limitations. The most serious limitation is that theory does not offer any real explanatory information about the world. What theory does provide are descriptions, rather than explanatory assertions: "The possibility of describing the world by means of Newtonian mechanics [or scientific theories] tells us nothing about the world" (TLP, 6.342). Any theory is like a network superimposed upon reality and through which we interpret that which we see. For each different network through which we perceive reality, we will arrive at a correspondingly different description. And while this description may characterize the perceived reality or picture in terms of the mediating network (net, grid), our perception is constrained by virtue of the limiting factors connected with our particular orientation: "The possibility of describing a picture like the one . . . with a net of a given form tells us *nothing* about the picture. (For that is true of all such pictures.) But what *does* characterize the picture is that it can be described *completely* by a particular net with a *particular* size of mesh" (TLP, 6.342). Wittgenstein calls the concept that the laws of nature *explain* elements of the natural world an illusion ("Tauschung"). In fact, it appears that theory tells us more about itself than about that which it objectifies. Hence, Wittgenstein claims that theory is more of a psychological process than it is logical by virtue of its being a discursive product of human perception and language.

This claim indicates the particular difficulties inherent in those postmodern theoretics, which deny the reality of any object whatsoever. In such a case, it is manifestly clear that the theoretical process becomes solipsistic at best, with the object of description being the theoretical orientation of the perceiver—or, in other words, the critic or theorist herself. And in such fashion, both objectivity and subjectivity are called into question, thereby denying any possibility of meaningful knowledge as distinct from the theoretical approach. This is to say that theory, in fact, tells us more about the orientation of the theory than about the actual form, or logic, of the world.[8] And yet, as Montefiore points out, the rejection of a particular world view (perhaps that of a hegemonic logocentrism) does not necessitate the loss of all meaning: "There are times when a near loss of meaning may give even greater force to an utterance. But loss of meaning is not mere absence of meaning. Rules can only be broken if, first, they are recognized as there to be observed" (62)—hence the importance of avoiding the limiting condition of theory, on the one hand, and the rejection of all limitation whatsoever. As Quigley notes, Wittgenstein has us "resist the tendency to absorb the multiplicity of language into some reductive explanatory schema" (217) while avoiding the pitfalls of extreme skepticism.[9]

Of course, the vast amount of theorizing found in the *Tractatus* itself severely undercuts Wittgenstein's earlier limitations on the value of theory. Insofar as the *Tractatus* is concerned, theory is invaluable; however, it is essential to understand theory's limitations and not to attempt to go beyond those boundaries.[10] Cora Diamond notes that the idea that there are no philosophical doctrines or theories can be understood in that one "can say that the notion of something true of reality but not sayably true is to be used only with the awareness that it in itself belongs to what has to be thrown away" (8). This is analogous to the fact that the *Tractatus* can be a useful tool provided we understand the limitations of its propositions and learn to go beyond them. Wittgenstein goes so far as to make such an assertion at the end of the *Trac-*

tatus: "My propositions serve as elucidations in the following way: anyone who understands me eventually recognizes them as nonsensical, when he has used them—as steps—to climb up beyond them. (He must, so to speak, throw away the ladder after he has climbed up it)" (TLP 6.54). Erik Stenius's discussion of this passage is elucidatory. He explains that such philosophical theorizing, while indeed "nonsensical," may prove to have a use value nevertheless, assuming that one reasons correctly (17, 224).

Insofar as theory is concerned, in the later *Philosophical Investigations,* Wittgenstein makes two major departures from his earlier approach elucidated in the *Tractatus.* While both changes are conceptual, one shift can best be seen in content, the other in tone and degree. The first, and most expected, is the rejection of the previous Tractarian privileging of logic as a means of explaining the world. This privileging had provided Wittgenstein with an alternative philosophical approach to theoretical reasoning. In rejecting the idea that logic has an objective or absolute nature and in noticing that logic is just one language game among many, the later Wittgenstein places logic in the same category as other theoretical approaches to knowledge. Such a shift may be seen as analogous to the poststructural shift away from a prior privileging of a logocentric absolutism.

Wittgenstein's other shift, that of tone and degree, is of equal concern for both literary critic and theorist. Within the scope of the later work as represented by the *Philosophical Investigations,* theory is treated much more harshly than in the early writings.[11] Wittgenstein came to realize that not only is theory incapable of explaining the world, but that it is not even a sufficient means of providing a complete description of the world. The limitations of theory are presented much more clearly and comprehensively in the later work. Interestingly, this can be seen simply by looking closely at the change in Wittgenstein's style and method. Whereas in the *Tractatus* Wittgenstein assertively presents various theoretical stances (hence the tendency for scholars to refer to the various points of the *Tractatus* as theories, e.g. the theory of projection, Wittgenstein's theory of meaning, the picture theory, etc.), in the *Investigations,* we find a method of observation.

Throughout the *Investigations,* Wittgenstein very carefully avoids the tendency to present his observations and thoughts dogmatically. Ideas and remarks, humbly presented in an epigrammatic style, tend to suggest directions for the study of language and reality, rather than insisting upon one set course of Tractarian analytic study (logically, hierarchically, and dogmatically laid out): "For we can avoid ineptness or emptiness in our assertions only by presenting the model as what it is, as an object of comparison—as, so to speak, a measuring-rod; not as a preconceived idea to which reality *must* correspond. (The dogmatism into which we fall so easily in doing philosophy)" (PI, 131). The primary goal of the *Tractatus* is seen to be misdirected in light of the actual goals of investigating the everyday nature of a lived reality.[12] It is more efficacious to question and investigate the "entanglement in our rules" of the *Tractatus* than to continue to lay down additional preconceived rules that are erroneously perceived as absolute and objective.[13] Wittgenstein notes that the "crystalline purity of logic was, of course, not a *result of investigation:* it was a requirement" (PI, 107), keeping him from seeing the actual nature of reality. Quigley points out that, in the later work, Wittgenstein resists any kind of totalizing, all-embracing theory that absorbs multiple phenomena into unifying frameworks (211).

The tendency to theorize is particularly problematic in the domain of literary criticism. Warren Goldfarb explains that "the nonuniformity of our criteria for understanding and their intertwining with much else in our physical, social, and mental lives represents differences from the [more uniform] models we have of states and processes in physical science" (642).[14] Of course, this is not to disparage categorically literary theory per se, much of which could hardly be classified as theory insofar as Wittgenstein is concerned. Rather, what is to be avoided is that branch of theorizing that imitates the narrowing absolutism of science. New Criticism, structuralism, and Frye's allegorical work, along with their claims towards universality, would situate these theoretical approaches within the scope of a Wittgensteinian reproval.

Unfortunately, Wittgenstein's rejection of theorizing within the bounds of philosophy has led literary critics to automatically assume that the implications for literary theory are dire. W. J. T. Mitchell asserts that Wittgenstein will "cure us" of our fascination with philosophy and our desire for "a secure foundation of theories and methods for us to follow" (361). Quigley stresses the importance of Wittgenstein's philosophical technique and emphasizes the limitations of theory (rather than the process of theorizing) for literary criticism (209–37). While it is the case that theory is unequivocally rejected for philosophy, it is essential that any transference of Wittgensteinian philosophy to literary theory or criticism be achieved with care. It is not altogether clear that a Wittgensteinian approach to literature would deny the usefulness of all literary theory. However it is true that the limitations of any specific theory must be clearly delineated. Wittgenstein emphasizes the importance of being clear regarding the limits of diverse language games in order to avoid ending up "entangled in our own rules" (PI, 125). Only by means of such boundary delineation will we be able to avoid such confusions and thereby be able "to shew the fly the way out of the fly-bottle" (PI, 309).

The importance Wittgenstein places on the avoidance of theory and the necessity for close observation is particularly evident when he shifts from his more humble, suggestive (and inquiring) remarks to an almost harsh and impatient insistence that we must change our methods if we hope to avoid the "superstitions . . . produced by [our] grammatical illusions" (PI, 110). This is to say that a Tractarian insistence on looking at reality by means of the limited blinders of a logical grammar leads us to logical truths that are, in fact, illusions and superstitions. Wittgenstein asserts that these illusions can be dispelled by a reliance on a process of observation and description—in other words, investigations. On this topic, Wittgenstein is inflexible and insistent:

> *look and see* . . . To repeat: don't think, but look! (PI, 66)

> And we may not advance any kind of theory. There must not be anything hypothetical in our considerations. We must do away with all *explanation*, and description alone must take its place. (PI, 109)[15]

> Here it is *difficult* to see that what is at issue is the fixing of concepts. A *concept* forces itself on one. (This is what you must not forget.) (PI, 204)

His insistence on the dangers of theory can be seen throughout the *Investigations* in his use of repetition, voice shifts to the second person, an emphatic underlining of words and phrases, and surprising shifts in his choice of diction. We are told that philosophy is "diseased" due to its one-sided theoretical diet (PI, 593), that we are conceptually confused (PI, 232), that we may learn "to pass from a piece of disguised nonsense to something that is patent nonsense" (PI, 464), and that we are flies who need direction in order to find "the way out of the fly-bottle" (PI, 309) of narrowly constraining theories. The way out is by means of the methodology proposed—that of close investigations.

Wittgenstein primarily presents his methodology by means of various examples. He eschews the explanatory and more theoretical approach of the *Tractatus* and chooses to clarify his new philosophical method of investigation through the discussion of a number of different examples (the best known being that of Jastrow's duck-rabbit [PI, 194 ff.]). "We now demonstrate a method, by examples. . . . Problems are solved (difficulties eliminated), not a *single* problem" (PI, 133). Throughout the *Investigations*, Wittgenstein presents his method by demonstrating it in his descriptions of the various examples presented. While presenting various interpretations of the examples, he chooses to look more closely at the examples themselves in order to gain a clearer view than any view that is largely informed by the limiting effect of preconceived notions, which invariably serve to cloud our perspective. By means of formulating theories or hypotheses, we are likely to misinterpret what we hope to understand by virtue of not seeing certain aspects of the objects under analysis (PI, 63, 212).[16] We avoid these problems when we realize the limitations of any descriptive or interpretive response, regardless of how precise or logical its language might be.

In light of the diverse games to be investigated by the literary critic in a Wittgensteinian close reading of a text, diverse perspectives become so much the more important. And here we repeat that an awareness of the value of multiple orientations is not an endorsement of a critical anarchy that does not differentiate between the viability of different approaches. The critic must observe the text closely in order to ascertain which language games the text participates in. Only after such investigations can the critic determine which critical strategies or theoretical approaches might best engender useful and meaningful entry into the particular work. A grammatical or linguistic approach might be helpful in addressing the language games present in either a contemporary language poem or much of Gertrude Stein's writing. However, in the specific case of Stein's poetry and prose, an explicitly lesbian feminist approach would, as well, prove useful. The text and its context determine the appropriateness of particular strategies. The critic needs to be prepared to learn strategies outside the realm of contemporary literary theory—particularly for those texts that demand alternative approaches.

It is essential here to reiterate that Wittgenstein's use of the term "theory" is not always synonymous with the diverse postmodern references to theory. It is nevertheless true that theory is often used by literary critics and others to refer to preconceived interpretive frameworks aimed at providing a clearer view of the world (or some aspect of the world in the guise of a text)—perhaps as in the cases of structuralism or New Criticism; however, "theory" is also used to refer to investigatory speculations and observations that strongly parallel the descriptive methodology urged by Wittgenstein. This latter use of the term "theory" has been popularized by feminist theorists, New Historicists, and many theorists working within the framework of the social sciences (such as Baudrillard, Foucault, Lyotard, and Bourdieu). While we certainly would not want to call postmodern theory Wittgensteinian, a growing number of theorists consider themselves influenced by Wittgenstein's philosophy. The diverse range of such theorists and critics (M. H. Abrams, Richard Rorty, Reed Way Dasenbrock, Henry Staten, and Marjorie Perloff) indicates that there is no set form as yet defined or formulated explicitly as a Wittgensteinian literary theory or criticism. This could be due to a number of factors, such as a diversity of interpretations and readings of Wittgenstein or a variety of ways in which such interpretations are implemented. However Wittgenstein does assert that there are correct and incorrect descriptions of the world. Accordingly, from a Wittgensteinian orientation, we would acknowledge that there are, as well, correct and incorrect readings of Wittgenstein's work. However, this is not to say that there need be only *one* correct reading.

The story of the blind people and the elephant graphically clarifies the Wittgensteinian view that, within any language game, there are criteria upon which to determine correct and incorrect play. In this story, the criteria or rules of play are determined by biological science and human language. As the story goes, an elephant wanders into a village inhabited only by blind people. A number of the villagers come out and encounter the beast. One grabs hold of the trunk, exclaiming that the creature is like a huge snake. Another villager explores a leg and asserts that the animal is like a tree. A third person feeling an ear describes the elephant as smooth and flat, perhaps a flying creature. The point of the story is obvious: each of the villagers is correctly describing the part of the animal with which s/he has come in contact. The descriptions are correct, albeit partial. However, we can imagine an incorrect description. Perhaps one of the villagers, instead of touching the elephant, gets turned around and ends up investigating a stray dog. His description might be accurate concerning the dog, but would not necessarily be correct regarding the elephant (e.g., "The elephant is small and furry, like a toy poodle").

Wittgenstein explains that truth or certainty are determined conditionally by the foundational rules of language games (such as the definitional rules of the elephant language game), such that unlikely situations may occur, but they may reflect fundamental changes in the language games (OC, 403).[17] Were the aberrant description to be accepted as correct, that would mean that our understanding of the term "elephant" had changed. And, therefore, there would be a change in the elephant language game.[18] "When language-games change, then there is a change in concepts, and with the concepts the meanings of words change" (OC, 65). Wittgenstein makes it clear that we can arrive at certainty regarding the world, and this certainty is decided by the terms of our language games. To use a mathematical example, a particular equation might be solved several different ways, all with the same answer. The different approaches merely look at the equation from different angles. Were a solution to yield an altogether different answer from that of the original equation, the answer would be determined to be incorrect within the rules or constraints of the calculus game being played. Of course, the divergent solution might very well be correct within a different calculus game (PI, 226e–227e), for the rules of any game determine how the game is to be played. Wittgenstein notes that "what counts as an adequate test of a statement belongs to . . . the description of the language-game" (OC, 82). In other words, a description of the language game of calculus or of biology would determine the accuracy of the equation's solution or the descriptions of the elephant.

The multiplicity of viewpoints current in contemporary literary theory points to the value of such a descriptive methodology. Guetti writes that "one of the most important attributes of a descriptive investigation, in other words, is that it makes allowances, and nowhere is this capacity more important than in literary studies" (1985, 66). The viability of a Wittgensteinian approach herein is manifested particularly by virtue of its openness and flexibility. Wittgenstein makes this clear in his assertion that even his methodology is not a set absolute that is unchangeable or unitary, but rather a process that is organically diverse and evolutionary:

> Instead, we now demonstrate a method, by examples; and the series of examples can be broken off.—Problems are solved (difficulties eliminated), not a *single* problem.
> There is not *a* philosophical method, though there are indeed methods, like different therapies. (PI, 133)

Such an awareness of the diversity of methods could be seen as support for the sort of critical pluralism called for by a number of contemporary critics such as M. H. Abrams and Richard Shusterman. Both Shusterman (1986c, 96–98), and Abrams (83–87), note the importance of a critical pluralism in light of the diversity of critical subjects, statements, and frameworks. However, the organicism of Wittgenstein's methodology mitigates against a pluralist view that would assume the viability and validity of all theoretical approaches. Such a pluralist orientation ignores the fact that each theoretical discourse is limited by its own boundaries which, in many cases, are sufficient determinants of the theory's efficaciousness, or lack thereof. This limiting situation indicates the necessity of investigating particular methods and theories in order to more fully comprehend their boundaries.

Just as Wittgenstein rejected philosophy in favor of doing a new form of philosophy ("One might say that the subject we are dealing with is one of the heirs of the subject which used to be called 'philosophy'" [BB, 28]), he also rejected theory (as understood within its original home of the sciences) as ineffective for non-sciences. However, this is not to say that theory mightn't serve a literary purpose were it to take an altogether different form (as Wittgenstein's philosophy takes an altogether different form from traditional Western philosophy). One example of such a new form that theory might take would be much of what goes by the name of feminist theory (which, in fact, might be more correctly identified as either applied literary criticism or as metacriticism). While theory, as defined by Wittgenstein, is rejected, a methodology that, according to A. W. Moore, "draws our attention to the flexibility, indeterminacy and open-texturedness of meaning, to the creativity of language-use, to the disparities between language and a rule-governed calculus, and to the inappropriateness of systematization and generality in theorizing about language" might be accepted and, in fact, encouraged (1985, 143). Quigley correctly notes this as the difference between a static theory and a dynamic process of theorizing (227-28). And this difference strongly parallels the difference Wittgenstein delineates between much of philosophy versus his methodology of philosophical investigations.

For Wittgenstein, there is no room for theoretical approaches to philosophical issues. Theory is rejected by virtue of its static and narrow focus. If knowledge, like the world and the universe, is ever expanding and evolving, then philosophy must accordingly work from a methodology that is continually broadening, rather than narrowing, in scope. Language games are not static, but change over time. It is theory that constrains us, "holds us captive," "entangles" us. Wittgenstein's way of conducting philosophy, his "way of looking at things," demonstrates a methodology for investigating the reality of the world while acknowledging that what is accidental and external changes across time and place. This fact that the meanings of words and concepts change is hardly a new discovery. Regarding the Corcyrean revolution, Thucydides noted that when a society changes, so too do the meanings of words.[19] Wittgenstein notes that the world is continually in flux and that the constraints imposed by the limits of particular theories are therefore incapable of fully comprehending the dynamic objects of their analysis. For Wittgenstein, theories posit some sort of static prototype that is then used as a rule against which reality is artificially measured: "Since we confuse prototype and object we find ourselves dogmatically conferring on the object properties which only the prototype necessarily possesses" (CV, 14e). And here we see the sort of difficulty that reflects the problematic situation of absolutist theoretics applied to the world or to any reality that is not static but dynamic.

Nietzsche, Marx, Freud, and Einstein questioned the foundations upon which much of our tottering logocentrism rests, with the continuing critiques of the postmodern era posing their somewhat anachronistic death blows.[20] Much of the postmodern debate concerning the reality of the world as it has been depicted in art and literature has served to demonstrate the absent, or at best shaky, grounds upon which a privileged and homogeneous logocentrism was based. We now see that the reality we had previously perceived and struggled to understand is, in fact, little more than the discursive construct of our own limited interpretive frameworks. Where that framework posited a unitary and absolute homogeneity, what was therefore perceived by means of those theoretical constraints were those objects which were able to fit those prescribed boundaries.

Literary criticism and the canon of literature in English present many examples of this process of limiting theories. When the determining constraints were those of New Criticism, for example, the valued literary works of the day were those texts which fit the prescribed framework most readily—namely those works fraught with irony and ambiguity, such as the poetry of the early seventeenth century. The much more complex poetry of William Blake was devalued by the New Critics (a devaluation evidenced in his omission by critics who preferred to work with texts more suitable to the New Critical enterprise) and did not find a secure place in the literary canon until the allegorical readings of Northrop Frye rescued it from obscurity. An analogous situation has occurred over the course of the past two decades of critical scholarship by feminists and others concerned about the disenfranchisement of literatures by working-class, minority, female, gay and lesbian, and colonial and postcolonial writers. Traditionally, such literatures have been devalued by literary critics whose critical stances did not call into question the hegemonic effects of such biased interpretive discourses. The postmodern response has been largely to clarify that the logocentric homogeneity upon which the critical discourses of the modern and early postmodern periods are based is just one societal construct of no greater validity than any other constructed interpretive discourse.

However, while the contemporary critical dialectic seems to jockey back and forth between traditional and postmodern orientations, between perceiving the text as a unitary whole capable of correct interpretation and as a heterogeneous construct defined by its larger context and open to a wide variety of diverse interpretive discourse (all equally valid and invalid), and between traditional views seen as true and absolute and contemporary critical discourses that demonstrate the hegemonic privileging evident in those earlier critical stances, it is not clear that the uprooting of the logocentrism of the modern period necessarily leads to the denial of all certainty or to the utter impossibility of any meaningful center in our lives, in our societies, or in our literatures.

Wittgenstein emphasizes the importance of discerning the various language games in relation to the objects of our investigations. In particular, he refers to the heterogeneity evident in literature and works of art: "These expressions may mean various kinds of thing" (PI, 526). In order to more easily traverse the "multitude of familiar paths [which] lead off" (PI, 525) from any expression, it is essential that we be familiar with those games in which the text participates. As Wittgenstein points out, "the question is one . . . of noting a language-game" (PI, 655). It is this process of language game discernment that indicates the most appropriate approaches or paths to take in/to a text. For Wittgenstein, while there are a "multitude of paths," all paths are not equal. Specifically in relation to a work of art, Wittgenstein asserts that "there is understanding and failure to understand" (PI, 526). In light of the diversity of language games evident in most texts, it becomes crucial for the critic to be able to approach the text from multiple directions (e.g., critical or interpretive approaches). As Wittgenstein notes, there are times when we need to "see the problem from a completely new angle. . . . One of the most important methods I use is to imagine a historical development for our ideas different from what actually occurred" (CV, 37e).

However, it is not always the case that a critic will be capable of seeing/entering/interpreting the text from a new angle. It is conceivable that a text might be so alien or distant that a critic would have no means of entry due to inadequate familiarity with any of the text's language games. One such example (discussed in greater detail in Chapter 3) might be a feminist approach to a poem produced within a culture and language that is outside the bounds of the phallocentric/feminist dialectic (such as a traditional Navajo chant). In such a situation, the only alternative for the critic situated outside the bounds of the Navajo language game who wants to approach such a text is to reposition herself such that she gains entry into a language game in which the text participates. The importance of avoiding such critical misconstruals will become clear as we investigate more closely Wittgenstein's own philosophical approach towards aesthetics (which for Wittgenstein included both the criticism of art and literature).

Wittgensteinian Aesthetics

By the 1930s, Wittgenstein had departed from his earlier thoughts regarding the transcendental nature of aesthetics. Having come to understand that any human judgment is necessarily constrained by the limitations of language and perception (understanding), he observed that this was also the case for aesthetic judgments. He further observed that works of artistic production (visual, musical, and literary), as the products of human activity, are a form of life, as is the case for any other element of human society. In these respects, Wittgenstein believed that the subject of aesthetics was larger than commonly thought and "entirely misunderstood." As in the case of philosophy, he repeatedly emphasizes the importance of avoiding explanation altogether and of looking more closely in order to provide a more accurate descriptive analysis of the objects (works of art) one hopes to understand better.[21]

In a series of lectures given at Cambridge during the summer of 1938, Wittgenstein focused on the practice of aesthetics (a term he uses for critical views of art, music, and literature). In a compilation of notes taken by students of his at the time, he points out that aesthetic judgments do not offer explanations of works of art by virtue of the noncausality of the judgments. Aesthetic judgments "take the form of criticism" rather than that of causal explanation (L&C, 14–15, 21). His main concerns here are the conceptual confusions in aesthetics, which are analogous to those in philosophy. These confusions arise due to the limitations inherent in the application of theoretical approaches outside the realm of science. He acknowledges the value of theory and experimentation for the sciences, but notes that such paradigms of science are less effective when inappropriately applied to philosophy or aesthetics. "What we really want, to solve aesthetic puzzlements, is certain comparisons—grouping together of certain cases" (L&C, 29). The appropriate methodology for aesthetics is the same as that already discussed in this chapter—that of descriptive investigations.

What is essential for the aesthetician is to investigate the work of art with the end result being, insofar as it is possible, an unclouded and comprehensive description. And this investigation must also situate the work and critic in their respective historical contexts: the work insofar as it represents a form of life and the critic in order to minimize unnecessary bias. Wittgenstein emphasizes the importance of investigating our perceptions and their derivations to "destroy a variety of misconceptions" and to prevent potentially avoidable preconceived judgments. Both the work of art and the critic's perception of it are products of their own times and cultures. In an essay on Wittgenstein's theory of art, Carol Hunts writes that artworks are expressive "by way of their playing a certain role in the community [and] of fulfilling the needs and expectations of both the artist and the audience" (160). She continues, explaining that "art (aesthetics) is intimately intertwined with other forms of life, so that to understand art, or to experience it with some degree of informed appreciation, we have to understand many things about the way we live" (172). Therefore, if critical language-game recognition and entry are the intended goals, then the critic's perception needs to be sufficiently unconstrained by the limitations of any preconceived theoretical approach. One must observe closely and then describe (not explain), and much of that description should focus on forms of life as manifested in the various language games in which the work of art or text participates. Wittgenstein asserts that "in order to get clear about aesthetic words you have to describe ways of living" (L&C, 11)—a process that necessarily involves situating texts in their worlds.

Regardless of whether our attention is turned to the work itself, our perceptions of it,[22] or our critical vocabulary and perspective, our focus is on the (objective) text insofar as it is a part of actual life. What is particularly important here is that the text (object of critical study) does not lose its own subjectivity as presenter of its textual world (which in turn represents the real world from which the text emerged). Wittgenstein observes that not only artwork, but also aesthetic judgments reflect the cultures in which they arise. "The words we call expressions of aesthetic judgement play a very complicated role, but a very definite role, in what we call a culture of a period. To describe their use or to describe what you mean by a cultured taste, you have to describe a culture" (L&C, 8). Aesthetic judgments and taste change across times and cultures. A poet in medieval England would certainly have very different expectations than we have about what constitutes a "good" poem. As

Wittgenstein notes, "An entirely different game is played in different ages" (L&C, 8). What this means for the aesthetician or critic is that she must learn the culture from whence a work of art derives in order to understand it clearly, because "what belongs to a language game is a whole culture" (L&C, 8). However, any interpretive perception which she might have will necessarily be affected by her own cultural biases. This is unavoidable, but the critic can, nevertheless, minimize the problems inherent here by attempting to situate a work within its own time and culture,[23] and by realizing that her perception will always reflect her own culture and background. Hartley Slater emphasizes that "aesthetics, surely, centrally involves *participation* with Art [and] the aesthetic value we attach to certain things is shown by the place of those things in our lives" (37). What is particularly crucial here is for the critic to have access to the work of art. She must be able to traverse those paths which provide entry into the language games of the artwork.

The historical contexts of both critic and work of art are to be understood as a language game. This is to say that within any particular culture (or critical context), there are rules that are expected to be followed, or at least responded to in one way or another. By discovering the rules involved, one's aesthetic judgment becomes "more refined." "Learning the rules actually changes your judgement" (L&C, 5). By becoming more familiar with the Navajo culture, one would see the products of that culture differently, and according to Wittgenstein, such judgment would be preferable ("more refined").[24] And here again, we are investigating the language game called Navajo; we are not attempting to come up with theoretical explanations. Richard Shusterman clarifies such a Wittgensteinian stance in his argument regarding the inapplicability of systemic and generalist theories for aesthetics: "Wittgenstein, by showing that our concepts need not have clear, fixed, and definite essences in order to be usable and adequate, and by further insisting that aesthetic concepts are especially vague and flexible and thus inherently resistant and unsuitable to essentialist definition, has shaken this assumption" (1986c, 95). While Wittgenstein acknowledges the appeal such explanations hold for us ("The attraction of certain kinds of explanation is overwhelming. . . . They have a peculiar charm" [L&C, 24–25]), his emphasis is nevertheless on the importance of observation.

There is one significant exception, however, to the process of language game discernment insofar as aesthetics is concerned. Wittgenstein asserts the existence of works of art which cannot be properly measured against the respective language games of their time and place. These works are what he terms the *"tremendous* things in art"—those works which cannot be reduced to the level of a mere product of their times nor completely explained in terms of cultural language games. Wittgenstein explains such exceptions (such as a gothic cathedral or a symphony by Beethoven) in terms of their place within the language game called art. Most works of art can be appreciated in terms of their "correctness," insofar as they meet the criteria (follow the rules) or standards established for their respective language games. The question here is one of degree—to what extent does a particular work of art measure up to its standard? Where "great" art is concerned, "the entire *game* is different" (L&C, 8). Wittgenstein argues that such works need to be responded to differently because the game and its rules are different.

Such an acknowledgement of the distinction of such *"tremendous things in art"* should not be misconstrued as a tacit acceptance of any sort of hegemonic absolutism. Wittgenstein is not lending his support to the colonialist homogeneity of a traditional Great Books approach to the literary canon. Rather, he is noting that there are works of art and literature whose dominions extend beyond the bounds of their respective societal language games. Wittgenstein is clearly providing a means of challenging traditional canonicities without resorting to the extremes of either a total skepticism or a valueless relativism. For Wittgenstein, "great" works, irreducible to the determining language games of their time, cannot be defined, or limited, by those discursive structures alone. For example, to define or measure the poetry of Emily Dickinson against the dominant language games of nineteenth-century New England (language games generally phallocentric at best and blatantly misogynistic at worst) would be not only to limit her poetry, but to force it into those very interpretive discourses the poetry rejects. As Wittgenstein emphasizes, we must "seek [our] reasons for calling something good or beautiful" (CV, 24e), thereby clarifying the constraining biases against which art is judged. In the case of art and literature, Wittgenstein refers to the role played by the word "beautiful" as idiotic ("dumme") and to the underlying grammar of the word "good" as peculiar (CV, 24e, 52e). Traditional axiological stances are seen by Wittgenstein as inadequate by virtue of the limitations of their theoretical biases. A Wittgensteinian approach to literature differs radically from the traditionalist stances of critics such as Allan Bloom or E. D. Hirsch. Wittgenstein calls on us to continually re-evaluate those criteria by which we gauge works of art, but this re-evaluation is not to say that we throw out evaluation altogether. Rather we evaluate by means of noting those language games in which the work participates, the degree and success of such participation (just as we might evaluate whether an individual played well in a given game of chess).

Descriptive Investigations

A WITTGENSTEINIAN-BASED critical (or aesthetic) method parallels Wittgenstein's philosophical method—namely that of descriptive investigations. And this strategy of descriptive textual investigations is applicable not only in regard to literary works, but also regarding critical and theoretical work. In light of the contingent nature of any evaluative determination, literary critics must investigate literary criticism and critical theory in terms of their respective language games in order to begin to discern possible critical fits between critic and text. Such critical investigations (the act of closely observing critical work) can help avoid the problematic, and all too frequent, situation of critics interpreting literary texts even when the entryways to those texts diverge from the means of entry being critically imposed. Wittgenstein was acutely aware of the error of forcing a reading on a text or on the world—and this was his specific complaint about theory. It is essential that critics be aware of their own critical language-game play to be able to discern the suitability of particular critical or theoretical approaches to a text. While Wittgenstein emphasizes the necessity of avoiding the narrowing effect of theory, it is clear that such a denigration of theory specifically applies to those "preconceived ideas to which reality *must* correspond" (PI, 131). Wittgenstein unequivocally rejects the limiting constraints of such theory insofar as it artificially skews our perspective and interpretation of the world. Such a rejection of theory is analogous to the poststructural rejection of the logocentric absolutism of earlier critical orientations such as New Criticism or structuralism. However, what Wittgensteinian philosophy most helpfully offers to postmodern criticism is a powerful mediation between the two contemporary extremes of a hegemonic foundationalism, on one side, and a historically situated skepticism on the other.

From a Wittgensteinian perspective, the literary critic or theorist would understand the value of the postmodern dismantling of earlier limiting approaches to literature. And yet, such a dismantling would be seen as the dismantling of a specific structure, not of the possibility of structure per se. Wittgenstein points this out clearly: "When we think of the world's future, we always mean the destination it will reach if it keeps going in the direction we can see it going in now; it does not occur to us that its path is not a straight line but a curve, constantly changing direction" (CV, 3e). It is only when we define the world, or a text, in terms of a specific set of rules, which are proven inadequate or faulty, that the reality of the world or text is called into question. Hence the usefulness of the language-game model for the purposes of a contemporary literary criticism and theory. The changing of the rules of logocentrism, for example, does not lead to the absence of rules, but rather to the changing of the game, just as the path changes its direction.

What such a mediation means for literary criticism is paramount. Rather than a poststructural denial of the possibility of meaning conjoined with the attendant proliferation of interpretive strategies, or a traditionalist reaffirmation of a narrow and unitary meaning, the Witt-

gensteinian critic understands not only the existence of textual meaning, but, more importantly, the fact that such meaning is discoverable as
a diverse and living multifluity of semantic use.[25] This affirmation of
meaning, far from being narrow or unitary, acknowledges the necessity
of historically situating the text within its respective language games.[26]
Further, a reliance upon the philosophy of Ludwig Wittgenstein provides the literary critic with a descriptive methodology by means of
which she will differentiate the diverse language games of a particular
text. The concept of limits is especially important regarding the boundaries of the text. These boundaries are established by the text's language games and, as such, need to be clearly delineated by the critic in
order to help determine the boundaries of her investigations. Such an
investigation might indicate that, in one case, the laundry list of a writer
is significant to a reading of his text and, in another case, that such a list
would be utterly unproductive to the critical endeavor.

In addition to the concern regarding the limits of language games,
the language-game heuristic provides an organic model helpful in clarifying how texts and interpretative strategies vary over time. Such organicism also speaks to the diverse uses of the term "theory" both
within the bounds of literary criticism and in other fields as well. The
changing concept of theory offers a means of entry for those theoretical
discourses generally disparaged as insufficiently theoretical or sophisti-
cated by theorists grounded more fully in a Eurocentric philosophical
tradition. Wittgensteinian philosophy, which veers away radically from
the main currents of philosophical discussion, proves to be a significant model for helping literary theory in an analogous directional and
definitional shift away from a logocentric hegemony of philosophically-
based theory. So, yet again, we find literary criticism and theory relying
upon the guidance of philosophy. The difference here is that rather
than turning to a member of the philosophical elite, we turn to the
work of an individual whose philosophy rebels against such elitism.[27]

However, rather than completely unsettling or denying any possibility of ascertaining a specific textual meaning or direction (by what
Cornel West refers to as the "hegemony of epistemic antifoundational-
ism" [24]), the philosophy of Ludwig Wittgenstein helps us to gain our
bearings as we realize the likelihood that our "path is not a straight
line but a curve, constantly changing direction" (CV, 3e). And yet, as
Wittgenstein clearly asserts, the fact that our "path is not a straight
line" does not necessarily lead to a poststructural conclusion that there
is no path at all. The pathways into texts—literary and critical—exist.
The job for the critical theorist and literary critic is to discover those
pathways—pathways hidden from the critic following the alternate
routes of her own preconceived critical biases.

2 Critical Descriptions, or Moving beyond Freud: A Wittgensteinian-Based Psychological Criticism

THE CONJOINED ACT of reading and responding to a text is a profoundly psychological behavior, analogous to the process of reading and responding to one's surrounding everyday world, and yet discussions which address issues of psychology in relation to literary critical concerns tend to apply a variety of theoretical constructs (derived in varying degrees from the pioneering work of Sigmund Freud) to the critical endeavor rather than focusing on the underlying epistemological psychology of criticism itself. A reliance on the work of Ludwig Wittgenstein in the field of the philosophy of psychology offers the critic interested in the psychological ramifications of textual entry a new approach that is outside those bounds predetermined by the theoretical limits of modern and postmodern psychological criticisms. While such an approach is new for literary criticism, it is not entirely new within the field of psychology. A recent conceptual system, initially developed by Peter G. Ossorio, which rejects current psychological theories and methodologies, is descriptive psychology. Through a close look at both Wittgenstein's discussions of psychology and the development of descriptive psychology (influenced in part by Wittgensteinian philosophy), we will begin to discover a new psychological method of descriptive criticism by which literary (and other) texts can be opened and understood.

In light of the proliferation of postmodern critical theories, a preliminary question that needs to be addressed is the extent to which a new method is not only useful, but in fact needed. The answer to this concern is simple: what a Wittgensteinian-based criticism provides is not another theoretical approach that is, by definition, circumscribed by its own limiting constructs,[1] but rather a *method* that is both dynamic and responsive in its actual applications, comprehensive in its applicability towards a wide range of texts, and expansive in its potential results. Jane Gallop suggests that feminism "promises" to expand psychoanalytic criticism by informing it historically and politically (315). And yet such expansion can only occur within the prescribed definitional limits of psychoanalysis—limits beyond which psychoanalysis becomes no longer itself. A new descriptive method of psychological criticism enables the critic to move beyond those problematic psychoanalytic boundaries that forbid entry in/to certain texts. This is not to say that psychoanalytic criticism is to be avoided. On the contrary, we use psychoanalytic tools (albeit differentially) in a descriptive method— thereby avoiding the rigid limits of the theory in order to approach divergent texts such as those written by Native American Indian authors. What is needed is not yet another theoretical construct through which we can note to what extent various literary texts fit the pattern of our superimposed critical grid, but a method of approach that foregrounds essential psychological concerns which tend to be overlooked by most critical approaches (ostensively psychological or otherwise).

Within a psychologically-oriented descriptive criticism, the critic approaches a literary text as a psychological entity whose psychology is accessible to readers/critics—thereby assigning to the text a status above that of a mere object waiting to be explicated. And this privileging of the literary text (which includes both the actual written text and its context or respective language games) over the critic—who becomes one who serves the text (in making the text accessible to other readers) rather than one who masters it—necessitates a categorically different method of critical approach. What this means most significantly for literary criticism and theory as a whole is that psychology becomes central to the critical endeavor as issues of perception, description, interpretation, and valuation (all central to the critical practice) are viewed as inextricable from individual, textual, and social psychology.

To arrive at this end, I first introduce Wittgenstein's views on the interrelated processes of perception, thought, speech, description, interpretation, and valuation as they relate to human psychology. Once this initial foundation has been established, the more recent developments in descriptive psychology are discussed along with their applicability to literary criticism. This introduction to descriptive psychology is followed by a description of a new methodological approach that provides an orientation to texts which, on the one hand, diverges from theoretically-based psychological criticisms, while, on the other hand, privileging a psychological focus as essential to sound and complete critical readings. The chapter ends with an application of such a method to a poem by Navajo poet Luci Tapahonso. In selecting a poem generally resistant to psychoanalytically-informed criticisms (the Navajo language game being significantly outside the bounds of the psychoanalysis language game), I demonstrate that the domain of psychological criticism can be broadened to open up virtually any text.

Wittgenstein's Philosophy of Psychology

WITTGENSTEIN UNDERSTOOD that the processes of speech, description, interpretation, and valuation are profoundly psychological processes. So his investigations into human communication and behavior (or language games) led him to consider developments in psychoanalysis and experimental psychology. His overriding concern with psychology mirrors his frustrations with philosophy. For Wittgenstein, both philosophy and psychology tend to superimpose preconceived theoretical grids through which their respective objects of study are examined. The problems with such an approach, for Wittgenstein, are twofold. First, the limiting factors involved in such a theoretical orientation constrain and skew one's view so that the resulting conclusions are at best limited and at worst meaningless beyond the bounds of the observed circumstance. Not only does a theoretical approach establish certain preconceived limits to one's investigations, but even more problematic is the fact that such a method, rather than providing a remedy to human psychological needs, perpetuates particularly hegemonic worldviews, which serve to devalue difference (or whatever does not fit into the preconceived theoretical grid). Terry Brown discusses the struggles psychoanalytic feminist critics have in their attempts to "break from the narrow Oedipal frame by positioning ourselves in an other way of thinking" (38). The option of positioning oneself in an "other" way of thinking is nevertheless problematic in the displacement of feminist criticism as "other" to the centrality of Freudian and Lacanian theoretics. As we shall see, a descriptive approach to literary texts provides a method for critics which is not bound in/to a reactive struggle for dominance with phallogocentric theories.

One metaphor that Wittgenstein uses as descriptive of our world is that of weaving—an analogy that incorporates both the sense of diversity as well as the idea that the multiplicitous elements of the world are interlinked or interwoven. The problem with the limits involved in a particular approach to the world (say, psychoanalysis) is that while we see this one pattern in the weave, we ignore or do not see other patterns (perhaps even more prevalent or significant). Wittgenstein writes:

> Seeing life as a weave, this pattern (pretence, say) is not always complete and is varied in a multiplicity of ways. But we, in our conceptual world, keep on seeing the same, recurring with variations. That is how our concepts take it. For concepts are not for use on a *single* occasion.
> And the pattern in the weave is interwoven with many others. (RPPI, 672-673)

This is not to say that any noted pattern is by definition problematic—merely that it is limited and that its uses need to be framed within this limiting context. As Wittgenstein notes, we tend to pick up on a certain pattern and then continue to look for the same or similar patterns elsewhere. While this conceptual practice does have its uses, the difficulty presents itself when, due to our preconceived notions (or pretences), we miss other, perhaps equally important, elements interwoven in the pattern.

Postmodern critics have correctly noted the limitations of traditionalist criticisms; however such destabilizations of earlier critical frameworks are reductive and solipsistic in their continual reaction against a previous theoretical order. While the boundaries which circumscribe the patterns of the past are becoming patently clear, contemporary poststructural approaches nevertheless maintain the centrality of earlier criticisms in a reactive dependence on those discursive structures of a more traditionalist modernity. Rather than considering alternative patterns, the focus is on other elements of the weave in relation/reaction to the initial pattern—a process that perpetuates the centrality of the debated origin. Wittgenstein repeatedly stresses the interrelationship between part and whole and that any view of the part must take into account the part's relationship to the whole. In a particular case, a similar pattern might signify completely different meanings based on the pattern's context. For example, Ellie Ragland-Sullivan notes: "Lacanian discourse theory teaches that all discourse organizes itself around a difference" (82). Such a view is enormously useful in approaching those texts whose language games reflect underlying discursive subject/object hierarchies of power. But are we to assume that such discursive distinctions are evident in all languages and all cultures? In a language such as Navajo, both subject and object are grammatically conjoined within the verb in a symbolic ordering that rejects a categoric, hierarchized differentiation between subject and object.[2] Therefore a reliance on Lacanian discourse theory might not be the most useful strategy in entering Navajo language and literature texts.

Our readings of the world, of individuals, of relationships, of texts, reflect more than anything else back on ourselves as a depiction of our own conceptual boundaries. Wittgenstein clarifies this situation in a discussion of divergent readings of a smiling face. "First and foremost, I can very well imagine someone who, while he sees a face extremely accurately, and can, e.g., make an accurate portrait of it, yet doesn't recognize its smiling expression as a smile. I should find it absurd to say that his sight was defective. And equally absurd to say that his subjective visual object just wasn't smiling, although it has all the colours and form that mine has" (RPPI, 1103). For Wittgenstein, our reading does not alter the actual situation of a smiling face. Rather, it presents our perception and interpretation of that face. However, Wittgenstein is very careful not to make a value judgment regarding the "correct" reading or interpretation of the face. One reading varies from another, but, as Wittgenstein comments regarding a variant reading, "I should find it absurd to say his sight was defective." Divergent readings do not necessarily indicate more or less accurate readings. The important question for Wittgenstein is not which reading is more correct, but which reading, in a particular case, is the most useful. If the goal is to address the problematics of a phallogocentric discourse, then feminist readings of literary texts might be the most useful. If the aim, however, is to note underlying psychological conditions in a text, then a psychologically informed interpretive approach would be called for. But where the intended aim is to elucidate the various language games in which a particular text participates (as a means of providing easier entry into that text for diverse readers), then the investigations into the text need to precede the critical selection process—that determining process that discovers, constructs, and/or imagines those pathways between readers and texts.

Such a methodology, which insists on the primacy of critical investigations prior to critical determinations, underscores Wittgenstein's discussion of the related processes of perception, thought, speech, description, interpretation, and valuation. Wittgenstein explains that these processes, while related, are nevertheless "different inner processes" ("vershiedene innere Vorgänge" [RPPI, 656]). And none of these processes are purely objective; all involve a psychological response on the part of the reader/critic. Perception is the one of these processes which can be potentially neutral (when seeing is merely a physical response rather than the more complex process of "seeing-as"). We perceive Jastrow's duck-rabbit picture to be an image on paper, but we see it *as* either the depiction of a duck or a rabbit—making the conceptual connection between the physically perceived picture and what we perceive it to look like.

All of the other processes noted above accordingly involve varying degrees of psychological complexity on the part of a reader or critic. As Wittgenstein points out, even the process of description is complicated:

> Mere description is so difficult because one believes that one needs to fill out the facts in order to understand them. It is as if one saw a screen with scattered colour-patches, and said: the way they are here, they are unintelligible; they only make sense when one completes them into a shape.—Whereas I want to say: Here *is* the whole. (If you complete it, you falsify it.) (RPPI, 257)

Remaining on the supposedly uncritical domain of description, Wittgenstein clearly identifies the interpretive and evaluative determinations involved in our desire to make sense of our perceptions as we "complete them into a shape." However, Wittgenstein stresses that what is in the world is complete and does not need us to make it complete or other than it is. Our efforts thereby serve to limit and make what is in the world less than it is and, in fact, twist the truths in the world into falsities. The analogy for literary critics and literary texts is clear. Neither the world nor texts need critics to complete them. They are whole and complete. Our job is not one of correction, creation, or completion, but rather that of discernment and recognition.

Wittgenstein's admonitions throughout his works serve to warn us of the dangers of a critical and theoretical hubris which, more than anything else, lessens the depth and diversity of those literary texts we read, teach, and critique. As Wittgenstein explains his aim: "What *we* do is to bring words back from their metaphysical to their everyday use" (PI, 116). And this process is crucial if our desire is for our words (our interpretive readings) to be meaningful and useful: "Where does our investigation get its importance from, since it seems only to destroy everything interesting, that is, all that is great and important? (As it were all the buildings, leaving behind only bits of stone and rubble.) What we are destroying is nothing but houses of cards and we are clearing up the ground of language on which they stand" (PI, 118). If this sounds similar to the various poststructural theories and criticisms, which focus on the uprooting of the critical constructs of modernism—it is; however, this "deconstructive" process (qua Wittgenstein) is not an end in itself, but deconstructs modern *and* postmodern theories and criticisms alike to clear the way to literary investigations which privilege the literature and reader over the critic. This shift in emphasis transforms the critic/theorist into one who serves, rather than masters, both literature and readers (students and instructors) in a recognition that criticism's primary role is to make literary texts more readily and more deeply accessible to greater numbers of diverse readers.

The Descriptive Psychology Approach

WITTGENSTEIN SOUGHT to clarify the foundational problems in the domains of philosophy, mathematics, and psychology; the descriptive psychologist notes such foundational problems specifically in the field of psychology and works from a categorically divergent set of assumptions. Peter Ossorio writes: "The most important precondition for descriptive psychology was a deep and pervasive dissatisfaction with the then [1964–65] current psychological theories and psychological 'science,' and with the philosophical views for which they stood proxy" (1985, 19). The overarching concern of the descriptive psychologist differs from the general presuppositions inherent in the foundations of psychological "science" in that we perceive, read, and interpret language, persons, behavior, and the world in terms of our own concepts of the world. Therefore, any sort of globalizing theoretical or experimental approach towards human perception and behavior is inadequate as a means of understanding the behaviors of actual human persons. Persons live in and respond to their own respective worlds, not to some objective construct of the real world. Acknowledging that our worlds are constructs, the descriptive psychologist works with a client in relation to the client's perceived/constructed world. Rather than trying to get a client to live in some preconceived world of psychology, the descriptive psychologist works to help the client to understand his/her world more clearly while attempting to reconstruct that world to give the client more behavior potential, both perceptually and actually. The Wittgensteinian influence is clear. The language games which constitute the client's world are those with which the therapist and client must work—not language games inferentially derived (theoretically or experimentally), which might not coincide or even relate at all to the client's language games.

Wittgenstein writes that "the world is everything that is the case" (TLP, 1). This "real world" (as it is termed in descriptive psychology) is the totality with which we engage partially and differentially. And since "every conception, observation, or description of 'the real world' or any of its parts or aspects is someone's conception, observation, or description" (Ossorio 1978, 33), the real world for any individual is "the world which includes him as an observer" (Ossorio 1978, 57). Therefore, there are different worlds which vary according to the person, time, place, and culture. For Peter Ossorio, the founder of descriptive psychology, the rightful domain of psychology consists of "what actually happens" in the human world (or the worlds in which humans manifest their subjectivity as persons). In a categorical rejection of theorizing in psychology (which parallels Wittgenstein's rejection of theory outside the fields of the physical sciences), Ossorio asserts: "There is no place for a Person in the world of psychoanalysis, the world of operant conditioning, the world of systems theory, the world of rote-memory learning, or any of the traditional 'naturalistic' theories within the behavioral sciences" (1978, 182). The never-ending Lacanian struggle to assert one's subjectivity in the world, from the early mirror-stage onward, can be seen as emblematic of the difficulty Ossorio notes throughout psychology: namely that human beings can only be helped to behave more effectively in the world if they are perceived as persons. Mary McDermott Shideler explains that "in Descriptive Psychology, we define a person as an individual whose history is, paradigmatically, a history of deliberate actions" (91). Such a perspective is impossible in those psychologies which take a "scientific" approach that differentiates theory and methodology and thereby views individuals as objects rather than as persons. Ossorio urges the importance of disengaging from the "deformities and deficiencies of our traditional intellectual framework," and stresses that an effective psychology grounded in the real world must be "directly responsive to the fact of persons and behavior and to our intellectual, practical, and scientific needs in respect to them and to give these concerns complete priority over any concern for preserving traditional or current scientific or philosophical theories, methodologies, vocabularies, customs, practices, or social norms" (1978, x, xi).

A look at several foundational maxims of descriptive psychology will help clarify the extent to which this approach to human behavior displays a categorically divergent view of persons and the world—a view that we will later see to be particularly useful to literary criticism.

Maxims

1. *The world makes sense, and so do people.* They make sense *now.*
2. *It's one world.* Everything fits together. Everything is related to everything else.
3. *Things are what they are and not something else instead.* And they do not need something else to *make* them what they are.
4. *Don't count on the world being simpler than it has to be.* (Ossorio 1985, 26–28, 21–26)

In the first maxim, Ossorio asserts: "*The world makes sense, and so do people.* They make sense *now.*" In other words, there is significance to the world and to people, and if we have difficulties seeing the connections and "sense," then that does not indicate that the world or persons are not making sense, but rather that *we* are having difficulties ascertaining that meaning. Ossorio and other descriptive psychologists have explained that most psychological approaches to the world superimpose their own perspectives on reality which predetermine problematic behaviors—namely those behaviors that do not fit the preconceived notions of appropriate behavior.

Three major theorists whose work has been enormously influential in literary criticisms informed by psychology are Freud, Adler, and Jung. Mary Kathleen Roberts notes that the overriding problem with these men's views of the world and human behavior is that of limits. In the case of dream interpretation, Roberts sees human behavior potential as being limited by the "narrow range of dream interpretations [which] fit within the constraints of the theory"—regardless whether the reading privileges Freudian instinctual gratification of repressed infantile desires, Adlerian power and superiority as related to lifestyle maintenance, or Jungian psychic integration and wholeness achievement (41–42). Ossorio's position is that such readings of dream interpretation are necessarily limited by their own preconceived boundaries, which determine the sense of dreams. For Ossorio, the world does make sense, but that sense is much more complex than such reductive theories might lead us to believe. And the world makes sense *now*. It is not that the world may make sense at some time in the future but that for now it is too fragmented and chaotic. To the descriptive psychologist, the world does make sense *now*—we simply need to look at it more closely and comprehensively.

This brings us to the second maxim: *"It's one world.* Everything fits together. Everything is related to everything else." In this maxim, Ossorio contrasts a holistic and unified view with the fragmentation and dichotomization evident in most conceptual frameworks of knowledge: "Consider just the dozens of theories of learning, of motivation, of personality, of psychopathology, and so on" (1985, 27). The descriptive psychological approach counters the "technical frameworks of scientific theories [with] common sense" (27). We do know that the world is one, and that everything does fit together, albeit differentially and multifariously. This fairly obvious point (particularly evident in our shrinking global "village" of postmodernity) is considered essential by descriptive psychologists to their understandings of clients and client relationships in the world. Connections and convergences are emphasized instead of focusing on artificially isolated categories and supposedly distinct systems. Such an approach places persons and psychology *in* the world and stresses the importance of interrelationships (Wittgenstein's family resemblances), not only between people, but also between the various conceptual frameworks, rather than seeing these frameworks as necessarily distinct or incompatible. Such connections are patently clear to literary critics, who tend to feel comfortable with such epistemological overlap and regularly draw upon the insights and discoveries of scholars in other fields (e.g., psychology, philosophy, linguistics, biology, etc.).

The third maxim emphasizes the importance of dealing with the world as it is, rather than approaching it by means of conceptual frameworks that impose a globalizing or universalizing theory against which the world and people are evaluated and interpreted. Ossorio states: *"Things are what they are and not something else instead.* And they do not need something else to *make* them what they are." A descriptive psychological approach to persons and the world would first investigate the reality of a person (those language games which define her and in which she takes part), and then interpret her in relation to *her* world. Ossorio criticizes traditional psychology for constructing worlds that are then used to evaluate and understand the real world and persons in the world. Such traditional approaches see people not as active subjects (persons) in the world, but as relatively passive players (pawns, if you will) in the games of psychological theories. The extent to which individuals' lives fit the rules of those games determines the clinical interpretation and evaluation of the individuals' health or lack thereof. And yet, just as theorists construct theoretical worlds, so do individuals construct their own worlds.

Within the bounds of descriptive psychology, the health of individuals is determined by the extent to which their worlds differ from the real world and by their behavioral successes or failures in that real world. Therefore, the individuals' worlds and the real world are investigated individually and comparatively, instead of providing a totalizing conceptual framework which is no less a construct than a person's own world/concept. As Ossorio points out: "In psychology, the traditional solution to the problem of achieving universal applicability is to define the subject matter as something else instead, while at the same time reifying the concepts of one's own framework" (1985, 28).

Not only are psychological theories limited by their own preconceived conceptual boundaries, but they are also distorting in their totalizing assumptions, which are inevitably reductive in their readings of persons in the world. Ossorio's fourth maxim reminds us of the complexities of the real world. *"Don't count on the world being simpler than it has to be."* While simplification is clearly useful in certain cases, poststructural critics have vociferously cried out against the problems inherent in totalizing, absolutist readings of texts. Ossorio's concerns regarding psychological theories parallel such concerns in critical theory, and yet it is all too telling that the criticisms of some postmodern critics nevertheless rely heavily on the work of such traditional theorists in psychology as Freud, Adler, Jung, and Lacan. As we shall see in the final section of this chapter, a reliance upon contemporary descriptive psychology will provide the literary critic with a psychological methodology more suitable to the readings of diverse texts (literary and otherwise).

In order to see how a Wittgensteinian-based psychology could be applied to textual criticism, a brief look at the actual application of descriptive psychology in clinical practice is necessary. Psychoanalytically-based critics have drawn attention to literary works such as Edgar Allan Poe's "The Purloined Letter"—seeing the conjoined processes of deductive and creative thinking as analogous to the psychoanalytic manner by which a client's words, behavior, and dreams are interpreted in order to fit the prescribed framework (be that more traditionally Freudian or more poststructurally Lacanian). The descriptive psychologist, unlike the psychoanalytically-based critic, does not begin with a particular conceptual framework against which a text or client is evaluated. While the descriptive psychologist does look for patterns, a preconceived pattern or model is not superimposed upon the facts. Instead, the facts are closely observed in order to arrive at patterns *from* the facts. As Carolyn Allen Zeiger explains: "It is a matter of recognizing the pattern that fits the facts or what pattern the facts make, NOT fitting the data to the pattern" (175). First, one observes and describes, then one critiques both what is observed and the observations themselves (178). As Zeiger notes, this model is an observational one, as distinct from the sort of inferential model seen in Poe's short story or in the Sherlock Holmes stories.

One literary detective whose work seems to fit the descriptive psychological method is Agatha Christie's Miss Marple: "Her way of operating or thinking is not making tight logical inferences to make accurate predictions. . . . Her focus is on making sense out of people's behavior, what people do and why they're doing it" (Zeiger 170–171). As Zeiger explains, Miss Marple seems to follow the commonsensical view of the world embodied in Ossorio's maxims. The world may be strange, but nevertheless it does make sense. There are several specific elements of Miss Marple's method of solving mysteries:

1. She simply engages people in ordinary conversation.
2. Her self-presentation is innocuous.
3. She is a keen and constant observer.
4. She steps into and joins the person's world, and forms a relationship with that person.
5. She listens attentively, understands, and demonstrates her understanding and appreciation of the person's position or situation.
6. She elicits people's reasons for cooperating, and she acts on those reasons.
7. And she knows her limits. (Zeiger 161–168)

Miss Marple, like the descriptive psychologist, works to find the patterns which exist within a person's world as the means for solving the mystery.

How does this method work clinically? Since descriptive psychology holds that individuals, peoples, and cultures construct and maintain worlds, the descriptive psychologist first works to discover and understand a client's world, and then works to assist the client to reconstruct the client's world as a means toward achieving greater behavior potential. As Mary Kathleen Roberts notes: "The objects, processes, events, and states of affairs in the real world provide us not only with possibilities, but also with limitations on what we can and cannot do successfully" (19). However, these limitations may be real (as in the case of a stated job requirement which the applicant has not met) or merely perceptual. The descriptive therapist helps the client perceive the world in ways that provide alternative possibilities previously unrecognized: "To the extent that the client can share the new way of seeing the therapist offers, it becomes potentially real that the world might be that way. To the extent that the client acts on this reformulation, the world and his place in it are changed" (Roberts 26–27).

Two techniques used to discover the client's world are dream interpretation and mutual storytelling. These strategies are also used as methods of reconstructing the client's world as a means of increasing the client's perceived and real behavior potential. Insofar as literary criticism is concerned, both the strategies of descriptive observation and world construction/reconstruction will be seen as patently useful for close readings of literary texts.

A Descriptive Literary Criticism

WHAT A RELIANCE upon both Wittgenstein's philosophy of psychology and the developments of descriptive psychology signifies for literary criticism is a new method of psychological criticism that is rooted in literary worlds rather than in the preconceived frameworks of Freudian, Jungian, or Lacanian theoretics. Of course, this is not to say that such approaches are without their uses, nor that they are incorrect. The problems with such preconceived theories lie in their actual limits, which preclude their aspirations towards any sort of totalizing absolutism. If we follow the lead of Wittgenstein and descriptive psychologists, we will ground our criticism and theory in the real world of literary texts. As Wittgenstein points out:

> One cannot guess how a word functions. One has to *look at* its use and learn from that.
> But the difficulty is to remove the prejudice which stands in the way of doing this. It is not a *stupid* prejudice. (PI, 340)

Wittgenstein underscores the importance of focusing first on the words as they are used. And while our primary focus is on the word, this is not to say that we are advocating a return to either a New Critical or deconstructive privileging of the text. For Wittgenstein, the word only has meaning when it is in use. We could thoroughly study an engine that is idling and never discover its actual purpose. A Wittgensteinian-based criticism starts with the word in use (the word as spoken, the sentence and passage in its context, the text in the world) and attempts to arrive at a relatively clear and complete description of the word, noting its language games and family resemblances. What is avoided is the imposition of preconceived theories upon the text. However, close investigations into a particular text might, in fact, indicate that a particular theoretical framework (say a Lacanian semiotic reading) might illuminate the text most efficaciously. But we do not start with the framework and then apply it to the text. As Wittgenstein reminds us, we must remove these prejudices—but that is not to say that the prejudices are "stupid" or without their appropriate uses.

A look at how a descriptively-based psychological criticism would open up a text can best be seen in an actual example. But first, several elements of such a method need to be delineated. Following both Wittgenstein's aphoristic style and Ossorio's brief maxims, certain facts informing a psychologically-oriented descriptive criticism may be noted:

1. The real world, persons' worlds, and textual worlds are different yet overlapping categories.
2. There are real objective texts, just as there is a real world. (Each individual text presents its own distinct textual world.)
3. A person who reads a text brings it into his or her own world.
4. The critical process begins with observations and investigations.
5. Criticism consists of constructing and reconstructing worlds.
6. Readers/critics perceive and interpret textual aspects and facts.
7. The limits of a critic's view determine the possible range of his or her criticism.

While a detailed discussion of each of these critical facts is beyond the bounds of this chapter, a brief explanation of each is necessary.

The real world, persons' worlds, and textual worlds are different yet overlapping categories. We have already seen the difference between the real world (defined by Ossorio as the world that we *all* live in and are a part of) and persons' worlds (the worlds persons perceive themselves to be a part of). The world of a text provides us with a third category that embodies its own distinctive language-game mix and yet necessarily shares language games with person worlds (particularly that of the author) and the real world. In descriptive psychology, dreams and story-telling are used clinically as descriptive tools that not only represent the client's world, but also can serve as means for therapeutic world reconstruction (Roberts 26–41). It is the case that a writer creates a work of literature out of her own world; however, the limits of the writer's world are not necessarily the limits of the world of the text. Literature is not merely a representation of the real world, nor is it merely a depiction of the writer's world. There is a reality to a work of literature (or any type of artistic creation) that extends beyond the bounds of either the author's world or the real world. Of course, the extent to which a work of literature diverges from the person world of the writer varies from case to case. Certain works are grounded in the reality of the writer, while others seem to expand beyond those bounds.

The second fact builds upon these distinctions between world categories in its acknowledgement that *there are real objective texts, just as there is a real world, and that each individual text presents its own distinct textual world.* Even though a work of literature is created by a person living in the world and therefore reflects the respective person world and real worlds of the writer, nevertheless, the completed work (like a birthed baby) takes on a life of its own—albeit significantly informed by its creative worlds of origin. And just as there is a real world from which a person constructs his world, there is a textual world from which a critic constructs her critical world. And this critical world is the domain of the critic or reader—the subject of the third fact: namely, that *a person who reads a text brings it into his or her own world*. This is not to say that a text that is read is completely constrained by the bounds of the reader's or critic's world, but simply that, in the reading process, the reader must be capable of engaging with the text. Wittgenstein notes the importance of such engagement when he writes that "there are problems I never get anywhere near, which do not lie in my path or are not part of my world" (CV, 9e). In other words, the reader must have some language games in common with those of the text in order to be able to enter the text/to bring the text into her world. And this overlap reflects the degree of family resemblance and familiarity between reader and text.

The fourth fact focuses specifically on the critical process: *The critical process begins with observations and investigations*. This fact underscores the empirical beginnings of the critical act. Criticism, as distinct from theory, begins with observations of and investigations into some object (a literary text in the case of literary criticism). Whereas critical theory begins in the realm of the abstract and then works to apply its theoretical constructs to actual cases, literary criticism begins with the real world of actual texts and then works to discern patterns, resemblances, and distinctions that might help readers to enter those texts more readily. In other words, the critic is the individual who creates the signposts and pathways into texts for diverse readers. Hence, the fifth fact: *Criticism consists of constructing and reconstructing worlds*. Just as individuals construct and reconstruct their own worlds (their readings/interpretations of the real world) from day to day, and at times, from moment to moment, so do literary critics construct and reconstruct their critical worlds (their readings of texts). And the critical worlds created by critics are worlds which interrelate and interconnect the real world, persons' worlds (of the critics and authors), and literary textual worlds. This critical process of world construction is built upon the framework of a critic's observations of a text, her recognitions of patterns, resemblances, and distinctions, and her interpretation of the significance of these aspects of the text.

The sixth fact emphasizes that what the critic works with is not the actual text itself, but rather the aspects of the text perceived by the critic: *Readers/critics perceive and interpret textual aspects and facts*. Jastrow's famous duck-rabbit picture, discussed by Wittgenstein in the *Philosophical Investigations*, can help clarify this sixth fact. The duck-rabbit picture is a drawing which can be "seen as" either a duck or a rabbit depending on how the perceiver looks at it. The existence of the picture is a fact. That it can be seen as a duck or a rabbit is a fact. However, what one *sees it as* represents the aspect of the picture that one *sees.*[3] Wittgenstein explains that what we "perceive in the dawning of an aspect is not a property of the object [in this case the duck-rabbit picture], but an internal relation between it and other objects" (PI, 212e). In other words, we see/perceive actual objects and events in the real world, but this is a different (albeit related) process from that of perceiving relations between objects and seeing them as something else (e.g., seeing the duck-rabbit picture as the representation of a duck). As Wittgenstein points out, " 'When I read a poem or narrative with feeling, surely something goes on in me which does not go on when I merely skim the line for information.'—What processes am I alluding to?—The sentences have a different *ring.* I pay careful attention to my intonation. Sometimes a word has the wrong intonation, I emphasize it too much or too little" (PI, 214e). The skimming of the line is the process of perception, of seeing. The reading with feeling involves both processes of perceiving the words and seeing them in a certain way. This is the critical process of seeing textual facts (the words) and textual aspects (the words in a certain way).

The seventh fact addresses those constraints which establish the boundaries circumscribing both the perceptual and interpretive ranges of a critic's textual reading: *The limits of a critic's view determine the possible range of his or her criticism.* To return to the relatively less complex case of a person, a person's world is circumscribed by the real boundaries of the real world and by the constructed boundaries created by the person's concept of the world. The boundaries of these two worlds (real and constructed) are analogous to the boundaries of critical worlds. The critic's world is circumscribed by the textual and real boundaries of a textual world and by the constructed boundaries created by her concept of the textual world she is critiquing. This critical world is more complex than persons' worlds in that additional levels of remove from the real world are involved in the critical reading of a person's literary depiction of his world. The predominant worlds that delimit the boundaries of any critical endeavor include the real world (as foundational to all other worlds of human construction), the writer's world (here I will note, but not discuss, the possible differentiation between the writer's person world and author world—both of which are brought to bear on his created literary work), the textual world, and the critical world (both the real/constructed world of criticism and the world of the individual critic).

With this explanation of several facts governing the critical process from a descriptively-based psychological approach, we can now turn to the manner in which these facts might be applied in actual cases of literary criticism. One primary, and crucial, condition for this new psychological entry into literary texts is that the critic must begin her reading with observations that are not constrained by a preconceived interpretive theory the text is presumed to fit. Regarding the clinical use of dream interpretation, Roberts notes:

> Each theory preempts the kinds of problems a person may be recognized as solving. If a person takes a particular theory seriously and remains within the givens of the theory in interpreting dreams, he will have an unnecessary limitation on his behavior potential because only a narrow range of dream interpretations will fit within the constraints of the theory. (42)

Accordingly, the critic must not limit her initial observations or readings, and thereby miss potentially meaningful patterns beyond the bounds of a particular theoretical approach. Especially in light of the complex web of constraints prescribed upon the literary world of a text and upon the person world of a critic, a descriptively-based criticism rejects the additional constraints of preconceived theories as problematically premature in their proscriptive impositions. Only after the process of observation and investigation does the descriptive critic consider possible fits between the literary text and particular critical theories. But such an informed connection cannot be drawn until the critic is sufficiently familiar with the diverse language games in which both text and theories participate.

Once such a familiarity has been achieved or discerned by the critic, then the move towards a critical evaluation can take place. The evaluative process of literary criticism involves axiological determinations regarding a text's successes and failures. From a psychologically-oriented descriptive approach, a critic would evaluate a text with regard to its successful participation in its respective language games (a participation that determines the readability of a text—in other words, the possibility of ready engagement with the text by readers through their participation in those language games played out by/in the text) and the degree to which the literary work is constrained by the limits of the real world and person (author) world language games (limits that would constrain entry into the text by readers from cultures and times different from those of the author/text). A specific example will help illuminate this process and how it can provide an alternative psychological reading of diverse texts.

A Textual Case Study

THE PARTICULAR TEXT I have chosen is a poem by Navajo poet Luci Tapahonso, "Last Year the Piñons Were Plentiful" (*A Breeze Swept Through*). In investigating the critical possibilities of a descriptive psychological approach towards a poem whose language games are categorically divergent from those of most texts read psychologically, we will see that psychological readings of texts can be extended to a wide range of literary works—perhaps to any literary text. Several sections of the poem follow:

> and it made no sense right from the beginning
> (the blue moonlight slid down the long center curve of his back
> as he got up to take a drink of water)
>
> ·
>
> i have no choice, she told herself
> leaving her nightgown on the floor
> and her husband waiting at lunch
>
> ·
>
>   they left on the dark horse towards two grey hills
>   late in the afternoon
>   and weren't seen again that spring.
> it doesn't make sense, her husband said,
> she seemed happy.
> but happiness had nothing to do with it
>   and years from now
>   her grandchildren will understand, saying
>   back then, those things
>   always happened.
>   that was last year, the piñons were large
>   and the winter—so cold, so cold
>   beneath toadlena mountain,
>   the white desert
>   shining with snow. (26-27)

In taking a specifically psychological approach into Tapahonso's poem, the descriptive critic acknowledges the fact that the poem is primarily a product of Tapahonso's person world and, as such, participates in those language games which are a part of Tapahonso's world. As we have seen, persons' worlds are differentiable from the real world. Accordingly, a descriptive psychological criticism investigates not only the real world language games played out in "Last Year the Piñons Were Plentiful," but also the person world language games of Tapahonso evidenced in the poem. And the recognition of Tapahonso's psychology in her poem assists the critic's investigations into the distinctive psychology of the poem (its textual world).

Certainly a recognition of the poem as part of the Navajo language game is crucial in any meaningful critical reading. As Ossorio notes:

"Every human behavior is *essentially* the historical realization of cultural patterns" (1983, 16). Literary texts as the products of human behavior are also historical realizations of cultural patterns or language games. Therefore, knowledge of those patterns and language games is fundamental to any critical evaluation of texts participating in those games. Among many other elements in the Navajo language game or culture is a tradition of teaching stories, myths, histories. These stories, which partake of the mythical and the historical, convey to the listener a sense of his or her place in the world as a Navajo, as a human, as a man or woman; and this place is made specific in lessons regarding how one is to live, be, walk in the world.

One recurrent theme in these teaching stories, myths, and histories centers around the topic of marital infidelity. These stories, found in both the oral tradition and in more recent literary works, do not exhibit a postmodern acceptance of such behavior as beneficial to either the individuals or to the community.[4] Throughout Navajo literature, adultery is presented as problematic, as dangerous to the individual's own well-being (physically and spiritually) and to the cohesiveness of the community—the stability of the family being seen as essential for community stability. However, this disparagement of adultery is interestingly conjoined with a realistic awareness of the weaknesses and imperfections of human beings in the world (yes, adultery is to be avoided, and yes, it will nevertheless occur). Of course, this recognition of the existence of adultery is not tantamount to any sort of approval of such behavior—simply the recognition of human frailty, and adultery as one manifestation of such frailty.

A second element of the Navajo worldview which is essential in approaching Tapahonso's poem is the nonphallocentricity of Navajo culture. This is not to say that men are valued any less than women within the tribal worldview, but rather that the participation of men *and* women in community affairs is seen as necessary to the well-being of individuals, families, and the tribe. A corollary to this is that sexual relations are also not gendered within a Navajo worldview—hence, there are stories, myths, and histories that focus on the infidelity of men and women. Unlike most Western cultures, for the Navajo, a woman's infidelity is not less acceptable than a man's. Both are analogously problematic.

As this brief look at Navajo culture demonstrates, the descriptive critic must gain sufficient familiarity with the poem's language games of origin in order to be able to enter the poem meaningfully—or, as Wittgenstein puts it, to construct pathways or bridges between critic and text. Of course, a reading of the real world of the Navajo is not identical to the Navajo world of Luci Tapahonso. This admission points out the strength of the psychologically-oriented descriptive critic.

Whereas New Historicists and cultural critics focus on the real world surrounding a text (thereby investigating real world language games which may or may not participate in the actual work of literature), this psychological approach acknowledges that a focus on the real world is inadequate and that the critic must go deeper—into the psychology of the writer's person world and then into the psychology of the text itself.

While a close critical reading of Tapahonso's poem is beyond the bounds of this chapter, several aspects of the poem's psychology or world can be noted. First, the poem's world is not restricted to the specific scenario depicted in the poem. Throughout the poem, there are markers which point outward from the one specific case to earlier historical times and other analogous cases ("back then, those things / always happened"), to the future ("years from now"), and to the reader in the very personal, almost confidential, tone of the familiar storyteller confiding private information to the listener ("leaving her nightgown on the floor / and her husband waiting at lunch"). Here we see that the poem has an open, inviting demeanor—an openness or inclusivity further demonstrated in its acceptance of the wife's (and we assume our own) imperfections ("her grandchildren will understand").

Tapahonso's poem demonstrates a high degree of trust—opening to the reader cultural and personal themes still problematic for most contemporary readers. And yet, the poem's vulnerability is not without protective markers which clearly identify the poem within its Navajo context (reservation geography—toadlena mountains, sage and rabbit-brush, gallup and newcomb, two grey hills and piñons; and cultural indicators—horses and a trading post)—a context that serves to prevent any ethnocentric misreadings that would attempt to ignore or remove the poem's cultural identity. And just in case a reader/critic might be tempted to overlook these protective markers, Tapahonso slyly provides an example of such error or ignorance (willful or otherwise) in the confused husband who simply doesn't understand why his wife had the affair, who doesn't see how cold it was that winter ("it doesn't make sense, her husband said, / she seemed happy. / but happiness had nothing to do with it"). And like the husband, criticism will continue to miss the points of connection within and between works of literature until efforts are made to really get to know those works.

Instead of focusing exclusively through narrow theoretical orientations (like the husband who misreads his wife's behavior in terms of his own world rather than in light of her own), it is time for critics to redirect their attentions to new methodologies which are more responsive to a wider range of literary texts. Peter Brooks is correct in his assertion that "psychoanalysis matters to us as literary critics because it stands as a constant reminder that the attention to form . . . [is an] attempt to draw the symbolic and fictional map of our place in existence" (348).

But such a map will not assist our travels into literary works beyond the limits of our psychoanalytic worlds. For Wittgenstein, the difficulty with psychological theories is not that they are without their uses, but that the assumption of their global applicability is false. Psychological readings can open up any literature, including American Indian literatures—but not without such a methodological expansion of the boundaries of psychological criticism. And this is where a descriptive method of psychological entry is essential—particularly if we are, in fact, interested in noticing the winter cold and the plentifulness of the piñons.

3 Theoria as Praxis, or Shifting Mythologies: Wittgenstein and Feminist Literary Criticism

FEMINISM IN THE POSTMODERN ERA presents, in itself, the very site and sign of the struggles of an age unsure of itself and yet desperately attempting to locate and establish (fabricate?) nonoppressive discursive structurings within society. Poststructuralism has proffered certain theoretical and methodological responses useful to the dismantling (deconstructing) of phallocentric totalities previously believed to possess absolute and objective status. The problem posed for feminism is that even the very existence of feminism, as a meaningful locus for a critique of phallocentrism, is called into question by contemporary postmodern theoretics. Chris Weedon begins her volume, *Feminist Practice and Poststructuralist Theory,* with the assertion: "Feminism is a politics . . . directed at changing existing power relations between women and men in society" (1). Herein lies the essential conflict for a postmodern feminism: the poststructural dismantling of the various discursive practices in our society is a process that questions all discursive structures. Even feminism is accordingly disrupted and called into question. And yet, the conflict between an essentialist and phallogocentric positivism, on the one hand, and poststructural criticisms, on the other, can be, if not resolved, certainly surmounted. A reliance on the later philosophy of Ludwig Wittgenstein provides a language and methodology for resolving the "conceptual confusions" that arise both within and between diverse critical and theoretical approaches to literature.

Perhaps Wittgenstein's greatest concern was the extent to which our "conceptual confusions"—most notably those that assume a perceptual and evaluative objectivity—blind us to the reality of our world. What Wittgenstein repeatedly stresses is that our assumptions of analytic objectivity are more accurately our objectifications of the world (and people) and as such reflect more our own psychology than actual facts about the world. The problem is objectification—not a particular type of objectification, but the practice in and of itself. For example, Wittgenstein conjectures that it is "meaningless to say 'there are humans who see'" since we, generally, do not objectify ourselves or that which we have established as normative. However, "it is not meaningless to say there are humans who are blind" (RC, III. 331), since we assert our own subjectivity in our objectification of some other. As Wittgenstein notes, we describe our own seeing capability by differentiating ourselves from others and establishing our capacity as the privileged norm: "There are people who behave like you and me, and not like that man over there, the blind one" (RC, III. 334). This sort of differentiation and objectification is foundational to the larger societal language games with which we have been reared—particularly those of a misogynistic phallogocentrism. But as feminists, we are equally culpable when we recreate an objectifying language game after our own fashion. The game does not need refining, but overhauling. Perhaps, as Wittgenstein urges for philosophy, an entirely new game is needed.

But the call for a categorically new game is a dangerous one. It does not mean learning to play the old game better or even differently, but learning new rules of play altogether. And such required learning tends to be disconcerting since it points us forward into uncharted seas and lands. As Wittgenstein tells us, "we must always be prepared to learn something totally new" (RC, I. 15). What this means for literary criticism is that a revisionist gynocriticism, privileging those texts written by and about women, while important in redressing the burdensome limitations of an earlier "phallocriticism," nevertheless repeats the same sort of limits only differentially. The problems inherent in any set determination of canonically approved texts exist regardless of the criteria (or underlying grammar) used in establishing that canon. Is a categorically new literary criticism and theory possible, one that avoids the troubling boundaries of modernist and postmodernist criticisms while being more responsive to the changing needs of readers and texts? As we shall see in this chapter, a Wittgensteinian-based literary criticism points us towards uncharted territory as criticism becomes less the insecure assertions of critical subjectivity and privilege and evolves into more humble and yet more secure signposts guiding readers' ways into literature.

Descriptive Boundaries

IF WE ARE to approach a text in the spirit of Wittgensteinian investigations, our methodology must include our entry into the discursive relations of the text as manifested in its language games. Such an orientation grounded in the respective language games of a text enables the critic to move beyond the questionable limiting constructs that artificially divide text from context, reading from interpretation, and critic from reader—pat divisions that obscure the meaningful overlap (useful or problematic) of categories that are by definition inextricably linked and interwoven. Wittgensteinian philosophy provides the literary critic with both a terminology and methodology with which to begin to establish the boundaries of the respective language games in which literary texts and criticisms participate as a means of discriminating between more and less useful fits between text and critical approach. Most important insofar as this discussion is concerned is the Wittgensteinian concept of limits. For Wittgenstein, the concept of limits does not possess a sense of devaluation; rather, it indicates definitional or otherwise descriptive boundaries beyond which one language game becomes another. For example, from a feminist perspective, one would differentiate feminist discursive structures from those we might term phallogocentric.

As is the case for all postmodern theories and criticisms, there is no one correct feminist method or stance, but rather a diverse and changing range of feminisms. As this chapter demonstrates, these divergent strands of feminism are, nevertheless, powerfully linked as members of the larger language games of feminist scholarship and feminism per se. Wittgenstein's discussion of "family resemblances" within and across language games proves enormously helpful in clarifying the diverse ways by which literary theories, criticisms, and texts interrelate foundationally (on the level of grammar) and superficially (in the actual behavior of play). Feminist discursive structurings present a corrective revisioning and reordering of those societal discourses which assert a patriarchally hegemonic view of the world, often held to be the only correct view of the world. The term "phallogocentrism" points to the patriarchal bias of such discourses as evident in joining phallus and logos in one term. Phallogocentrism epitomizes the dogmatic absolutism of both phallocentric and logocentric language games, which from a feminist standpoint prove to be inextricably linked in a collusive denial of gender difference. The distinction between phallogocentric and feminist discursive structures and practices, in Wittgensteinian terms, demonstrates the limits or borders between these divergent language games.

Postmodernism has undermined the certainty by which we granted objective truth-value to those societal structures now understood to be historically produced and reinforced. From a theoretical standpoint, feminist discursive strategies have successfully decentered patriarchal discourses from their previously privileged status as the only games in town. Postmodern theories have helped us to understand why such games are at best anachronistic, if not the hegemonically elitist tools of oppression they may in fact have been (and all too often continue to be).[1] As we shall see in the course of this chapter, several elements of Wittgenstein's philosophy will clarify our navigation between seemingly contradictory theoretical positions. One clarifying element is the fact that feminist criticism (and any other critical approach) is limited by its preconceived definitional boundaries, and, accordingly, its use-fulness is determined by those boundaries. Only by means of a descrip-tive process of language game recognition and discrimination can critics most usefully differentiate between more and less effective strategies of textual entry and analysis—a process that is essential if criticism is to move beyond the reductive solipsism of both modernist and postmod-ernist theories and criticisms that all too often do little more than pro-vide a textual legitimation of their own epistemologies.

Questions rarely asked, but demanded by a Wittgensteinian ap-proach, include the actual usefulness of a particular approach in/to a particular text, the problematic privileging of the text as a means of critical legitimation, and the extent to which a certain critical reading proves less useful as an opening up of the text and more a psychologi-cally reassuring assertion of critical legitimation, subjectivity, and priv-ilege in the world. If our desire is for feminist (and other) criticisms to enable readers toward more meaningful (i.e., useful for a particular reader at a given moment with regard to a particular text) and accessi-ble entries in/to texts, then the work of literary theorists and critics be-comes more that of a guide or signpost. Rather than as a dominant subject explaining an objectified text to an equally objectified audience, the role of the descriptive (or Wittgensteinian) critic is that of a partici-pant engaging with and in the text's language games—entering the world of the text and taking on the responsibility of enabling other readers to do the same.

Wittgenstein notes that a signpost may dictate a direction that leaves no room for doubt, but that it need not do so (PI, 85). Often a signpost merely indicates a directional option that is open for interpretation and choice by the reader. Wittgenstein explains that rules for language games (such as the underlying critical theories upon which actual criti-cal work is based) are like signposts. The rules (or theories) determine the general direction and define the language games themselves, but the play or applications remains neither completely fixed nor wholly de-terminate:

> Does the sign-post leave no doubt open about the way I have to go? Does it shew which direction I am to take when I have passed it; whether along the road or the footpath or cross-country? But where is it said which way I am to follow it; whether in the di-rection of its finger or (e.g.) in the opposite one?—And if there were, not a single sign-post, but a chain of adjacent ones or of chalk marks on the ground—is there only *one* way of interpreting them? (PI, 85)

For example, in one particular case, the signpost might indicate the usefulness of a radical feminist reading, but this is not to say that a rad-ical feminist pathway might not be taken differentially (e.g., perhaps semiotically, deconstructively, or even psychoanalytically) or that an entirely different direction might be taken. But only through Wittgensteinian descriptive analyses will the critic be enabled to make such discriminations in meaningful ways—namely, in terms of their usefulness.

Insofar as literary critical practice is concerned, the Wittgensteinian language game heuristic is a helpful means towards understanding the significance and value of poststructural critiques of subjectivity (emblematic of the dynamic nature of language games) and feminist assertions of subjectivity (representative of the more constant foundational grammars of those games). Accordingly, the language game heuristic provides us with (1) a language for asserting grounds and certainties that are neither static and essentialistic nor logocentric and patriarchal but organically linked in their inextricable relation to particular language games; (2) a view of literary texts that circumvents the need to define boundaries between some abstracted text and its surrounding context since the language games of a literary work generally cut across such critically imposed boundaries (though they need not always do so); and (3) heightened descriptive power, for when we investigate a work of literature in terms of its language games and family resemblances to (and differences from) other games, both the depth and breadth of our view of the work are increased.

Insofar as feminist criticism is concerned, the Wittgensteinian tools of the language game and family resemblance provide a means by which we can move beyond even the discursive limits of feminist language games to investigate languages and realities in the world that are by definition nonphallogocentric (e.g., the Navajo language game). By and large, feminist theory, criticism, and philosophy present a privileging of woman as a response to prior phallocentric devaluings of woman. Just as postmodernism requires the presence of a modernist discourse for its very existence—an existence we must assume will fade away as it reduces and deconstructs modernism to a groundless and pointless trace, thereby erasing itself—so is feminism codependently interwoven with the very phallocentrism it rejects. Wittgensteinian investigations can enable us to discover, comprehend, and speak about gendered realities that are neither phallocentric nor feminist in their underlying discursive relations. Through the recognition of resemblances between our gendered discourse and the language games of other peoples (e.g., the Navajo), we can discern pathways in/to those games and begin to develop new theory, philosophy, and methodology for categorically new ways of living and being in the world.

Perceptual Boundaries

WITTGENSTEIN REPEATEDLY stresses the importance of our seeing "something that throws new light on the facts" (CV, 39e). Here we see what may be the most vital element of literary criticism, and in particular feminist literary criticism, insofar as a Wittgensteinian orientation is concerned. As Wittgenstein notes: "If we imagine the facts otherwise than as they are, certain language-games lose some of their importance, while others become important. And in this way there is an alteration— a gradual one—in the use of the vocabulary of a language" (OC, 63). Each critical approach to a text (written and lived) provides a particular stance or orientation that enables a reader to perceive aspects of the text which might be missed otherwise, and for Wittgenstein, such perceptual shifts relate to changes in language use and practice in the world. Wittgenstein writes: "It is incredible how helpful a new drawer can be, suitably located in our filing cabinet" (CV, 39e). New drawers for literary critics might be new critical approaches to pursue in relation to works of literature. Wittgenstein stresses that, while we will never be able to remove all of our perceptual limitations, we can be sufficiently aware of them that they do not severely impede our views of the world (or of texts). Alice Jardine underscores that we must first "understand that the strategies available for use against the symbolic function . . . necessarily operate according to different economies in different cultures, even within the hegemony of Western culture, thus affecting *perceived* limits of representation" (229). Wittgenstein anticipated Jardine's concern in his repeated emphasis on the importance of viewing the world from diverse standpoints in order to provide a more complete picture. It is our narrow orientations (theoretical or pragmatic) that continue to limit our perceptions, descriptions, interpretations, and evaluations of literary texts (and other aspects of the world). With regard to philosophy, Wittgenstein tells us,

> I find it important in philosophizing to keep changing my posture, not to stand for too long on *one* leg, so as not to get stiff.
> Like someone on a long up-hill climb who walks backwards for a while so as to revive himself and stretch some different muscles. (CV, 27e)

The feminist implications of this quotation for literary criticism and theory are obvious. Since literary criticism and theory have been almost exclusively male-oriented for so long, it is time that the unused "gynocentric" muscles be stretched and strengthened. This necessitates that what has been ignored, forgotten, and buried be foregrounded in a move to restore balance to the field. The past three decades have seen a tremendous privileging by feminist scholars of works written by and about women. This is what Elaine Showalter termed "gynocriticism." Many forgotten works of women authors have been rediscovered. Male-authored texts have been given alternative readings, and traditional evaluative standards have been called into question. As Linda J. Nicholson notes, feminists "have argued against the supposed neutrality and objectivity of the academy, asserting that claims put forth as universally applicable have invariably been valid only for men of a particular culture, class, and race" (5). Nicholson goes on to explain that feminists have asserted that the claims of reason and objectivity are historically bound and "reflect the values of masculinity" (5). Janet Todd echoes Nicholson's concerns when she asserts that "if theory has taught us anything it is that we are all theorized and that historical discourses of different kinds are never transcendental truths" (137).

Wittgenstein certainly came to believe that such "truths" were, indeed, historically and culturally bound. But Wittgenstein goes even further: he asserts that our readings of the world generally reflect more about ourselves and our own agendas than about those aspects of the world we choose to observe. For example, we might observe a cultural practice that we find different and perhaps even "sinister" ("finstere"). Wittgenstein states: "What is sinister, deep, does not lie in the fact that that is how the history of this practice went, for perhaps it did not go that way; nor in the fact that perhaps or probably it was that, but in what it is that gives me reason to assume it" (RFGB, 16e). For Wittgenstein, we must continually question, and question again, our presuppositions regarding the world (and texts)—especially since it is often the case that even our textual support and evidence proves to be "non-hypothetical" and "psychological" and therefore more meaningful about ourselves and our orientations than about the objects of our observations and criticism (RFGB, 16e). Wittgenstein wants us to discover the world as it is, rather than as one might assume it ought to be. "We want to establish an order in our knowledge of the use of language: an order with a particular end in view; one out of many possible orders; not *the* order" (PI, I, 132).

However, such an awareness of the inherent limitations in any theoretical approach does not resign us to a relativism that denies the possibility of differentiating between more and less useful readings. Since "interpretations by themselves do not determine meaning" (PI, I, 198), and meaning can only be ascertained by looking at a word's use and by removing "the prejudices which stand in the way of doing this" (PI, I, 340), Wittgenstein acknowledges that we can never remove all of our interpretive biases. However, he believes that in order to read a text descriptively and clearly we can (and should) remove those biases which serve as impediments to our investigations and "note" those language games essential to our investigations (PI, I, 654–655), and these language games could include not only those in which the text participates, but also those of our own critical biases.

What this means for a feminist literary criticism is that our methodologies, interpretations, and even the feminist orientation itself must be investigated and questioned as a means of determining to what extent and in regard to what language games feminist inquiry might be most efficacious. Any theoretic, in Wittgenstein's schema, even one which possesses a wide range of usefulness, is potentially suspect in that it imposes its own constraints upon any investigation. When any literary critic approaches a text from a particular standpoint, only those elements within the bounds established by the critical approach are visible to the critic—a condition that has often led to the devaluing of a work which did not sufficiently fit one's theoretical expectations. The works of the metaphysical poets were positively valued within the New Critical framework, while the works of the Romantics were devalued. The deconstructive orientation finds the works of the Romantic poets very suitable for deconstructive analysis, and New Historicism has become influential for interpretations of Renaissance and eighteenth- and nineteenth-century works. However, a Wittgensteinian question would be whether the successes of the various critical approaches make them generally useful for all works of literature. The Wittgensteinian response would be to investigate any work of literature as fully and as closely as possible by means of language-game and family-resemblance recognition and by removing those interpretive strategies or theoretical approaches resistant to the particular text.

Critical Boundaries and Luci Tapahonso's "What I Am"

IN THE ACTUAL critical application of theories, diverse theories prove more or less suitable in certain situations. Each language game provides its own set of discursive practices and rules which determine its larger context, such that, across diverse frameworks, we can see the discursive realities both hailed and bemoaned by various postmodern critics and theorists. The important point raised within this concept of the language game is that particular theoretical approaches are neither essentialistic nor objectively correct for all texts. Certain critical theories and methodologies might prove to be more useful in opening certain literary texts than might be the case for other approaches. The language game analogy allows us to perceive more clearly the fact that any one theoretical approach to the world (or any particular interpretive stance) is necessarily limited and may be inadequate where our desire is to see the world (or a text) and its respective entryways more clearly.

Particular language games may not permit the breadth desired for a certain reading; therefore Wittgenstein's focus on family resemblance proves useful as a means of discussing the relationships which straddle diverse language games. While there are language games which are distinct from other games, it is more likely the case that most language games coincide or overlap with others in various ways. And analogously, elements or participants of language games may take part in more than one language game at one time. To look at a literary example, the poetry of Luci Tapahonso participates in the women's literature language game, the American poetry language game, the American Indian literature language game, and the storyteller language game. Each of these particular language games may share various rules of play with the other games such that a familiarity with one game might facilitate entry into the others.

A brief look at one of Tapahonso's stories can help us to see the value of Wittgensteinian investigations. Tapahonso ends her recent book *Sáanii Dahataa̱, The Women Are Singing: Poems and Stories,* with the short piece, "What I Am." This is the most explicitly self-conscious work in the volume, and yet its revelatory self-consciousness is protected by pathways hidden to readers unfamiliar with the Navajo language game. In other words, the reader is only permitted real entry into Tapahonso's story via certain pathways, such as those of family, matrifocality, tribal unity, tradition, and faith—pathways that represent the underlying grammatical (or foundational) rules that define the Navajo language game as presented in Tapahonso's writing.

The significant concern for the non-Navajo critic is how to approach a literature whose language games are categorically divergent from those language games more familiar to most critics. This is not to say that there is no relational overlap—a condition that is necessary to our entry in/to any text. As Wittgenstein writes, "It is just *another* language game; even though it is related to [it]" (PI, I, 64). But only through our close scrutiny of the language games essential to the critical process (e.g., the language games of the critic's world, the author's world, and the textual world) can we discern those pathways in/to texts most accessible to us. Since it is often the case that critical strategies useful in opening certain texts prove less useful towards other texts, Wittgenstein's emphasis on our own approaches or requirements of those texts is enlightening: "The more narrowly we examine actual language, the sharper becomes the conflict between it and our requirement" (PI, I, 107). Insofar as literary criticism is concerned, the more narrowly we examine the language games actually played by a particular text, the more readily will we be able to discern where our critical methods and theories ("requirements") prove impediments to textual entry.

Postmodern revisionist criticisms (such as cultural, feminist, or New Historicist criticisms) serve to redress the problematic limits of earlier literary approaches, but Wittgensteinian investigations into critical language games might indicate that some texts resistant to earlier criticisms and thereby ignored or devalued might be resistant to revisionist readings as well. The past two decades of feminist scholarship have produced a tremendous amount of criticism on the poetry of Emily Dickinson, but I would argue that the majority of these readings are relatively un-helpful in guiding our entry into the world of Dickinson's very perplex-ing experimental poetry. A slim volume by avant-garde language poet Susan Howe, *My Emily Dickinson*, penetrates Dickinson's work much more deeply by virtue of Howe's greater familiarity with particular language games played out in Dickinson's poetry.[2] It is crucial that feminists investigate those language games participative in literary texts as a means of determining which approaches to take towards those texts—and a feminist reading might not always be the most useful.

One language game in which a feminist assertion of female subjec-tivity is largely unnecessary is the Navajo language game. The Navajo are traditionally matrifocal and matrilineal, with one's maternal rela-tives (representing the clan which gives one birth—indicating a very intimate relational connection) given priority over the paternal (repre-senting the clan one is born for—indicating a greater relational dis-tancing).[3] For the Navajo, a strong sense of self is inextricably linked with a sense of belonging in the world—a relationship with the group that is alien to our "western" dialectical split between individual and group in which the very assertion of subjectivity is contingent upon one's differentiation and dissociation from some "other." This latter type of discursive relationship is not the case for most Native peoples, and may even be seen linguistically. For example, in the Navajo lan-guage ("Dine' bizaad"), both subject and object are contained within the verb via linguistic markers, thereby preventing the relational sepa-ration between subject and object—a linguistic reflection of the rela-tional aspect of Navajo life which describes each individual as connected to all of creation.

Such conversive relations are evident throughout Luci Tapahonso's writing. In *The Women Are Singing*, it is the most explicitly auto-biographical piece that is also the most humble and selfless. Such an assertion of self conjoined with a humble selflessness would prove para-doxical within the bounds of a Western phallogocentric discourse, but in terms of the Navajo language game, Tapahonso's writing is both hers and not hers. As she notes in the introduction to the book, "This writ-ing, then, is not 'mine,' but a collection of many voices that range from centuries ago and continue into the future" (xii). This recognition is categorically different from the acknowledgements commonly found today in most published volumes (although there is a family resem-blance). Tapahonso's poetry and prose are inextricably bound up with a conscious sense of self that embodies all of who she is—an "all" very abstruse for non-Native peoples to comprehend. We cannot approach Tapahonso's writing directly by following our own critical approaches, but must follow the pathways she provides for us.

The final story in the book, "What I Am," appears to be a collection of three different stories, each related to different members of the Tapahonso family. The first focuses on a night in 1935 when Kinłichíi'nii Bitsí's son Prettyboy arrived home late the day before she died. The second story (the longest of the three) tells about Prettyboy's death in 1968 and then retells the story of Kinłichíi'nii Bitsí's death from the perspective of her daughter, Prettyboy's sister. The final (and shortest) story begins: "Nineteen hundred eighty-seven. The great-grandaughter of Kinłichíi'nii Bitsí said . . ."; then follows the great granddaughter's (Tapahonso's) story about her trip to Paris. In order to comprehend Tapahonso's story, we must first hear the stories of those who came before. This requirement (or rule of this particular language game) is further underscored in the middle story—for to understand Prettyboy and his death, we must hear again the story of the death of his mother, Kinłichíi'nii Bitsí. In this rendition, the story is told by Tapahonso's mother (as it had been told to her by her mother), bringing the story closer to Tapahonso, who ends the final story with her return from Paris to her mother and grandmother.

Tapahonso's "What I Am" begins with her elder relatives on the maternal side and, after what seems like merely a brief aside (the trip to Paris), returns to the mother and grandmother. "What I Am" takes us full circle to return where we began as we learn that entry into the story requires not a linear discursive approach, but a more roundabout conversive style evident not only in the actual conversations within the story, but even in Tapahonso's conversive narrative style, as if she is telling us her story comfortably over a cup of coffee back in Shiprock, New Mexico. Regarding her imminent trip to Europe, she writes, "I was nervous and couldn't sleep. I felt like changing my mind, but my mother had already spent all that money. She promised she wouldn't cry at the airport, then she did. I know that my little sister teased her about it" (91). And yet in these few words, Tapahonso comfortably welcomes her reader into her world of the everyday Navajo—not the problematized and nostalgized Native American worlds depicted by mixed-blood writers such as Louise Erdrich, Paula Gunn Allen, or Gerald Vizenor. There is an ingenuity about Tapahonso's writing that is refreshing. Her directness and honesty open up her world to her readers, provided we make the initial efforts to approach that world and language game. It is the necessity of our own critical efforts that might mislead the reader into misconstruing "What I Am" as either simplistic and superficial or indirect and wandering. But such misinterpretations would devalue the literature simply by virtue of its failure to play our Western language games.

We read that the grandmother told her daughter, "Having a mother is everything. Your mother is your home" (91)—ideas crucial to the Navajo language game and poignant to the children, grandchildren, and great-grandchildren of Kinłichíi'nii Bitsí, whose premature death informs their lives and worlds down to the identity of her great-granddaughter. The significance of Kinłichíi'nii Bitsí's death is such that it has profoundly informed generation upon generation of her family. The Navajo say that those who live to old age are blessed. Kinłichíi'nii Bitsí was not blessed in this way. Her daughter, Tapahonso's grandmother, tells the story of her mother's death. She recounts the story of her brother Prettyboy's arrival at her home with the news about their mother:

> Finally, as he came up to our hogan, I went out and I could see that he was crying. He wasn't watching where he was going. The horse led my brother who was crying. I watched him, and then he saw me. I called out, "Shínaaí, my older brother!" He got off the horse and ran to me, crying out, "Shideezhí, nihimá adin. My younger sister, our mother's gone!" My heart fell. We cried. The wind stopped blowing and we went inside. (90)

In one brief paragraph, Tapahonso communicates volumes about the unnatural trauma of Kinłichíi'ni Bitsí's death. We read that "the wind stopped blowing" and that Prettyboy was led by his horse. For the Navajo, this ordering of the horse (an animal) controlling Prettyboy (a human) would point to the unnatural conditions and results of Kinłichíi'nii Bitsí's death.

An event that can help explain the profundity of this short passage occurred a number of years ago in a beginning Navajo language class. The teacher was asking us questions about our relatives. When she got to me, she asked where my mother lived. Since my mother is dead, I replied, "Shimá adin." The teacher, an older Navajo woman, looked at me directly (not standard procedure for the Navajo) with an expression that spoke volumes to me. She then said very gently, "Susan, you never say that in Navajo. One always has a mother." The words I spoke, similar to those uttered by Prettyboy, 'nihimá adin," indicate what in our world would be akin to serious psychological problems, for without a mother one is out of balance with oneself and with the world (Mother Earth). For the remainder of my semesters studying the Navajo language, I would speak of my living mothers (step-mother, older sister, aunt). This story helps us to enter the Navajo language game as Prettyboy's words ("nihimá adin") become infinitely more profound and ominous.

Kinłichíi'nii Bitsí's life and death are essential to our entry into Tapahonso's writing—perhaps important elements in her becoming a poet as a means of restoring the balance of time and life by giving Kinłichíi'nii Bitsí her due time in this world through her great-granddaughter's words. Only after we have gotten to know Kinłichíi'nii Bitsí, her son, daughter, and granddaughter are we able to begin to approach Tapahonso in the realization that the three stories are her story—

all necessary to our entry into Tapahonso's reality. We cannot know Tapahonso without approaching her through the interwoven language games of her family, her people, her history. Tapahonso ends her tale of a trip to Paris:

> It was while I stood on top of the Eiffel Tower [where, Tapahonso previously tells us, she prayed] that I understood that who I am is my mother, her mother, and my great-grandmother, Kintichíi'nii Bitsí. It was she who made sure I got through customs [having taken corn pollen for prayers] and wasn't mugged in Paris. When I returned, my grandmother was at the airport. She hugged me tightly. My mother stood back, then came forward and held me. I was home. (92)

And here Tapahonso comes full circle, the circle complete with daughter, mother, grandmother together, ending a volume of poetry and story that originates with Tapahonso's elders. In fact, she writes, "I view this book as a gift from my mother and father, both of whom embody the essence of Navajo elders—patience, wisdom, humor, and courage" (xii).

In these few pages, we have entered the Navajo world of Luci Tapahonso's writing via familiarity with certain rules of the Navajo language game—rules that facilitate our critical engagement. This is not to say that these are the only rules useful for such engagement, but that some language-game familiarity is crucial to any meaningful criticism. To prematurely superimpose the grid of a critical approach or theory upon Tapahonso's story would be to impose limits that can only lessen her work by hindering deeper entry into the actual language games played out in the text. Wittgenstein's metaphor of an idle engine strongly speaks against any interpretive theory that does not firmly place a work in its historical, authorial, and literary context.[4] Neither a critical theory nor a literary text can be properly evaluated when divorced from its actual use in the world. But more importantly, our criticism must include our entry into those textual worlds to avoid the sort of distancing objectification Wittgenstein counsels against in philosophy.

Feminist Boundaries

FEMINIST SCHOLARS have argued against such problematic limitations. In fact, the phallocentric biases inherent in much literary theory has led many feminist critics and writers to express a strong distaste or distrust for theory per se, seeing it as yet another hegemonic tool of the fathers used to devalue those works not firmly situated within the boundaries prescribed by particular interpretive constructs. In her essay,

"The Politics of Poetics," Tey Diana Rebolledo presents a direct critique of theory: "I personally find it difficult to have theory be what dictates what we find in our literature. I prefer to have the literature speak for itself and as a critic try to organize and understand it. Perhaps from a more open perspective our own theoretical critical analysis will arise, rather than finding the theory first and imposing it upon the literature" (350). While Rebolledo does not provide us with a clear methodology for permitting a text to "speak for itself," we can readily see strong parallels to a Wittgensteinian approach. However, a completely "open perspective" (entirely free from theoretical bias) may not be possible. Rather, what does seem possible is to achieve a "more open perspective" freed from the larger barriers to our investigations.

The criticisms against theory have been voiced most strongly by third world feminist writers and critics who have found much of contemporary theory inadequate in its distortions and misreadings of third world texts. Bell Hooks emphasizes that "discursive practices and the production of knowledge are easily appropriated by existing systems of domination" (132), and rather than providing a means of opening up a text, serve to discredit and devalue those works which do not readily fit the prescribed (and valued) discourse. Regarding Chicana literature, Rebolledo stresses that "our critical discourse should come from within, within our cultural and historical perspective" (354), and Barbara Christian, an African-American critic, states that theory must be rooted in practice—otherwise "it becomes prescriptive, exclusive, elitist" (340). Both of these concerns, the necessity for critical inquiry to take into account the "cultural and historical perspective" of writer, text, and critic, and Christian's proscription against prescriptive theorizing, reflect the very concerns of descriptive critical investigations. Jane Marcus explicitly states that such a process of contextualization has strengthened her critical arguments and "reinforced [her] commitment to the historical" (1988, 288). What Wittgensteinian philosophy offers to such a "commitment to the historical" is a methodology that is not only responsive to the diverse aspects of texts, but, more importantly, a practice that refuses to critique and evaluate texts from a distance—rather choosing to enter those texts by means of a respectful and attentive familiarity with the texts' language games. As Rebolledo urges, a criticism that comes "from within." This is not to say that only Native peoples can read and interpret Native American Indian literature (or, in the case of Rebolledo, Chicana literature, or of Hooks, African-American literature), but that critical responsibility, qua Wittgenstein, demands sufficient textual language familiarity of the critic—regardless of her cultural background. Otherwise, as Wittgenstein warns, "the *deep* aspect of this matter readily eludes us" (PI, I, 387).

This is where Wittgenstein's discussion of family resemblance proves useful, particularly in regard to critical entry of seemingly impenetrable texts (perhaps Native American Indian literature for non-Native readers and critics). Family resemblance is a concept that specifically deals with the crossing of limits, the blurring (and clarifying) of categories, and the relationships between language games and between the participants of language games. Many feminist critics have noted the necessity of recognizing the diversity of feminisms. This recognition acknowledges both the differences which exist between diverse feminist language games and the interconnections joining all feminisms under the larger discursive structure of a political response to a patriarchal hegemonics. A reliance on the concept of family resemblance (and difference) provides us with a terminology and a perspective that consciously address critical concerns regarding issues of subjectivity and difference in the world and in literature. Wittgenstein begins his discussion of family resemblance in the early sections of the *Philosophical Investigations* by clarifying that different language games need not be completely distinct from one another and may, in fact, overlap to the extent that they appear to be the same or similar (either on the foundational level of grammatical rules or on the surface level of play or application and aspects or appearance).

The example used by Wittgenstein is that of "the proceedings that we call 'games'" (PI, I, 66). He notes the diverse usages of the term "game"—from ball games to card games to chess and Olympic games. While some elements of particular games are common to others (e.g., winning and losing), this is not to say that such elements are common to all (not all games involve winning and losing). Wittgenstein points out that, often, the boundaries surrounding and dividing language games may be indistinct or overlapping (as in the case, perhaps, of Gloria Anzaldúa's use of the term "mestiza" to refer to individuals of mixed cultural heritage). Wittgenstein writes that when we look at different language games, we

> see how similarities crop up and disappear.
> And the result of this examination is: we see a complicated network of similarities overlapping and criss-crossing: sometimes overall similarities, sometimes similarities of detail. (PI, I, 66)

By means of a further example, Wittgenstein points to the overlapping fibers of spun thread. While there are diverse fibers interwoven, there may not even be one common fibre extending throughout the thread's entire length (PI, I, 67), but we would still recognize the unbroken thread as one piece.

Analogously, we might look at women's literature as one very encompassing and complex language game, and yet we might not be able to discern any one specific thread common to all women's literature, even though we would recognize each work as participatory in the larger game. For example, a feminist critic with no familiarity with the Navajo language game, might find entry into Tapahonso's story through the pathways of family resemblance—perhaps noting the prevalence of women in the text, the privileged status of the mother, and the respect accorded women by the men. While such insights might not have the depth available to a critic with greater familiarity with the language games participant in the text, nevertheless, such relational resemblance provides a useful means of entry into the text. Of course, such readings are limited by virtue of their own preconceived critical boundaries— boundaries that are useful where there is sufficient grammatical overlap with the textual language games.

Mae Gwendolyn Henderson argues the importance of developing a model for literary criticism that "seeks to account for racial difference within gender identity and gender difference within racial identity" (117). The model she discusses relies heavily on "Mikhail Bakhtin's notion of dialogism and consciousness" with the attendant effect of a discursive heteroglossia (118). Henderson points out that, for her, a feminist analysis of literary texts must include both the identity (static and definable) of gender and race and the differences (changing) which reject strict categorization. Henderson's use of Bakhtinian analysis strongly parallels the Wittgensteinian concept of "family resemblance," which acknowledges both similarities within families (categories or identities) as well as differences within those categories. Henderson's discussion of the "multiple *dialogic of differences* based on [the] com- plex subjectivity" (119, emphasis in original) of the black female points out the necessity for critical recognition and analysis of the diversities involved in the specific case of African-American women. What a Witt- gensteinian approach adds to Henderson's perspective is the recognition and analysis of both similarities and differences which exist within *and* between or across families ("within a family there is a family resem- blance, though you will also find a resemblance between members of different families" (CV, 14e). But even more importantly, a reliance upon the philosophy of Ludwig Wittgenstein provides the critic with a method for a *deep* criticism that focuses not merely on the heteroglossia of language game play but furthermore provides a means of addressing the more enduring differences at the foundational level of language game rules and grammar—those very rules which determine what moves are possible at the surface level of a Bahktinian dialogic heteroglossia.

Alice Jardine has noted the need for "rethinking a feminist ap- proach to cultural translation [that] involves finding new ways of sus- taining what women have come to know through experience without reducing experience only to what we know" (18). The difficulties she points out in relation to a comparativist criticism are those which stem from cross-cultural investigations that impose alien theoretical con- straints upon certain texts. Wittgensteinian investigations, rooted in the language games of those texts, speak to Jardine's concerns. The Wittgensteinian stress on the necessity of noting language games and families of games provides a means of responding to diverse assertions of subjectivity (identities defined according to the rules of particular language games) as well as to the diverse and shifting manifestations of such subjectivities in the world (in other words, the actual moves in a language game). Where women's realities (both in the world and in texts) have been ignored, buried, or otherwise devalued in terms of the dominant phallogocentric critical language games, Wittgensteinian investigations discover those realities in their own worlds, thereby restoring the previously disrupted balance (that balance which reflects the very real presence of men *and* women in human worlds, lived and literary), much as Luci Tapahonso's writing restores the balance of Kinlichníi'nii Bitsí's premature death. A Wittgensteinian-based descriptive criticism makes such restoration possible through actually entering the text and gaining a relational familiarity with the real world of the text. Insofar as a feminist agenda is concerned, such a methodology enables the texts to speak for themselves, providing a textual empowerment that permits the silenced voices of women to speak more strongly and directly than when funnelled through prescriptive readings (feminist or otherwise) imposed by outside theoretics.

As noted, even a feminist interpretive approach, usually illuminating towards most texts, cannot be assumed to be the most useful critical strategy to take towards all texts. Within a patriarchal context, a hegemonic dialectic between the genders must be investigated and understood as part of the grammar of such a discourse. The feminist response intends to subvert that dialectic in order to improve the oppressed conditions of women (both in the world and within the framework of literary and critical canons). The view of traditional Navajo gender relations as egalitarian (as depicted in the poetry of Nia Francisco, Elizabeth Woody, and Luci Tapahonso) might provide the sort of model useful for a wide range of feminist analytic work. This is where a Wittgensteinian approach can prevent potential critical misconstruings. By a close investigation into the language games in which a text participates, the feminist critic can more accurately discern which critical methodologies would be useful in opening up the text or if an altogether different approach is called for (as in the case of Tapahonso's story, "What I Am"). Such an investigation would further delineate the rules of play (of the respective language games) and the family resemblances between the text's games and other elucidatory games evidenced in other related texts.

Wittgenstein compares our perspectives on the world to "part of a kind of mythology" (OC, 95). What we perceive is not the reality of the world or of a text, but rather a reality filtered through our own interpretive biases. Of course, this is not to say that these biases are useless. As

Wittgenstein notes: "One cannot guess how a word functions. One has to *look at* its use and learn from that. But the difficulty is to remove the prejudice which stands in the way of doing this. It is not a *stupid* prejudice" (PI, I, 340). Our prejudices or preconceived orientations may be enormously useful in particular cases, but each case must be investigated in order to ascertain correctly which approach would be most efficacious. What Wittgenstein calls for is the removal of those approaches that impair our descriptive investigations in/to the language games of particular realities (lived and literary). In some cases, it might be best or proper to reject certain critical language games (for example, an essentialistic, phallogocentric New Criticism). Where the old literary or critical language game might be discursively phallogocentric, certain events (most notably those connected with feminism, such as feminist literary criticisms and theories) inform us of the value, perhaps even of the necessity, of rejecting the old game—perhaps no longer useful or, at the very least, certainly less useful than it may have been before. In other cases, we might find a particular critical language game to be valuable in most cases, but less helpful in regard to certain texts (such as a feminist critique of Tapahonso's story). As Wittgenstein admits, "Certain events would put me into a position in which I could not go on with the old language-game any further. In which I was torn away from the *sureness* of the game" (OC, 617). This may be a rejection of the game for all cases or simply the rejection of the game in a specific case.

While we do need to counter those theories, philosophies, criticisms, and mythologies that are inherently phallocentric with a responsively corrective feminism (as Wittgenstein notes, "the mythology may change back into a state of flux, the river-bed of thought may shift" [OC, 97]), it is equally essential that we apply mythologies meaningfully and that we also recognize where such applications might be less useful than the sort of descriptive investigations Wittgenstein urges. Rachel Blau Du-Plessis writes that "shifting focus, bringing the world into different perspectives, is the ontological situation of women because it is our social situation, our relationship to power, our relationship to language" (285). A Wittgensteinian-based descriptive criticism does just this— "bringing the world into different perspectives" by enabling the world (literary and real) to speak its own voices and its own realities through our access to its diverse language games. This approach to literature disengages the critic from the divisive oppositionality of contemporary critical debate, enabling her to focus instead on textual access, thereby serving as a guide for others in/to literary works, even those apparently resistant to our entry, such as the poetry and stories of Luci Tapahonso.

4 Native American Indian Literatures and the Problem of Canonization: A Wittgensteinian Critical Approach

WHY WOULD it be *unthinkable* that I should stay in the saddle however much the facts bucked? (Aber ware es denn *undenkbar*, da ich im Sattel bleibe, auch wenn die Tatsachen noch so sehr bockten?)
Ludwig Wittgenstein

The hypostatization of literary works into canonical texts has always served to privilege those texts over others resigned to positions of subalternity. And yet, most critical debates that argue for the inclusion of texts and authors previously discredited or ignored in the larger domain of literary criticism and pedagogy do not offer any acceptable alternatives to the reification of literary canons (which, by their very natures, are exclusionary). Traditionalist canons of American and British literature have tended to ignore or marginalize the literatures of female, working-class, minority, third world, and postcolonial writers. The responses of literary critics, particularly from the feminist, cultural, and New Historicist critical camps, have been to revision literary canons as much more inclusive institutions than they have historically been. However, such newfound inclusivity in our ever-broadening literary canon does not avoid the inherent exclusivity of canons per se. For example, the feminist rejection of a phallocentric literary canon has indeed served the purpose of broadening the standard canon to include more works by women authors and has created a new literary canon of literature by women. But again, as is the case for any canonical register of literature, those included are present at the expense of those who have been excluded—hence the breakaway feminist groups who have in turn rejected the women's literary canon as restrictive and developed other, more recent, literary canons of literature by lesbians, working-class women, disabled women, African-American women, Latinas, Chicanas, and so forth. The criticisms made by these groups are certainly legitimate and parallel the less specialized criticisms made by feminists in the seventies and early eighties. The problem, of course, is in the very nature of institutionalized valorization.

The proliferation of specialized, and increasingly narrow, literary canons does not circumvent the essential difficulties involved in any critical determinations of literary axiology and validation. This sort of problem can be seen most acutely in the case of American Indian literatures and the development of the canon of Native American literature. This new body of literature is now represented in those newer anthologies which aspire to greater degrees of cultural inclusivity. While such anthologies do serve to introduce Native American literature to a larger audience, they also serve to canonize selected authors and texts. In a discussion of Native American Indian literature, Arnold Krupat notes that "the canon, like all cultural production, is never an innocent selection of the best that has been thought and said; rather, it is the institutionalization of those particular verbal artifacts that appear to best convey and sustain the dominant social order" (310). Specific writers are chosen and given an authoritative presence as representative of "Native American literature."[1] As this chapter will make clear in relation to the particular case of the Native American literary canon, those texts that tend to gain academic approval are not always those texts that represent the living diversity of literature written by Native American Indian peoples, nor are they necessarily those texts most usefully taught to students, but merely those which are more easily accessed, read, and studied by critics who often have an inadequate familiarity with the breadth and depth of Native American Indian literary traditions (both written and oral), languages, and culture.

Limiting Canonization

The answer to the problematic hegemony of literary canons, in general, and the canon of Native American literature, in particular, is to categorically avoid the creation of such institutions in favor of a more dynamic Wittgensteinian method of literary selection that emphasizes the importance of the meaningfulness of texts for their respective reading audience. In other words, the readings for a class in Native American Indian literature taught in the Southwest might most effectively stress the literature of that region, while an analogous course in Alaska could emphasize works by Alaskan and Canadian Native peoples. Such flexibility in relation to text selection avoids the privileged rigidity inherent in the universalizing nature of literary canons. Robert von Hallberg, in a discussion of canons and canon-formation, suggests that canons reflect "feelings of power and helplessness among scholars of the humanities, . . . the competition of rival interest-groups, . . .

[and] a greater political stability, a sense of pending consolidation" that points to future changes in relation to literary canons (3).

As this chapter makes clear, a redirected focus for literary critics away from the anxious axiological assertions of an unmitigated textual privilege can enable the critic to begin a Wittgensteinian approach towards texts that acknowledges both textual and contextual diversity (in relation to the various definitional language games in which those texts participate) as well as those unifying elements (or family resemblances) within and among texts that cut across and overlap their differences. This may be accomplished through a critical refocus that emphasizes the scholar's service to readers and to the text. Instead of asserting the importance of specific texts or canons, we make textual selections based on their usefulness in particular cases. Wittgenstein stresses the importance of focusing on the actual use or applications of things in the world, rather than debating their abstractions on a theoretical level (regardless of the real world effects of theoretical abstractions such as literary canons): "It is necessary to get down to the application, and then the concept finds a different place, one which, so to speak, one never dreamed of" (PI, 201e). By shifting our focus away from the endless debates regarding canonical determinations, the issue becomes less one of exclusivity versus inclusivity on a global scale and more one of effective teaching and criticism in particular cases.

Accordingly, the very concept of a literary canon takes on a categorically different meaning with a position of less power (or, more specifically, less dysfunctional power, as in the institutionalized processes of critical [de]valorizations); it "finds a different place, one which, so to speak, one never dreamed of" as it becomes less strictly prescriptive and merely one of many tools available to literary critics—useful in some cases and not in others. We can best see this shift towards an emphasis on method in Wittgenstein's rejection of the problematic universalizing nature of theory: "But *none* of them was making a mistake except where he was putting forward a theory" (RFGB, 1e). Wittgenstein's point is that whenever we appropriate the theoretical process of the sciences for non-scientific work we are attempting to understand the world (or a text—literary or otherwise) by means of a particular interpretive stance—and therefore, whatever we see is limited by the boundaries imposed by the prescribed theoretical approach. Preconceived theoretical stances serve as grids through which we perceive texts, and these grids constrain our views of those texts in a way that predetermines both our evaluations of the texts and our selective privileging of them. For example, if what we are looking for is irony or ambiguity, our sight may be clear and perceptive; but, by virtue of the narrowing effect of the New Critical approach, as we look for such ambiguities in the text, we miss many other elements perhaps of greater significance to a full description of the text—thereby serving to privilege those texts that fit the New Critical grid and devalue those that do not.

For Wittgenstein, the meaningfulness of any text cannot be divorced from its place and use in the world. This is why the concept of the language game is so useful for literary criticism and theory—by virtue of the fact that the boundaries of the language games in which the text participates are not constrained by the written words in and of themselves. Language games cut across the boundary between the written text and its external context so that, within a Wittgensteinian orientation, such boundaries (between what is within and without a text) become unnecessary. Wittgenstein writes that "there is always the danger of wanting to find an expression's meaning by contemplating the expression itself, and the frame of mind in which one uses it, instead of always thinking of the practice" (OC, 601). A Wittgensteinian emphasis on text selection would necessarily focus on the particular uses of texts for actual classes and scholarship instead of making determinations based on canonical abstractions more rooted in our own theoretical orientations to the world and to texts than in actual real world applications. However, it is important to note that Wittgenstein's rejection of theory is not a rejection of the particular methodologies used by literary theorists. As is discussed in Chapter 1, the term "theory" is used in a broad range of contexts. Wittgenstein's rejection of theory is not a rejection of theory per se, but a rejection of the inappropriate use of the paradigm of scientific theorizing. Much of what we term critical theory is other than the static and abstract hypothetical absolutism which Wittgenstein rejects. Rather, the majority of our work could be more appropriately termed "metacriticism" by virtue of our larger discussions concerning issues of critical method, canonicity, and particular readings of texts. What Wittgenstein rejects is the universalizing absolutism of theory. Wittgenstein's delineation of the appropriate use of theory is connected with his realization that objective interpretation is impossible.

Therefore, the primary aim of literary critics ought to be the description of texts and their respective language games and family resemblances. He does not deny the importance of textual evaluation;[2] however, he emphasizes that such a close and thorough description must come before any sort of meaningful evaluation. Evaluations that are based on narrow and preconceived notions are insufficient for any meaningful textual discussion that would go beyond the limits imposed by the initial theory. Annette Kolodny suggests the potential problems that result from the often self-fulfilling prophetic nature of our preconceived biases. She points out that "to begin our criticism by *looking* for even the possibility of such underlying factors, however, would leave us in danger of discovering what might not be there—since the form of the question necessarily predisposes the outcome of the inquiry" (76).[3] While echoing Wittgenstein's rejection of preconceived theories, Kolodny then goes on to emphasize that we should "throw such assumptions out altogether and begin not with assumptions (acknowledged or not) but with questions" (79).

This concern for a clear and complete view of a text (both written and lived) is the oft-stated desire of many feminist literary critics who work from an agenda that, if not explicitly political, certainly relates to the broader concerns of the women's movement. As Jane Marcus points out, "the production of feminist literary theory is a result of our reading and writing practices as women in this culture" (1988, 282). A feminist political agenda works towards a fuller understanding and eradication of hegemonic patriarchal structures in society, as well as towards the empowerment of women (disempowered within a system that is based on a societal norm that is male). As Chris Weedon asserts, "as feminists we take as our starting point the *patriarchal* structure of society" (2). Here we see the feminist desire for a world that is less exclusionary (at least insofar as women are concerned) conjoined with the rejection of those preconceived biases (such as sexism) which are understood as essential to the literary and societal processes of exclusion. The desired end is a more comprehensive view of the world (or of literary texts) which would include, rather than ignore, the lives and accomplishments of women. And such a concern specifically targeting a gendered prejudice parallels the analogous concerns regarding racial, ethnic, and cultural biases. The problem noted by Wittgenstein is that any preconceived notions, regardless of merit, nevertheless serve to constrain our approaches to the world (or to literary texts).

The Native American Literary Canon

As HAS ALREADY been discussed, such interpretive problems often result from the limits of our critical and theoretical approaches. The real world effects of such limited investigations can be seen in contemporary canonical determinations as evident in Native American literature as it is generally taught in English departments. When we think of Native American writers, names such as Leslie Silko, Paula Gunn Allen, Gerald Vizenor, Louise Erdrich, and Joy Harjo come to mind. These diverse writers reflect different tribal affiliations, ethnic mixes, and geographic heritages. What all of these writers have in common is that they are mixed-race people (participatory in the mestiza language game discussed in Chapter 6), part Native-American and part other (usually Anglo). This fact, openly discussed in a number of the works of literature they have produced, is significant for several reasons. First, such mixed ethnicity portrays a distinctive reality and presence in the world that is neither purely Indian nor non-Indian—but rather represents a poignant dualism of being "split at the root" (to borrow a phrase from Adrienne Rich).

While this experience is both significant and profound in its consequences and lived experience, this mixed Native American/Anglo reality is not and cannot speak for the reality of those Indian peoples not "split at the root." And yet, unfortunately, the contemporary canon of "Native American literature" has, by and large, come to be defined by the works of these mixed-blood writers. One serious outcome of this is the devaluation of works by full blood writers—works that may be more resistant, by virtue of their language games being more alien, to most literary critics and theorists. The works of writers such as Nia Francisco, Luci Tapahonso, Elizabeth Woody, and Anna Lee Walters are much less familiar to contemporary readers and critics than are the more popular and legitimated writings of mixed-blood writers such as Louise Erdrich or Leslie Silko. To lose sight of the underlying grammatical difference between the full-blood American Indian language game and that of the Native American mestiza is to misrepresent and perhaps eradicate, or at the very least ignore, the reality of Indian peoples who have grown up within a cultural language game in which there is not the mestiza cultural split or dichotomy at the foundational or grammatical level. For many Indian peoples who are full-blood or who have been raised on the reservations, hegemonic dichotomizing forces appear to come more strongly from without (from the larger historical discursive structures) than from within the actual individual. The case for those of mixed blood is different.

In "The Experience of Mixed-Race People: Some Thoughts and Theories," Michelle M. Motoyoshi notes that interracial people truly live on the margins of society in that their very existence straddles at least two ethnic identities. Motoyoshi emphasizes the distinctive position held by such individuals and sees it as a strength, arguing that mixed-race persons "serve not only as models, but as prototypes," perhaps, for the future (89). While there are without a doubt language games that are particular to full-blood Indian peoples, there are, as Motoyoshi points out, also some profoundly meaningful language games particular to the experience of those "split at the root." Therefore, to confuse the mixed-race language game with that of full-blood peoples would be misleading at best. While there certainly are meaningful family resemblances between the Native American mestiza/o language game and that of full-blood Indian peoples, it is crucial that investigations at the grammatical level of these games, along the lines of those suggested by Wittgenstein, occur so that clear delineations can be properly drawn and ascertained.

Only through close descriptive investigations can critics avoid the misconstruings that, in part, lead to the canonical debates now current in the academy. Fredric Jameson alludes to such concerns in his essay, "Marxism and Historicism," in which he identifies a tendency to interpret other peoples in terms of our own identities, thereby failing "to touch the strangeness and the resistance of a reality genuinely different from our own" (43). It is much easier to approach texts with which we are more comfortable, namely those works whose language games coincide with some of our own language games. Such language game familiarity certainly accounts for the fact that mestiza Native American representations of Native American Indian culture have attracted much more critical attention than have the writings of full-blood Indian writers such as Luci Tapahonso or Anna Lee Walters. To be sure, these women present Indian realities that diverge significantly from the more popular portrayals which provide easier access for non-Native critics. The stories and poems of mixed-blood writers are much more accessible in that their language games more fully participate, on the grammatical or foundational level, in the rules of both Native American *and* Anglo-American language games, providing predominantly Anglo readers and critics with more of an opening. Thus, in Wittgenstein's words, "we remain unconscious of the prodigious diversity of all the everyday language-games because the clothing of our language makes everything alike" (PI, 224).

Not only do we end up having difficulty perceiving differences hidden by a common language (difficulties and conflicts made more apparent in the challenges of writers who choose to cross linguistic boundaries), but we then perceive similarities (perhaps nonexistent) which often prove to be the products of our own interpretive biases. And those works of literature which cannot be made after our own likenesses become those which are ignored or devalued. This has been generally the case for female, minority, gay and lesbian, and working-class writers. Unfortunately, the same devaluative game, albeit variations thereof, continues to be played out against those works which lie outside the bounds of our critical language games. Bell Hooks notes this problem in a critique of cultural studies—a field and practice which, like feminism, cannot be blithely assumed to be immune to the hegemonic expropriations by those connected with discursive power structures: "Cultural studies re-inscribes patterns of colonial domination, where the 'Other' is always made object, appropriated, interpreted, taken over by those in power, by those who dominate" (125).

To address such concerns where interpretations of the world or of the arts are not rooted in actual use, Wittgenstein reminds us to question the very grammar of our interpretive stances rather than simply to use our methodologies indiscriminately. The conflict which might arise between critical expectations and the reality of a text is related to "the position you are in if you look for definitions corresponding to our concepts in aesthetics or ethics. In such a difficulty always ask yourself: How did we *learn* the meaning of this word ('good' for instance)? From what sort of examples? in what language-games?" (PI, I, 77). We are continually urged by Wittgenstein to question not only the objects of our critical endeavors, but to question and question again our critical orientations—not just in and of themselves, but specifically in relation to their actual use. For example, New Historicist literary critical methodologies are very useful in opening up texts and clarifying important cultural aspects of those texts, but this is not to say that this particular critical strategy is *always* the most useful strategy in every case. We must continually remember to place both text and criticism in useful relations to each other, hence Wittgenstein's reminder that language is a "spatial and temporal phenomenon . . . not some non-spatial, non-temporal phantasm" (PI, I, 108)—an important reminder in relation to all prescriptive debates involving the various literary canons. Not only is language "spatial and temporal," but so are literature, criticism, and the teaching of literature.

Within a Wittgensteinian terminology, we would say that the range of language games present within the domain of English literature demonstrates both differences and similarities between and within language games (e.g., family differences and resemblances). In light of this diversity across literary language games, Wittgenstein's investigatory methodology provides us with a readier entry into texts than might be the case were our approach limited by the constraints of any particular critical orientation. Throughout much of his philosophical writing, Ludwig Wittgenstein emphasizes the importance of closely investigating whatever components of the world we hope to understand. This process of descriptive investigations has ready applications for any literary critic, since our activities are specifically those of close readings—be they the close readings of the text by New Critics, structuralists, and deconstructionists, close readings of what is below the text by semioticians and critics influenced by psychoanalytic approaches, close readings of critical response by reader-response critics, or close readings of the work's larger historical context by New Historicists, Marxists, Anglo-American feminists, and cultural critics.

Textual Entry and Nia Francisco's "Male and Female"

THE CRITICAL PROCESS of close readings becomes particularly problematic when difficulties arise in our attempt to see the work closely. Any number of factors could prove to be a major stumbling block here. Often we avoid such problems by choosing to critique works whose language games are already somewhat familiar. This situation serves to perpetuate the hegemonic valorization given to particular works of literature and denied to others—generally those with which literary critics are less familiar. This problem of textual entry can be most clearly seen in a specific example—namely, the poem, "Male and Female," by

Navajo poet Nia Francisco. After a brief discussion and introduction into the Navajo language game as it relates to issues of gender, I offer a Wittgensteinian-based critical entry into the poem. I demonstrate how such a methodology can enable any critic to approach and enter a wide range of culturally diverse works of literature without exclusive resort to the dialectically limiting orientation of any specific critical or theoretical approach. The critical entry into Francisco's poem is followed by a concluding investigation into the canonical implications of this method for both critics and the discipline.

The statement, *sǫ'ah naagháii bik'eh hózhó*, can be seen as emblematic of the Navajo way of life. While any translation into English is ineffective at best, we can roughly read the statement as follows: as we grow from birth to old age (*sǫ'ah*) we will walk (*naagháii*) according to (*bik'eh*) the way of beauty (*hózhó*). The words *sǫ'ah naagháii* represent thought and passivity, which are male principles for the Navajo, while *bik'eh hózhó* represents speech and activity, female elements.[4] The essential nonphallogocentrism of the Navajo way is evident in this phrase: *sǫ'ah naagháii bik'eh hózhó*. Even though in this sequence, "thought" and "man" precede "speech" and "woman," within a nonlinear Navajo context, for the Navajo, this does not indicate any inequality insofar as status is concerned. One could reverse the terms, as *bik'eh hózhó sǫ'ah naagháii*, without any loss or change in meaning. In fact, within a Navajo framework, while in various ways woman and man differ (generally insofar as function or roles are concerned), there is no hierarchical preference given to one or the other. Both First Man and First Woman were created concurrently at two sides of the First World (*Ni'hodilqil*). First Man was created at the conjunction of the East (connected with the color white and the dawn) and North (black; night). First Woman was formed where the South (blue; daylight) and West (yellow; twilight) meet. The East and dawn are connected with the male principle, which thus temporally precedes the female directions of South (daylight) and West (twilight). However, this does not indicate any male primacy.[5]

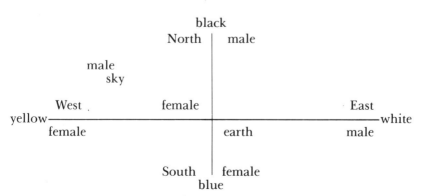

Just as the female directions follow the male directions, so do the male directions follow the female with North (night) coming after the West (twilight). The tribal structure of the Navajo is matrilineal, and the female principle, which is seen as active, productive, and reproductive, is highly valued (Witherspoon 141); however, this is not to say that woman is more valued than man. Were either gender to be granted primacy over the other, the circle of life would be out of balance. This points out the importance of balance and harmony. There is no sense of the dialectical competitiveness between the sexes so apparent within phallocentric societies. Nia Francisco's poem, "Male and Female," demonstrates this sense of gender balance:

> My people
> they believe
> in the mating
> of turquoise
> and white shell (47)

While these beginning lines of the poem may seem to be a straightforward representation of Western heterosexual relations, such a reading would grossly misrepresent the views depicted in the poem. The title does mention male before female and could accordingly be given a feminist reading which would point out such a patriarchal ordering. One could then note the colors, turquoise and white, as evidence of this hierarchical relation. From our Western phallogocentric language games, we expect to find colors such as blue and white in a poem representing a phallocentric heterosexuality. Blue (which is accordingly mentioned first) is traditionally used to identify babies as male, and white often signifies the expected purity or virginity of the woman. The fact that the "white shell" follows the turquoise and is presented as lower, by virtue of being relegated to a separate and lower line that is spaced further out, could indicate the secondary status of woman, who is supposedly seen as an afterthought, as marginalized other (*"and* white shell"). However such a reading grossly diverges from the poem's own discursive context.

Within a nonphallocentric society, language games do not include the hierarchically unbalanced relationship between male and female common in most Western cultures. Harmony and sense of balance pervade the Navajo culture or language game from the grammatical level of words, forms, or thoughts to the more visible level of everyday life. In other words, a Wittgensteinian reading or description of the poem, which would take into account the diverse rules of play of the poem's language game(s), would avoid a phallogocentric reading which would represent less the actual poem and more the language games in which the critic, not the poet, is a participant. Wittgenstein repeatedly emphasizes the importance of avoiding problematic interpretive or critical approaches that bar our entry into a text by artificially imposing an extraneous discursive patterning upon the text's language games. Such an approach proves problematic most clearly where the language games of critic and text scarcely coincide at all, as in the case of Navajo literature and literary critics who are not familiar with Navajo language, thought, and way. In such situations, the interpretation usually produces a reading that generally accords with the dominant culture or ideology—a practice that perpetuates the disenfranchisement of alternative realities and texts not in accordance with the dominant ideology.

The above brief reading of Francisco's "Male and Female," approaching the poem from the angle of Western phallocentrism, presents an interpretive analysis which might lead, from a Western feminist perspective, for example, to a devaluation of the poem as a simplistic representation of Western heterosexual relations. Other critical approaches developed within the Western tradition (be they supportive of, or in reaction against, that tradition) would analogously misread the poem after the fashions of their critical orientations. Francisco's poem could be read subversively with a feminist deconstructive reading that would emphasize the aporia and struggle between the dominant male term and the suppressed female term with the placement of the phrase "and the white shell" seen as evidence of the struggle of the female to release herself from the bondage of the male term. However, such a deconstructive interpretation would still present the poem in terms of the aporetic dialectic between two contrastive and combative constituents. While either of the above readings may provide insights into the poem (perhaps regarding its poetics, word choice, or apparent dualism), by not taking into account its basic grammar as a Navajo poem, the readings must be seen as partial and distant from the poem and its representative language game(s).

However, in a Wittgensteinian reading, the critic would need to be conversant with the predominant rules of those games in which the text is a participant. Such a critical reading of Francisco's poem would serve less as interpretation and more as translation across language games—providing the general reader with easier access to the poem. Much of the previous discussion regarding Navajo gender equality would help to provide a critical reading that would be more accurate in the sense of seeing the poem's language game(s) more clearly. This would indicate that the ordering in the title, with male preceding female, should not be read as an indication of any sort of hierarchical ordering. A Wittgensteinian approach would note that the actual title, "Male and Female," demonstrates a Navajo sense of balance and harmony with each term occurring on either side of the center, just as the two genders are seen as complements within the Navajo cosmology and way of life. Further analysis of the poem will clarify this even more.

Throughout the poem, there is an absence of the dialectical distinctions that we have come to expect from phallogocentric language games. In the first stanza, Francisco provides a muted first person ("My people") that immediately thereafter shifts to a less subjective third person inter-relationally including the poem's first-person persona (or Francisco herself) as a Navajo ("My people / they believe"). This is in the Navajo tradition of humility and inclusivity in story telling. Stories often begin with *ba' hane'* (it is said), and may alternate with the third person plural or singular (they say, one says). There is no specific identification of the speaker, an absence that serves to remove the sharp distinctions between a speaker (generally privileged through asserted subjectivity) and hearer (devalued through passive objectivity). Even the distinction between the narrative voice of the poem's persona and the objective status of the reader is categorically avoided by the absence of any strong first-person persona in the poem. The only indication of a possible first-person voice occurs in the first line ("My people")—a first-person allusion often avoided in Navajo by saying "Dine'," which would achieve the same result of identifying the poem as originating within the Navajo language game of which Francisco is a participant. This identification further avoids the dialectical separation of speaker and reader/listener by bringing together the voices of Navajo poet Francisco, of the poem's first person persona (muted, but present nevertheless), and of the Dine' in general.

The equation expressed in the title is described in the second half of the first stanza: "the mating / of turquoise / and white shell." Close investigation into the context of the poem clarifies that, traditionally, the color turquoise is used to signify, not a male image, but rather the female direction, while the color white signifies the male direction, East. At this point in the poem, we see that the placement of the terms in the title ("Male and Female") does not indicate any sort of hierarchization, for in the first stanza, female (turquoise) precedes male (white). The balance between the genders is emphasized in the reference to marriage. One gender is not represented as a subject who acts upon (marries) a passive object. Rather, in a Navajo context, there is a "mating," which does not privilege either woman or man. Francisco's poem continues to avoid any sort of dichotomous imbalancings by not even ascribing the mating of the genders specifically to human beings.

In the second stanza, there is an allusion to a human "mating" where Francisco says "they ['My people,' Dine'] only live it." But the pronouns (they, it) provide an open-ended reference that permits the reader any number of readings. The penultimate stanza ("naaldlooshii / naagháíi / naat'agii / nanise'" clarifies that, in the poem (as in the larger Navajo language game), we cannot even expect a problematic privileging of our human species. For the Navajo, mating is a fact of life for all of creation, from human beings and large mammals (*naaldlooshii*) to walking around and flying animals (naagháíi and naat'agii) to the simpler forms of plant life (*nanise'*). Dualism is inevitable—but this dualism does not signify any sort of discursive power imbalance. There are two genders, different from each other just as one direction or color differs from another direction or color. And as there is no priority given to one direction or color over the others, so is the Navajo language game grammatically nonphallogocentric and, hence, resistant to most interpretive discourses produced within the dominant patriarchal language game (this would include a range of both nonfeminist and feminist critical readings).

The poem's resistance to Western interpretive approaches is further underscored by the poem's devaluation of its own words and in its emphasis on practice over words. One way in which this is done is that the poem refuses to provide its own voice; "they believe" (*haníí teh,* so it is usually told), presents a voice external to the poem. The poem serves as a transmission of that which has been said elsewhere. Furthermore, the poem emphasizes practice and life and de-emphasizes words. We do have words (of the poem) and thoughts ("they believe"); however, these are expressed not simply in the poem, but more importantly in what is outside the poem—namely, everyday life. And here we see that the boundaries of the poem defy a strict analysis since it is unclear where the poem begins and ends other than in actual life. Words (the active principle signifying woman) and thoughts (passive and male) divorced from everyday life are meaningless ("No one knows / the meaning")—a concept that echoes Wittgenstein's emphasis on the meaningfulness of words *in use.* As Francisco writes in the second stanza, "No one knows / the meaning   in forms / of words / thoughts / or other wise." Meaning is expressed in life: "they only live it." And this emphasis on the power of living one's words (spoken or written) is demonstrated by the profound respect the Navajo have for language and its proper use. Within a Navajo framework, abstract debates regarding the differentiation (hierarchized or not) between speech and writing would be, if not meaningless, certainly much less important than the effects of words in the world. This strongly parallels Wittgenstein's emphasis that our language use must be grounded in the world, not abstract or separated from everyday life.

While a full discussion of the relational qualities of *Dine' bizaad* (Navajo language) lies outside the bounds of this chapter, what is important to mention here is the fact that much of what constitutes Navajo way and Navajo cosmology can only be expressed/translated in English with great difficulty—due to the significant differences between the language games (as manifested in the diverse languages and cultures). We see this distinction evidenced in that Francisco uses both the English and Navajo languages in her poem in order to communicate particular themes in her poem. Reed Way Dasenbrock notes two possible interpretations of bilingualism in multicultural literature (such as Francisco's use of Navajo and English). One is that the translation of particular terms or concepts may not be possible into certain other languages: "A refusal to translate generally indicates difficulty in translation" (1987b, 17). Also the increased difficulty for the reader (necessitating a familiarity with more than one language) forces the reader to work for textual access (14).

The importance of bilingual texts for many writers of diverse backgrounds leads to potentially serious repercussions insofar as canonical decisions are concerned. In a nation whose emblematic legacy is that of a melting pot and English-only movements, literary works that are bilingual are less accessible to readers than would be the case for those works in nations in which multilingualism is encouraged. Therefore, bilingual works, important to many writers like Nia Francisco who desire to communicate particular worldviews that are incapable of being communicated exclusively in one language (particularly one that is seen and felt as alien), become less marketable and are less likely to find their way into English courses. Gloria Anzaldúa emphasizes the importance of bilingualism for non-Anglo writers: "To speak English is to think in that language, to adopt the ideology of the people whose language it is and to be 'inhabited' by their discourses" (xxii). Maria Lugones further strengthens this point in an essay which she begins in Spanish:

> Empezare monologándoles en mi lengua ancestral para hacerle honor, para prepararme y prepararlas a hablar con comprensión de las deficultades de nuestros diálogos y para recrearlas con el precioso son de una de las lenguas vivas de esta país (46).

> [I begin with a monologue in my ancestral language to give it honor, to prepare myself and others to speak knowledgeably of the difficulties of our speech, and to recreate ourselves by the beauty of one of the living languages of this country.]

For feminist writers like Anzaldúa and Lugones, the issue is not that one language, Spanish, is less phallogocentric than another; but rather that the fluidity of crossed boundaries, made possible through a bilingual form of writing, furthers their rejection of the more limited and demanded monolingualism of the "fathers" (as defined by, for example, the state, the schools, or the publishing houses). While the bilingual language game evident in Francisco's poetry diverges significantly from that of Anzaldúa or Lugones by virtue of the languages used and what they signify (with Navajo being an indigenous language rather than a Eurocentric language), there are nevertheless meaningful family resemblances between the different bilingual projects.

In the second half of "Male and Female," Francisco demonstrates the decision not to write exclusively in English. The four final stanzas, all written in Navajo, have fewer than half as many words as do the first three stanzas, and yet the second half of the poem much more clearly and completely expresses what the first half only begins to approach. Francisco's poem communicates to the reader a categorically nonphallogocentric world view that is shockingly divergent in its simplicity ("they only live it") from the postmodern world in which life becomes seemingly more and more complex as the proliferation of theoretical constructs appears to outpace the actuality of their manifestations in the world. In order to depict a Navajo worldview, Francisco moves from English to Navajo, from more words to fewer, from an abstract explanation of belief, thought, and life to a simple presentation of examples, from longer stanzas to shorter ones, from speech to silence. In his lectures on aesthetics, Wittgenstein questions the efficaciousness of Eurocentric interpretations and evaluations of art from non-Eurocentric traditions—specifically in relation to African art (L&C, 8–9). He notes not only that such readings of the art are more than likely to be misreadings, but that those interpretations lead to devaluations of the work due more to critical ignorance than to any lack of merit in the artwork itself.

Interpretive Limits

AS WE HAVE SEEN in this chapter, it is crucial that critics reevaluate their respective discursive modes of interpretation as they might apply to literature such as Nia Francisco's poem. The deceptive ease or familiarity involved in any reading can be problematic, for it may enable us to overlook the dissimilarities or conflict between critic and text. Feminist critics have noted sharply erroneous readings of women-authored texts by male critics who overlooked concerns foregrounded by women writing about female experience, and minority feminists have castigated white feminists for omissions and misreadings particularly insofar as race is concerned. It is ironic that we rarely question our interpretive strategies unless challenged by other critics or by a seemingly impenetrable text that insists upon an alternate reading. However, such shifts away from our previously held interpretive stances come slowly and with great difficulty. Since our theoretical orientation enables us to see those elements of a text within our interpretive domain, we may completely miss the fact that those aspects of the text which we are seeing clearly only make up a small percentage of what actually constitutes the text— thereby leading to potentially problematic axiological determinations regarding that text. Our interpretation, perhaps quite clear and insightful, may in fact be shockingly limited, or even unsuitable for significant textual entry.

A situation that most poignantly comes to mind as a demonstration of the potential distances that present themselves between categorically divergent language games (in this case between the language games of Indian, mestiza-Indian, and Anglo worlds) occurred at a poetry reading given by a prominent Native American (mestiza-Indian) woman writer. The audience, predominantly Anglo, included a few American Indian students. At the end of the reading, one of the Indian students (from one of the Rio Grande pueblos in New Mexico) came up to me. She looked rather puzzled. I inquired if she enjoyed the reading. The student pondered my question for a moment and then, motioning towards the lectern, asked, "She's Indian?" In other words, the student, for whom functioning in our Anglo world is a continual battle—culturally (she's always lived on a reservation) and linguistically (English is her second language, Keresan her first)—did not recognize the writer as Indian; and, in fact, found the writer more alien than did the Anglo listeners. I would like to note the interesting fact that the Indian genealogy of the Native American writer who had given the reading is similar to that of the Indian student. While the actual tribes are different, the cultures of the two tribes are, nevertheless, very similar. But for the student, the writer was unrecognizable as an Indian. The speaker's assertive mannerisms, her nostalgia towards her Indian relatives and silence regarding her non-Indian family, and a very pointed dialectical presence in the world (as manifested in a combative feminist judgmentalism and anger) all identified the writer more strongly as an "Anglo" to the Indian student.

Here we see the difficulties that arise when communication is attempted across diverse language games. A woman writer who justifiably does have significant ties to American Indian culture through one parent ends up portraying an Indian way more recognizable to Anglo listeners and readers than to her Indian audience. As an epilogue to the story, at a recent scholarly conference, in a session devoted to Native American literature, one of the members of the audience quoted the aforementioned poet, noting that she was central to the Native American literary canon. This fact was accepted as a given by an audience largely unfamiliar with the wealth of literature written by Native American Indian peoples. Of the papers presented at that session (by and large representative of most such sessions to date), all were devoted to the writings of mixed-blood writers (the writer predominantly discussed in the papers was Louise Erdrich). While the papers were insightful and interesting, they nevertheless served to perpetuate a problematically limiting and marginalizing canon of Native American literature.

The difficulty that presents itself is not merely how to broaden the canon of Native American literature into a more inclusive canon of Native American Indian literatures, but rather how to follow Wittgenstein's advice to be sufficiently aware of our own orientations to the world and to literary texts such that we possess more self-knowledge regarding our own preconceived notions. Such awareness conjoined with a tendency towards a dynamic inclusivity rather than towards the more rigid exclusivity inherent in the nature of canons can assist critics in more comfortably entering and critiquing a greater diversity of literary works. As Wittgenstein notes, "I find it important in philosophizing to keep changing my posture, not to stand for too long on *one* leg, so as not to get stiff" (CV, 27e). When a literary work is looked at repeatedly through one view or critical approach, our readings become "stiff." Diverse approaches to texts will provide a readier means of avoiding the limiting constraints of canonical readings and canonical lists of texts, but such a method categorically diverges from the easier and more secure strategies of narrow theories and criticisms. The easiest, and most potentially problematic, means of entry into the dissimilar language games presented in diverse literary works is by using those interpretive strategies developed within the contextual environment of our own language games—the strategy presented by the mixed-blood Native American writer (that of portraying an Indian worldview through her own conflictual and dialectical model). While such entry through one's own language games does provide a standard against which to approach various works and is therefore a fairly simple approach, it is also limiting and biased in that it privileges those works whose domains either coincide, or can be forced to fit, most readily with our own.

It is particularly essential for literary critics not to fall prey to these tactics—albeit within the bounds of a politically acceptable critical agenda of canonical inclusivity. When feminists or cultural critics define "Native American" literature in terms of those particular works whose discursive structures provide us with the most ready access, we are establishing boundaries scarcely better than those previously established, which served to keep female, working-class, and minority writers out. Wittgenstein emphasizes that "to say 'This combination of words makes no sense' excludes it from the sphere of language and thereby bounds the domain of language. But when one draws a boundary it may be for various kinds of reason. If I surround an area with a fence or a line or otherwise, the purpose may be to prevent someone from getting in or out" (PI, I, 499).

To date, many works of literature have been categorically excluded from the literary canons in order to maintain a hegemonically-based status quo (be that a Great Books canon, a women's literature canon, or the canon of Native American literature). Wittgenstein makes it clear that there are many reasons why various categories or limits are established: "It may also be part of a game and the players be supposed, say, to jump over the boundary; or it may shew where the property of one man ends and that of another begins; and so on. So if I draw a boundary line that is not yet to say what I am drawing it for" (PI, I, 499). In other words, insofar as Wittgenstein is concerned, the mere existence of a boundary or restriction is not sufficient in and of itself to indicate a problem of hegemonic exclusion. If certain works are not included within the burgeoning canon of Native American literature, that is not to say that similar exclusionary effects necessarily indicate similar causal reasoning. However, divergent intentions do not mitigate the overall effect of exclusion and omission. Such exclusions are unavoidable, insofar as Wittgenstein is concerned. We can never completely escape our interpretive boundaries, nor need we. What we can do is to investigate the limits of our critical orientations such that they are applied in an informed manner. As Wittgenstein emphasizes, "don't think, but look!" (PI, I, 66). And "in order to see more clearly, here as in countless similar cases, we must focus on the details of what goes on; must look at them *from close to*" (PI, I, 51). Such investigations might indicate that, rather than simply including a few additional texts into a class or critical paper, the solution might very well indicate a need to rephrase and rethink the fundamental questions we are asking.

What is crucial is that we focus on the use of the texts under investigation and inquire which texts would be most usefully investigated for each particular course or scholarly writing. In regard to selections of those texts valued as Native American literature, it may very well be that our definitional categories or boundaries (both Anglocentric in their orientation and hegemonic in their effects) are the problem. Wittgenstein's assertions regarding the importance of close investigations emphasize his point that "language is founded on convention" (PI, I, 355). As such, only by means of looking at both the larger context of discursive practices (including convention, history, and environment) and the discourse itself in its actual applications can we expect to see those discursive practices as clearly as possible. When any discourse or text is extracted from its use, the statements can be discerned but their meaning is not necessarily the meaning of the statement as understood within its respective contexts. For Wittgenstein, abstracted meaning is arbitrary and can lead to such problems as the positive valuation of a text that might be devalued within the boundaries of its own language game and culture, as well as the converse case of a text erroneously devalued by being evaluated on the basis of a foreign language game incapable of adequately accounting for textual diversity.[6] The situation of Native American literatures demonstrates such problems.

Broadening the Native American Literary Canon

CRITICAL ATTENTION has focused on selected works that have helped to define the grammar or rules for the Native American literature language game. While these rules may be helpful, it is essential, nevertheless, to realize that the rules upon which other works of American Indian literature are produced may be significantly different such that any evaluation of those texts based on the canon of Native American literature as it is generally taught today would be misleading. Arnold Krupat points out that "the Euroamerican attempt to think a Native American 'literature' has always been marked by the problem of Identity and Difference, a problem that . . . marks as well the attempt to develop a written criticism of this 'literature' " (1983, 3). Krupat goes on to note that "while we cannot avoid the explanatory categories of western culture, we can at least be aware of them and beware of them as we approach the 'literature' of other cultures" (10). Krupat is correct in that we cannot take ourselves out of our respective language game(s), but we can work to avoid those "western explanatory categories" which would otherwise impair our critical work. This is not to say that "western explanatory categories" are by definition problematic or useful, but rather that critics must discern those situations in which they could be usefully applied and those in which they would be misapplied.

Wittgenstein makes it very clear that the desire for explanations is where we go astray. Since we cannot remove ourselves from our own historicity, which necessarily biases our interpretations of the world (and of texts), Wittgenstein stresses that we ought to strive for descriptive analyses rather than explanatory interpretations. "Our mistake is to look for an explanation where we ought to look at what happens. . . . The question is not one of explaining a language-game by means of our experiences, but of noting a language-game" (PI, I, 654–655). When we begin to explain some language game that we are observing, we put ourselves in the role of subject-observer who is looking down upon some passive object that will be theorized and interpreted. However, if we hope to understand a text within its own cultural and linguistic historicity, then we, as observers, must go to the text (by entering those language games in which the text participates), rather than expecting it to come and fit into our critical worlds. When we, as critics, make the effort to learn from the text (and by "text" I am including the diverse range of language games and family resemblances which cut across interrelated textual and contextual discursive structures), we then are in a better position to begin the process of differentiation and integration within and across descriptive (rather than explanatory) categories. This process is that of critical investigations into the diverse language games in which works of literature participate.

Wittgenstein's writings on aesthetics are particularly adamant in his rejection of explanation and theory. He emphasizes the impossibility of objective or absolute evaluative stances and that any work of art or literature is necessarily evaluated in terms of the particular language games of the critic. In light of the differences that occur between critics, any interpretive axiology must vary from critic to critic. Wittgenstein asserts the futility of trying to establish any sort of objective axiological or interpretive schema. "You might think Aesthetics is a science telling us what's beautiful—almost too ridiculous for words. I suppose it ought to include also what sort of coffee tastes well" (L&C, 11). Of course, this is not to say that we cannot differentiate between a bad cup of coffee (say, one that has been burned or a cheap cup of instant coffee) and one that is good. In this case, the underlying grammatical rules of coffee making (say, freshly ground beans, properly roasted, and percolated the correct length of time) help us to determine the extent to which the coffee (or a text) plays well its respective language games. But this does not offer objective criteria for determining whether a cup of Ethiopian coffee is better that a cup of Mexican Altura—this is a matter of personal taste. The problem, Wittgenstein sees here, is the absence of clearly defined critical boundaries.

When the boundaries of our interpretive frameworks are unclear, we cannot account for and control the various biases and preconceived notions that affect our view. For Wittgenstein, this problem is the convolution of our personal tastes and prejudices with our determinations of textual language-game play. If our goal is to perceive and read a text as clearly and as closely as possible, then we must be aware of our own biases and of those language games played in/by the text. "In learning the rules [of the language games] you get a more and more refined judgement. Learning the rules actually changes your judgement" (L&C, 5). As this chapter has made clear, the assumptions involving language game entry are much more complex than generally perceived. Regarding Native American Indian literatures, a familiarity with the rules of the respective language games evidenced in those texts more commonly anthologized and studied, while crucial, is not sufficient to prevent critical misconstruings of other non-canonical texts: as in the case of the devaluation of Nia Francisco's poetry—a devaluation evident in the absence of her work from the more privileged texts generally included within the canon of Native American literature. In other words, a familiarity with those texts generally included within the canon of Native American literature (such as works by mixed heritage writers: Silko, Erdrich, Allen, Vizenor, etc.) might not be adequate for approaches to and entries into other Native American Indian texts (perhaps those by non-mestizo/a Indian writers).

The critic must go further and investigate other contexts and language games in order to approach those literary works for which our critical frameworks might be inadequate, thereby providing more responsive and meaningful textual selections for instruction and analysis. As Wittgenstein asserts, "It is necessary to get down to the application, and then the concept finds a different place, one which, so to speak, one never dreamed of" (PI, 201e). A Wittgensteinian approach to literary canons is categorically divergent from those approaches currently offered—be they traditionalist or revisionist. Such an approach disengages from such dialectical struggles by asking not which texts are to be included in (and excluded from) the literary canons, but rather which texts can be meaningfully read, studied, and taught in particular cases. And the answer to this latter question can, and ought to, vary from case to case. Here we see the power of the philosophy of Ludwig Wittgenstein in its resistance to debates that, while useful in raising important questions concerning the literary canon(s), prove to be little more than critically solipsistic in their actual effects. A reliance on Wittgenstein's work releases the critic from such academic debates by eliminating the need for institutional valorization altogether. Where the focus is on the application rather than on the larger concept, we do indeed find "a different place . . . one never dreamed of "—a place where canonical debates are meaningless in relation to the more significant determinations of use. Do all literary critics need to study the poetry of Nia Francisco? No. Do all critics of Native American literatures need to study her work? Also, no, but they might find it enlightening. Do I study and teach Francisco's poetry in my courses on Native American literature? Yes, because I find it useful to do so.[7]

5 Meaningful Differences, or The End of Doubting: Wittgenstein and Deconstruction

DURING THE PAST two decades, deconstruction and other post-structural criticisms have eroded the traditional distinctions between philosophy and literature (including both the work of literature itself and literary criticism and theory). From a deconstructive approach, philosophy is no longer understood as a literal and objective inquiry into truth and knowledge, but as a rich mine laden with a wealth of metaphors previously unearthed. The Renaissance, Enlightenment, and Romantic debates concerning the comparative valuation of literature versus philosophy are now understood to be fundamentally meaningless within the bounds of a poststructural framework. Deconstruction undermines the very foundation of the distinctions between philosophy and literature by questioning those categorically divisive postulates upon which the debates are based. Such hierarchized divisions are not only called into question by a deconstructive orientation, but also by the work of Ludwig Wittgenstein. However, we shall see that what may appear on a cursory reading to be similarities between the two approaches, in fact, conceal very serious differences. While Wittgenstein acknowledges important similarities between philosophy and literature that distinguish both from the natural sciences, he, nevertheless, is aware of the dissimilarities manifested in their respective uses. And where deconstruction rejects the possibility of arriving at any degree of semantic certainty, Wittgenstein clearly asserts that certainty is achievable within the bounds of particular language games as determined by their rules of play.

However, such differentiations between the two perspectives do not necessitate a categoric rejection of either view. Rather, what a Wittgensteinian approach suggests is that we clearly establish the limiting boundaries of the deconstructive language game as a means of critical discrimination: namely, that process of determining the suitability of a particular critical language game for opening up a particular text. As we shall see in the course of this chapter, the specific grammar of the language game of deconstructive criticism radically diverges from a number of Wittgensteinian concerns. After an extensive discussion regarding their respective dissimilarities (in order to clearly address the confusion of some deconstructive critics who desire to place Wittgensteinian philosophy within the rubric of deconstruction), it will be clear that, while Wittgenstein is not a deconstructor and deconstruction is not Wittgensteinian, a Wittgensteinian approach towards literary criticism not only leaves room for deconstructive readings, but encourages them where they would be most useful—namely, towards those texts whose logocentrism almost seems to insist upon the post-structural response of a deconstructive critique.

Writing, Language, and Meaning

THE DIFFERENCES between deconstruction and Wittgensteinian philosophy can be seen in their divergent views of writing, language, and meaning. Deconstructionists focus on writing per se and see the distinctions between types of writing as reflections of the disempowerment of the written word and of the privileging of either the spoken word or the meaning expressed by writing. The deconstructive privileging of writing (écriture) emphasizes that any writing is open to a deconstructive process of destabilization. Accordingly, philosophy, criticism, or any form of writing is accorded the same treatment as literature (which traditionally has been thought to be more metaphorical than other forms of writing). This leveling occurs because the grounds of any writing or sign system are fair game for the deconstructive project's challenging of a unified and coherent logocentric reality. Therefore, even philosophy is no longer seen as more logical, referential, or absolute than literature. Wittgenstein arrives at an analogous conclusion regarding the non-scientific nature of philosophy, but his process is significantly different from a deconstructive interpretation.

An especially important parallel between the deconstructive project and the philosophy of Ludwig Wittgenstein lies in their emphases on language and meaning. The divergences are also readily apparent. The deconstructor utilizes the method of close reading as a textually disruptive technique designed to demonstrate the groundlessness of our preconceived interpretations. This deconstructive groundlessness does not permit an unequivocal rejection of those interpretations in that they are essential to the entire project. A Wittgensteinian reader, by contrast, is predisposed to approach a text (and its larger historical context) in order to determine its boundaries as a means of ascertaining with greater precision which critical approaches would be most helpful in opening up the text. The textual boundaries are determined through a process which includes both a close and comprehensive descriptive analysis of the text, its language game(s), and its grounds (the rules of the game[s]). Rather than a rejection of prior interpretations, the Wittgensteinian approach attempts to establish the limits encompassing both text and critical method.

The deconstructive emphasis on writing can be seen in the assertion of Jacques Derrida (philosophic father of deconstruction) that writing has been erroneously degraded both in favor of speech (*parole*) and of meaning, within the framework of Saussurean linguistics. As such, written language is seen to consist of signs or signifiers primarily important insofar as they serve as the means to the more important signified. Language has been traditionally perceived as unimportant in and of itself and clearly subservient to meaning. Derrida rejects this hierarchy as false and insists that it reflects a hegemonic logocentrism that privileges both speech (seen as more natural) and meaning over writing. Gayatri Spivak explains that "it is this longing for a center, an authorizing pressure, that spawns hierarchized oppositions" which deconstruction subverts (lxix).

The deconstructive project follows on the heels of the Saussurean approach to language. In his *Cours de linguistique generale*, Saussure refers to the "dangers" and "tyranny" of writing to the more natural language of speech, which is adversely constrained by the bonds of writing. Derrida seeks to uproot this hierarchy by asserting the primacy of that which has been suppressed and subordinated: "To deconstruct is above all, at a particular moment, to reverse the hierarchy" (1981, 56–57). Within the deconstructive reading, writing becomes privileged insofar as conventional relations are opposed and turned on their heads— thereby contesting the original dualism. Christopher Norris notes this "strategic reversal of categories" when he explains that deconstruction "seeks to undo both a given order of priorities *and* the very system of conceptual oppositions that makes that order possible" (1984, 21).

The irony of this procedure is that even though hierarchies are called into question by the deconstructionist, and even though the suppressed term is re-evaluated as more important than previously thought, the dichotomous relation is left intact (albeit in its reinscribed form). The prior structuring is not, in essence, demolished, and the suppressed term never really gains a position of primacy. Derrida writes in *Of Grammatology* that "this does not, by simple inversion, mean that the signifier is fundamental or primary. . . . The signifier will never by rights precede the signified, in which case it would no longer be a signifier and the 'signifying' signifier would no longer have a possible signified" (324). As Derrida suggests, traditional hierarchized dichotomies—meaning over language, speech over writing, signifieds over signifiers, presence over absence, male over female—are questioned and the suppressed term is re-evaluated. But the problem for anyone seeking an actual eradication of these hierarchies is that the primary or privileged term is not re-evaluated in the same sense as is the secondary or unprivileged term. As Jonathan Culler notes, the "opposition that is deconstructed is not destroyed or abandoned but reinscribed" (133).

Reinscription suggests that the former oppositions are maintained even though the original meanings have been questioned. With the opposition or dichotomy intact, albeit in its reinscribed form, the raising of the lower term serves only to strengthen the position of the primary term. In fact, the entire deconstructive project is dependent upon the original logocentric structuring. Derrida acknowledges that the process is not one of "simple inversion." The secondary term will never precede the primary one, nor will they become equal since the dichotomy is essential within the deconstructive perspective. This inequality is essential to the Derridean sense of *différance* in which two distinct meanings (*differ* and *defer*) are brought together in order to emphasize their separateness. Hierarchies are disrupted insofar as their grounds are questioned and shown to differ from their prior assumptions, but the dismantling of the entire system (inextricably linked to the concept of sign) is deferred by virtue of its essential importance for the deconstructive process.[1] No alternative system is proposed, alternative semantic grounds are deferred (Norris writes that "meaning is always *deferred*, perhaps to the point of an endless supplementarity" [1982, 32]), and differences (albeit questioned) are merely reinscribed, rather than altered.

However, what is especially notable and of particular importance to this process is the violence involved. The traditional hierarchies are perceived as tyrannical, forceful, and dominating. Barbara Johnson refers to the "warring forces of signification" (5)—which indicate the battle, never resolved, but subverted in a deconstructive move that frees signifiers from their supposed signifieds and results in a condition of "play." Both Wittgenstein and Derrida emphasize the importance of play. However, whereas the deconstructive sense of play envisages a state of freedom from the constraints of a forced logocentric signification, play for Wittgenstein involves a range of motion prescribed by the limits of each particular language game. Ironically, both the deconstructive sense of play (or free signification) and a rigid absolutist logocentrism would be categorized in a Wittgensteinian framework as flip sides of the very same problematic—that of language going on holiday (PI, I, 38).

Using the example of chess, commonly referred to by Wittgenstein, we can readily see this connection. For Wittgenstein, we play chess by means of freely chosen moves, but such freedom is within the scope of those rules which define that particular game. Within the rubric of the language game, language is used and has life. The condition of a static absolutism, as represented within the chess example, would deny any possibility of play by virtue of dogmatically predetermining our every move, to the degree that every game would be the same. Not only would there be set rules, but even the players' moves would be bereft of any choice whatsoever. In such a situation, the game would have no life. To clarify this problem, Wittgenstein refers to the image of a lump of wood in the form of a human body (PI, I, 430). The "stupid block" is not alive, is not a living person; similarly, language frozen within the bounds of a logocentric absolutism is also not alive, is not a representation of language in everyday use, but language on holiday. The irony of language being outside the bounds of everyday use is that a deconstructive sense of absolute semantic freedom or "play" would, as well, manifest similar difficulties, from a Wittgensteinian perspective.

Freed of all constraints (continually questioned, rejected, and reinscribed), a deconstructive game of chess would approach the level of "play" of a game I observed as a college freshman during the annual "Reality Weekend." After an evening, night, and morning of unlimited consumption of beer (by many, not all, of the students), the traditional game of "beerball" would commence. It was played on a soccer field (but not restricted to the limits of the field) with a ball whose purpose was questionable (certainly far from clear). There were two teams whose memberships were ever-changing (any number could play and one could be on either team, neither, or both simultaneously at any given moment). There were no rules, although the players were encouraged to minimize bodily harm and to refrain from vital injury. Many found the "game" liberating and freeing (perhaps as a reaction to the rigors of the academic program at the college); others found the "game" dangerous and generally ridiculous. These two orientations could be seen as representing the diverse stances of deconstructive theory and Wittgensteinian philosophy towards the language game of poststructural criticism.

The analogy here with a chess game bereft of rules is obvious. The game (defined as chess by its rules) would no longer exist. The game could not be played deconstructively with all possible moves not only allowed but even encouraged—for in this case, the game would no longer be chess, but an altogether different game. As in the example of chess qua a static absolutism, the language and rules of the game are "on holiday." Both rules and moves are "liberated" from the bounds of the language game of chess. As Derrida asserts, "the center closes off the play which it opens up and makes possible" (1978, 279), so we reject that center (or the rules of the game). There may be a deconstructive sense of free "play" with chess pieces moving any which way, not even constrained by the limits of the board, but from a Wittgensteinian perspective, the denial or doubting of the rules of chess is neither reasonable nor possible within the basic grammar of the chess language game. "Imagine a language-game 'When I call you, come in through the door'" (OC, 391). One of the rules of this language game is that there is a door through which the person called is to "come in through." Wittgenstein asserts: "In any ordinary case, a doubt whether there really is a door there will be impossible" (OC, 391). The extraordinary case is that of deconstruction, where language is outside the bounds of everyday language use, where language is on holiday. While this condition is seen as positive by deconstructors, for Wittgenstein, when "language goes on holiday . . . problems arise" (PI, I, 38).

However, within the reality of a world conditioned by the discursive structures of a hegemonic logocentrism, the deconstructive project certainly offers a challenging alternative to a repressive traditionalism. Deconstruction addresses linguistic hierarchies and questions the significations upon which they rest (namely the lower level terms that the privileged terms dominate). By deconstructing traditional terms, values, and concepts, the deconstructionist implies that the privileged terms, values, and concepts are upset. But by maintaining the dichotomies as such, actual subversion never occurs, as can be seen even in the name of the project that includes the "construction" one struggles against. "Deconstruction" reflects within itself the stress of oppositional pulls that result in a violent movement that nevertheless consigns us to the status quo, as in a game of "beerball" between two inebriated teams—both battle against each other, but get nowhere. Neither team ever completely vanquishes its opponent, nor does either team really lose in this game of free "play." Within "deconstruction," we thus see the hierarchies of the reigning status quo being constructed (asserted) and then violently "destructed" (not destroyed, but shown to be groundless). Both processes are forcibly brought together into a new term ("deconstruction") that in itself maintains the duality of the endeavor.

One inevitable result of this process of deconstructive interpretation is that the project provides no means of differentiating between texts. In fact, one of the primary focuses of the deconstructive endeavor is to eradicate such distinctions. Any text is fair game for deconstructing—even those works of the deconstructors themselves. As Altieri points out, "Derrida, insomuch as he makes claims, remains trapped, like his master, Nietzsche, in an ironic or demonic version of the logic he wishes to deconstruct" (1976, 1398). Michael Fischer echoes this point in his assertion that deconstruction "mirrors the conditions that it rightly criticizes" (1985, xiii). The conditions upon which a logocentric reading is contingent are the very conditions which make a deconstructive reading possible. Wittgenstein speaks to this point in the *Investigations*. He notes that "the assertion of the negative proposition contains the proposition which is negated, but not the assertion of it" (PI, I, 447). This indicates that a deconstructive act of inversion/subversion does not, in and of itself, assert the logocentrism upon which the entire project is based. However, Wittgenstein states quite clearly that "if you tried to doubt everything you would not get as far as doubting anything. The game of doubting itself presupposes certainty" (OC, 115). This logocentrism, unquestioned, is rather contained within the bounds of the reactive nature of deconstruction.

Charles Altieri addresses the deconstructive rejection of a center by pointing out that the "rational, self-justifying formal systems" (which Derrida accepts as ontologically unavoidable: questionable but not destructible) are, in a Wittgensteinian perspective, publicly determinate ways of producing meanings (1976, 1414–1415), and as such "provide access to a different secure ground . . . found by remaining within the complex interrelationships of ordinary experience" (1409). Altieri emphasizes that Derrida points to grounds which are, in fact, interpretive fictions, and hence suitable for a deconstructive endeavor, but not suitable for a Wittgensteinian critical approach. Rather than viewing an indiscriminate deconstructing of texts as liberating, Wittgenstein sees this sort of situation as an argument or rationale for holding on to previously held beliefs, rather than as an argument for their rejection. This argument, applied to deconstruction, would read as follows: If everything can be deconstructed and shown to be questionable, then deconstruction itself must be open to doubt. And if the deconstructive endeavor is open to doubt, then there is no reason to categorically adopt a deconstructive stance.[2] Insofar as Wittgenstein is concerned, the doubting/giving grounds process has an end within the bounds of any particular lived language game. He argues that it is an illusion to imagine that doubting goes on forever (OC, 19). There is a point at which doubting stops—thereby avoiding the endless free play of signifiers perceived by deconstructors: "As if giving grounds did not come to an end sometime. But the end is not an ungrounded presupposition: it is an ungrounded way of acting" (OC, 110).

Wittgenstein makes it very clear that there are cases in which doubting would be either senseless, unreasonable, or logically impossible (OC, 2, 454). Within the framework of any particular language game, there are grounds (rules) upon which the game is based or structured. These grounds provide the means of ascertaining the truth of any given fact. "What counts as an adequate test of a statement belongs to logic. It belongs to the description of the language-game. The *truth* of certain empirical propositions belongs to our frame of reference" (OC, 82–83). What Wittgenstein is emphasizing here is that certainty can be arrived at within the framework of a particular language game. The rules of the game determine whether or not a statement is correct insofar as the particular game is concerned. Therefore, a clear understanding of the rules of the game is essential in order to be able to differentiate between what can and cannot be properly doubted. Within the language game of our earlier example of chess, it would not be meaningful to doubt the fact that each piece has certain prescribed moves. One could doubt a particular move made by a chess player and question why another move was not made, but one cannot meaningfully question the rules of the game *if* one chooses to remain within the rubric of the chess language game. One could change the rules, but that would alter the foundations upon which the game lies and would result in a different language game. Such an alteration does not deny the existence of certain rules of play, but rather changes the rules so that the game becomes altered.

Within the deconstructive project, some of the elements of particular language games are questioned and doubted. However, there is little distinction made between which elements serve as a foundational grammar to the game (e.g., the rules) and which are not requisite to all manifestations of the game (such as applications of the rules or interpretations of the game). For example, were we to investigate those works of literature which would fall within the Shakespearean sonnet tradition, the grammar or rules of the sonnet language game might establish that we look for fourteen-line poems comprised of three quatrains and a final rhyming couplet. However, while most of these poems would present a traditional heteropatriarchal love poem format, others (such as a number of Shakespeare's own sonnets) might not. In this case, we see certain rules followed—albeit in different manifestations.

In deconstruction, there is no questioning whether the hierarchized dualities are, in fact, *necessarily* contradictory, with dominating terms asserting their primacy over submissive terms. It is assumed (not doubted) that the lower or absent term needs assistance (like the proverbial "damsel in distress" of phallogocentric tales) and wants to lash out at the privileged term, and it is further assumed that the condition of "play" or perceived groundlessness is preferable to the prior hierarchies. But this "play" fails to provide a more balanced and secure haven for both those who have been previously privileged and those who have been previously devalued. Deconstructors are committed to the disestablishment of any structure (new or otherwise) by virtue of its hegemonic absolutism. Nor does a Wittgensteinian approach to literature provide a new structuring. It does, however, provide a descriptive method (more inclusive than that of deconstruction) capable of clarifying what is actually going on in and around a (con)text. This process will provide the descriptive knowledge (truth) necessary for any future alternative structuring.

Critical Misconceptions: Wittgenstein and Deconstruction

THE DECONSTRUCTIVE PROCESS of destabilization has led literary critics to draw parallels between deconstruction and Wittgenstein's rejection of the philosophical privileging of logic and metaphysics. Walter

Glannon writes: "There are affinities between Wittgenstein's repudia-
tion . . . of the metaphysical realism in the *Tractatus* and . . . the
rejection of the metaphysics of presence by deconstructionists" (263).
He further notes the similar emphases on language and on a text exclusive of the author (here noting Wittgenstein's avoidance of psychology). Samuel C. Wheeler III points out the common ground between
deconstruction and " 'analytic' philosophy both in presuppositions and
in strategies" (239), while describing Wittgenstein as a "conservative
deconstructor," and Jules David Law asserts that both Wittgenstein
and Derrida attempt "to *extend* the field of language by breaking down
its *internal* barriers" (143).[3] Michael Kevin Greene states that "both
Wittgenstein and Derrida employ methods which are comparable [in
that] both thinkers dismantle the traditional theories of language" (82).

Critics and theorists have correctly noted Wittgenstein's dismantling
of the "straight line" of an absolutist logocentrism, but have thereby
misconstrued his philosophy as deconstructive. As Christopher Norris
writes: "The effects of deconstruction are already at work in [the] twists
and contestations of Wittgenstein's text" (1984, 47). Henry Staten goes
furthest in his assessment of Wittgenstein's work as patently deconstructive: "Wittgenstein is unique among Derrida's predecessors in having
achieved, in the period beginning with the *Blue Book*, a consistently
deconstructive standpoint" (1). He even describes the *Investigations* as
Wittgenstein's "great deconstructive work" (2-3).[4] While it is the case
that there are important parallels between the deconstructive project
and the work of Wittgenstein, it is nevertheless essential that the distinctions between the two be drawn as clearly as possible in order to
prevent future misunderstandings and to correct the problematic conflation of the two endeavors.

While Wittgenstein does reject much of the metaphysical endeavors
of philosophy, he does not reject the possibility of grounds upon which
a different sort of system can be built. In fact, as he rejects the structures
of prior philosophy, he argues for the importance of a more organic
form that responds to the diachronic needs of a diverse and evolving
world, and he begins the investigatory work that is preliminary to the
actual unfolding of a new way of philosophizing. Austin E. Quigley
notes that "Wittgenstein's alternative to existing theory is not an anti-
theory, any more than his alternative to existing philosophy is an anti-
philosophy. It is instead a philosophical procedure displayed in action,
a philosophical technique variously exemplified, a philosophical process that refuses to become a reified product" (211-212). It is this Wittgensteinian methodology of investigation that displays the greatest
divergences from the deconstructive strategy. There are several areas of
Wittgenstein's later work which will help clarify where he significantly
diverges from the concerns and interests of the deconstructive approach—
regarding their divergent methodological approaches as well as their
foundational differences concerning language.

As Law and Glannon correctly note, both approaches emphasize the importance of looking closely at language. While Wittgenstein does not focus on the difference between written and spoken speech, as in the Derridean debate regarding the merits of the one over the other, both Wittgenstein and Derrida uphold the importance of the sign, seeing language as a crucial arena in which to address various philosophical problems. Wittgenstein explicitly states that such problems "are solved, rather, by looking into the workings of our language, and that in such a way as to make us recognize those workings" (PI, I, 109). Derrida focuses on language as a direct means of subverting the "tyranny" of logocentrism. And, in each of these diverse philosophical orientations, the investigations regarding signs are intended to provide a new perspective that will lead us to change our understanding of those signs. The deconstructive approach challenges the traditional interpretation in such a way that we are forced to acknowledge our previous errors of interpretation; however, we are not permitted to arrive at an alternative reading that completely eradicates the former reading, since the negation is dependent upon the initial assertion.[5] M. H. Abrams points out that "Derrida remains committed to absolutism" insofar as absolutes are the very problem against which deconstruction reacts (274). In other words, any deconstructive activity depends upon the presence of existing structures, which are then deconstructed. As Richard Shusterman notes: "Deconstruction . . . succeeds in breaking free from ontological positivist essences and distinctions only to be ensnared in a greater, negative essentialism" (1986a, 32).

Say that we look at an old building admiringly and comment: "How beautiful are these old homes modelled on traditional Dutch styles. See the delightful double doors and the carefully styled windows and roof." Our deconstructive companion follows our gaze, albeit with doubt. He looks more closely at the building, looking specifically for the weaknesses and fissures. "Ah, but see how old this house is! Notice the chipping paint, the broken windows, and the roof that leaks. And those double doors are dangerous—continually reminding children of their second-class status. One must imagine they must be forever bumping their little heads on the upper portions." Looking with our friend, we see that he has correctly described the house (according to his generally skeptical nature), and agree that it is nothing more than another decrepit and dangerous old structure no different from any other. As we leave our friend to his doubtful ponderings, however, we realize that we could look at any house in such a manner and that the inevitable result would always prove the same—an indiscriminate, but acute, awareness of the failings of any structure.

Wittgenstein would agree that it is important to scrutinize the object of our investigations as closely and thoroughly as possible. However, we must, as well, remember that Wittgenstein was not a deconstructor but a builder, an engineer, an architect. Where weaknesses in the structure might be noted, the Wittgensteinian response would be not to merely point them out and leave them as such, nor even to automatically assume that what we are perceiving are weaknesses in the structure itself, but to correct those weaknesses where problematic, to adjust our perspective in order to see more clearly that the building is actually sound and that the failings were erroneously perceived to be more consequential than they, in fact, are, and to recognize that what were perceived, in some cases, to be failings actually may serve meaningful functions which the previously held perspective did not allow.

Wittgenstein uses an example to clarify that many of the problems which we perceive are, in fact, problems created by our faulty perceptions. He looks at an individual who, rather than admiring the shadows of trees, disparages them for only being shadows and not the actual trees: "I could imagine somebody might admire not only real trees, but also the shadows or reflections that they cast, taking them too for trees. But once he has told himself that these are not really trees after all and has come to be puzzled at what they are, or at how they are related to trees, his admiration will have suffered a rupture that will need healing" (CV, 57e). Wittgenstein's point in this example is not that the shadows are actually trees, but that the rupture is the result of a conflict between the reality (the shadows are shadows, not trees) and one's previously held expectation (the shadows are trees). Here the deconstructive response would be to uproot an assumed hierarchy of tree over shadow in order to demonstrate that both tree and shadow are to be valued equally (not one gaining preference over the other). However, the deconstructed reading is nevertheless dependent upon the initial hierarchy as the motivating problem against which the new reading rebels. The Wittgensteinian response would differ in that the problem would not be to question the prior suppositions and then reinscribe them (though in a ruptured form), but rather to remove those prejudicial views in order to completely eradicate the conflict which arose due to one's erroneous preconceptions. Hence, Wittgenstein refers to his method as "therapy" (PI, I, 133) which will help us to understand our "entanglement in our rules" which we ourselves have laid down (PI, I, 125). What Wittgenstein is getting at here is that many of our confusions are not necessary confusions (actual conditions of reality), but are rather imagined confusions due to our faulty investigations and skewed interpretations. These limiting theoretical approaches (of which deconstruction is one) force us to see the world in a certain manner. We, therefore, only see those aspects which that framework permits us to see.

Since Wittgenstein asserts that the meanings of words are to be seen in their actual uses (PI, I, 10), we must acknowledge that the tree and the shadow, in the aforementioned example, are not one and the same. In other words, the actual use of both tree and shadow are very different. Whereas a deconstructive response to the tree/shadow example would be to reject the problematic privileging of tree over shadow through a deconstructive destabilisation of the assumed primacy of the tree, a Wittgensteinian response would be to question the initial assumption of hierarchized dualism and, rather than rejecting any primacy of the tree altogether, would investigate the significance of both the tree and the shadow within particular contexts. For example, were one hungry, it would make sense to privilege the fruit of the tree over the shadow-fruit of the shadow-tree. However, were one hot and tired during a summer day, the shadow would take greater precedence as a place to rest. When our preconceived notions remove our critical interpretations from any sort of grounding in the real world of trees, shadows, and texts, we end up grappling with difficulties largely the creation of those interpretive strategies.

Wittgenstein repeatedly emphasizes the importance of looking at the world (and this includes pictures of the world—written or otherwise) as closely and as *clearly* as possible. We must try to get away from our biased perspectives, which force us to see reality in certain prescribed ways. It is as if our directed perspective is due to "a pair of glasses on our nose through which we see whatever we look at. It never occurs to us to take them off" (PI, I, 103). Wittgenstein urges us to remedy our myopia, rather than merely acknowledging, in a deconstructive manner, that our vision is interminably myopic. It may be myopic, but often that myopia is due to wearing a pair of glasses that serve to further impair our eyesight rather than to improve it. This avoidable myopia leads us to misconstrue reality in such a way that we confuse shadows and trees.

Wittgenstein asserts that this constrained vision is the cause of our "conceptual confusions." Rather than looking clearly at the world, we permit our view to be clouded by our preconceived notions. According to deconstructionists, one notion that clouds our vision is that the world is necessarily divided between contradictory realities which present themselves within a dualistic framework (good/bad, inside/outside, speech/writing, philosophy/literature, male/female). While Derrida deconstructs the divisions between these dualities ("Il n'y a pas d'hors-texte"),[6] Wittgenstein discusses both the need to clear away our confusions and the importance of avoiding the ironclad expectation of contradiction. In the early analytic work of the *Tractatus*, Wittgenstein looks at the nature of logical contradiction. He explains that both contradictions and tautologies are fundamentally meaningless. Neither says anything about reality. However, this is not to say that they are nonsensical. They are important symbolically, just as is the number "0" in mathematics, but the symbolism represents nothing, or the absence of a positive or negative numerical valuation. "Tautology and contradiction are not pictures of reality. . . . Contradiction fills the whole logical space and leaves no point to reality" (TLP, 4.462, 4.463). The deconstructive response here would be to agree, and assert that this is the very sense of the deconstructive "play." Where there is no ontological foundation of meaning, there is no logically meaningful point to reality. There is only contradiction.[7]

It is here that Wittgenstein and deconstruction part company most thoroughly, for while Wittgenstein does point out that contradiction is meaningless (other than in its meaningful assertion of contradiction) and leaves us in an irreconcilable state of conflict, he stresses that certitude, progress, and forward motion are nevertheless still possible. "Different concepts touch here and coincide over a stretch. But you need not think that all lines are *circles*" (PI, 192e). Therefore, progress is possible—we do not always end up back where we started, circling around a static center we either logocentrically accept or reactively deny. If our language games are centered or grounded in their rules of play, then we can, in fact, arrive at the games' centers by approaching the actual play or rules in use. For Wittgenstein, there is a meaningful world; our lived realities are true according to the grammar of our respective language games; and contradiction is not the only alternative.

Wittgenstein's point is not that there should be no contradiction at all, but that there are clear limits for the proper use of a contradiction beyond which it is less useful. It is possible that we might doubt certain concerns, perhaps seeing them from seemingly contradictory standpoints, but our doubting opposition may be the result of our own misinterpretations of the world. In his later work, he notes the problems that arise due to a desire to force concepts and the world artificially together in the form of ostensive definitions. Since "an ostensive definition can be variously interpreted in *every* case" (PI, I, 28), it is essential to realize that *what is the case* is what is most important, and not our diverse interpretations or definitions. Wittgenstein emphasizes that meaning is to be found in the use of a word, not in any static definition or interpretation: "A meaning of a word is a kind of employment of it. For it is what we learn when the word is incorporated into our language" (OC, 61). When we look at a picture of a duck-rabbit, the picture does not change even though we may see it differently (as a duck one moment and as a rabbit the next). To remain focused on our interpretations/definitions is to remain on the superficial (or linguistic) level of the sign. Wittgenstein insists that we focus our attention on the actual use of the sign in practice: "There is always the danger of wanting to find an expression's meaning by contemplating the expression itself, and the frame of mind in which one uses it, instead of always thinking of the practice" (OC, 601). For Wittgenstein, any focus that does not include a thorough investigation of language in use ("practice") is misdirected, or, at best, inadequate.

The disquietudes of language are real and reflect the deeper conflicts of the world. Language, as a form of life,[8] is important and must be investigated, so that we do not mistake the sign for the reality. We receive "false appearances" from language that "bewitch" our intelligence. "One thinks that one is tracing the outline of the thing's nature over and over again, and one is merely tracing round the frame through which we look at it," as in the case of the points on a circle which only circle around the center (PI, I, 114). Wittgenstein repeatedly emphasizes how we get stuck within our respective interpretive frameworks. "Again and again a use of the word emerges that seems not to be compatible with the concept that other uses have led us to form. We say: but that *isn't* how it is!—it *is* like that though! and all we can do is keep repeating these antitheses" (CV, 30e). Wittgenstein stresses that these antitheses (like the *différance* of deconstruction) are not the result of an essentially antithetical world, but rather the result of the conflict between the reality and our requirements of it (PI, I, 107). And this conflict can be removed or avoided by "turning our whole examination round" (PI, I, 108), so that we "do away with all *explanation,* and description alone must take its place" (PI, I, 109).

A deconstructor might interject at this point that this is just the concern of deconstruction: free play, traces, linguistic unreliability, relative semantics, words *sous rature,* the futility of final explanation. A Wittgensteinian response might be that, yes, we must look at the world and language "from close to" and that, yes, it is necessary to investigate the conflicts we perceive (and often create), but, no, this is not to say that there is no meaning at all. Michael Fischer correctly emphasizes that we must not forget Wittgenstein's "constructive lesson" (1986, 97) that *"essence* is expressed by grammar" (PI, I, 371). By investigating the foundational grammatical rules of language games, we can determine meaning as prescribed or delimited by those rules. And we investigate these rules by noting their actual use. In other words, we can not get at that meaning or essence by focusing only on the linguistic sign. Any logocentric essence ascertained by "contemplating the expression itself" would be misleading and quite ripe for any deconstructive attack. It is the use of an expression that is meaningful.[9] "One cannot guess how a word functions. One has to *look at* its use and learn from that. But the difficulty is to remove the prejudice which stands in the way of doing this. It is not a *stupid* prejudice" (PI, I, 340). In these three brief sentences, Wittgenstein emphasizes several crucial points regarding the complex situation of preconceived orientations to the world. He begins his thinking here by asserting that we can only arrive at the functioning of a word by observing the word's use. An uninformed "guess" is just that—uninformed or "stupid."

However, Wittgenstein is careful to note that while it is important to remove those prejudices "which stand in the way" of such observations and understanding (*"look at* its use and learn from that")—a process he acknowledges to be understandably difficult—he is not saying that we must remove all prejudices indiscriminately, nor that all prejudices are "stupid" (i.e., unclear, uninformed, or misguided). The deconstructive project, which proffers a particular approach to a text, may be narrow insofar as it is prejudicial in its theoretical orientation, but may, as well, prove to be a sharp and clear representation (albeit with its limited scope) of that text. A Wittgensteinian approach demands the sharpness and clarity found in many close deconstructive readings, while stressing a broader and less prejudicial investigation in order to determine the actual limits of both text and critical approach. What is essential is to look at the world and language (as a reflection of the world) without the preconceived notions which adversely constrain our investigations.

The forced imposition of such preconceived notions on our readings of the world (and texts) can be seen in the violence and force which I noted in the deconstructive struggle against the hegemonic absolutism of logocentric readings of texts. The difference is that Wittgenstein wants to preventively remove, rather than reactively subvert, these interpretive frameworks which insist upon a hegemonically imposed violence. The deconstructive response lends credence and weight to those interpretive frameworks by acknowledging their significance as a force to be struggled against. Such violent deconstructive reactions primarily serve to reinforce the original positions, rather than to effect a disengaging shift away from those previously held interpretive stances Wittgenstein sees as limiting. For Wittgenstein, the interpretive stances or theoretical approaches are the problem since they create their own imaginary tyrants and then insist upon doing battle with oppositions that might not even exist. In the *Investigations*, Wittgenstein says that concepts are "fixed" and "forced" upon us. Objects that are seen according to an interpretation are "squeezed" and "forced" into forms they do not really fit (PI, 200e). Our desire or wish to impose such preconceived views upon objects, facts, words, and expressions is referred to as a "despotic demand" (PI, I, 437). Bell Hooks and many other feminist critics argue against such demands made by earlier logocentric literary criticisms, which they have pointed out are not only logocentric, but, in fact, phallogocentric in their devaluing of women's writing. In the case of deconstruction, a despotic logocentrism is exposed in an aporetic revealing/unveiling that proves to be the primary aim of the deconstructor.[10] A Wittgensteinian approach goes further by virtue of investigating the language games of the various literary and critical texts in order to discern the appropriateness of particular critical approaches to literary works.

For a Wittgensteinian, the traps set by language must be revealed (CV, 18e), and often this necessitates that we "apply words in ways that conflict with their original usage" (CV, 44e). Such a conflict could manifest itself in a critical reading of a poem that might describe various aspects of the work which escape the notice of most theoretically-bound critics, or a deconstructive reading that would emphasize the need to subvert and then reinscribe perceived hierarchies. But, unlike the resultant deconstructive reinscription, the end for a Wittgensteinian is to see the facts (as displayed in the text and its larger contexts) in a new light and with greater clarity than previously. This might indicate that previously held theoretical stances are invalid or useless, and might point to problems which are, in fact, imaginary rather than real. "Once the new way of thinking has been established, the old problems vanish; indeed they become hard to recapture. For they go with our way of expressing ourselves and, if we clothe ourselves in a new form of expression, the old problems are discarded along with the old garment" (CV, 48e). Only by means of "getting hold of the difficulty *deep down*" (CV, 48e), by going beyond the actual text to its many and various contexts (language games), will a critic be able to view the work anew and describe or evaluate it more comprehensively.

Wittgenstein emphasizes that such valuations change across cultures and times. Both Richard Shusterman and Austin E. Quigley see a recognition of the historicity of culture as essential to the Wittgensteinian method and as radically divergent from a deconstructive view. Quigley writes: "It is in their differing estimates of the power, importance, and diversity of historical constraint that Derrida and Wittgenstein most strongly diverge" (220–221). Shusterman emphasizes the importance of critical pluralism in light of three themes he notes in Wittgenstein: radical indeterminacy of aesthetic concepts, logical plurality of critical discourse, and historicity of art and art appreciation (1986c, 108). Such an historical pluralism indicates the need for critical responses to acknowledge divergent readings, rather than to dictate a particular interpretation (deconstructive or otherwise). Wittgenstein writes that "at different times we have different ideals of exactitude; and none of them is supreme" (CV, 37e). To merely exchange meanings and subvert the hierarchies is to lose all meaning and to be lost in a deconstructive world of "free play."[11] For Wittgenstein, meaning is not only possible but essential to the continuation and existence of language games.

There simply are things which we must accept and not doubt: "That is to say, the *questions* that we raise and our *doubts* (*Zweifel*) depend on the fact that some propositions are exempt from doubt, are as it were like hinges on which those turn" (OC, 341). If we want to open a door, we must accept the existence and functioning of the hinges. "We just *can't* investigate everything, and for that reason we are forced to rest content with assumption. If I want the door to turn, the hinges [like the rules of language games] must stay put. My *life* consists in my being content to accept many things" (OC, 343–44). Wittgenstein is not denying the value of doubt, nor is he saying that we must accept everything. Rather we must learn to discriminate between what is usefully doubted and what is usefully accepted. By investigating further (the text, its larger context, as well as our critical approach), we can hope to arrive at much deeper and more complete descriptions. As Wittgenstein reminds us, "One keeps forgetting to go right down to the foundations. One doesn't put the question marks *deep* enough down" (CV, 62e).

Textual Language Games: A Text Case Study

WE MUST REMEMBER what may very well be Wittgenstein's most important caveat: "The meaning of a word is its use in the language" (PI, I, 43). Therefore, in order to flesh out the distinctions between the deconstructive and Wittgensteinian approaches that I have been discussing, I will look at the first stanza of Emily Dickinson's poem, "My Life had stood—a Loaded Gun," in terms of both approaches. Since deconstruction is much more familiar to most literary critics, a brief deconstructive reading will be offered first, followed by a somewhat longer (though still brief) Wittgensteinian reading.

In a deconstructive reading, we might note that the poem begins with the following first line (there being no title): "My Life had stood— a Loaded Gun—" (825). While Dickinson emphasizes the importance of the speaker's life, the presence of the gun points to a death or arrested life. The gun is loaded and pointing forward as indicated by the dash following the word "gun." The combination of the threateningly loaded gun and the fact that the life is standing still rather than moving indicates a condition of death rather than of life. This inactivity or passivity is further underscored when Dickinson writes that the activity of the later stanzas only occurs after the speaker of the poem is carried away. And all future activity is undercut by the repeated ruptures between the stated actions and the unstated but implied powerlessness presented throughout the poem. While there is roaming and hunting and speaking, these activities are only achieved in tandem with the owner or master ("We roam" and "We hunt") or for the sake of him ("I speak for Him").

The tension between life and death, activity and inactivity, power and powerlessness is underscored by the poem's final assertion of destructive power. But while there is the power to kill, it is a derived power, since there is no power to kill oneself or die. At this point, the poem seems to reflect back on itself, with the poem incapable even of ending itself. There is neither the power to die nor the power to live. The poem and its speaker remain stuck in a state of limbo or aporia; there is no reconciliation, just the forcibly violent condition of a loaded gun that does not fire and a deadly life unable to die. The poem, like its speaker, is caught between the unrealizable hopes for a resolution and for closure. Read deconstructively, the poem (inevitably mirroring its critical approach) ends where deconstruction begins, in an unending process of assertion and subversion (each reflecting back upon the other). And the poem's progress (or lack thereof) illustrates that of deconstruction. The refusal of closure is symbolically manifested in the inevitable duality of opposition—oppositions certainly evident even in the life of a reclusive woman poet, both absent from the world and imprisoned by it, yet freed through its crevices.

In this cursory look at Dickinson's poem, liberty is seen to be a direct result of the aporetic struggles against an externally imposed discourse of control that merely appears powerful. While such a reading does shed light on the text, nevertheless, it is constrained by its own critical boundaries, which prevent views of the poem beyond those prescribed limits. A Wittgensteinian approach demands the critic go further—considering other avenues of approach or entry in/to the poem as a means of descriminating between them and enabling a potentially more meaningful (i.e., useful) reading. Such an openness and comprehensiveness would include the possibility of situating the poem within its authorial, socio-historical, geographical, psychological, and/or linguistic contexts. This would indicate the advantage of critics having a greater familiarity with as many as possible of the language games in which a particular literary work participates. For example, in the case of "My Life had stood—a Loaded Gun—," some of the language games with which a critic would want to be familiar might be the female poet language game, the nineteenth-century American poetry language game, the New England poet language game, the Civil War literature language game, the reclusive writer language game, the hunting poem language game, the feminist language game, and the experimental poetry language game. A familiarity with any of these language games (which would include the games' various rules of play) would provide the critic with diverse means of access to Dickinson's poem. Such familiarity or participation in certain language games should not further bias the critic's interpretive or evaluative stance, but should aid his or her descriptive powers by permitting a closer and more comprehensive view of the poem (as opposed to the more limited view afforded by either a narrowly constrained theoretical approach or a less comprehensive description due to unfamiliarity with most of the language games in which the poem participates).

However, prior to any evaluative stance regarding either poem or criticism, the investigation or description of the poem's language game(s) or form(s) of life must take place, since observation is necessary in differentiating between the essential and inessential aspects (rules and play) of the poem; this is necessary as a means of making later evaluative responses, such as the extent to which a poem succeeds in playing particular language games. Unlike a deconstructive stance, Wittgenstein strongly affirms the existence of a center or grounds upon which certainty is based. "There is something universal here; not just something personal" (OC, 440). However, the center is not some sort of *a priori* absolute we are forced to either accept or struggle against in deconstructive fashion. Our center(s) is/are as multifarious in essence and organically evolving in character as is/are the language game(s) of which each center is determinate. This centering is provided by those rules of the game which are essential (necessary to the existence of the game). If we are investigating the language game of Dickinson's poem "My Life had stood—a Loaded Gun—" then, the text serves as the center of observation. All other elements involved in the investigation must be continually referred back to the central text, for the text (and its larger context) determine the other language games, whose secondary investigations must necessarily inform any comprehensive reading.

The poem begins without a title and, based on Dickinson's handwriting, has been dated around 1863. The Civil War dating of the poem certainly rings true in light of the images of the loaded gun, of hunting and killing, and of being in service to a "master." While many of Dickinson's poems focus on the theme of death, the collection of militaristic or hunting images in this poem stands out as representative of this period of national strife and violence. This sense of discord, played out throughout the poem, even more poignantly portrays the radical condition of an Emily Dickinson—a nineteenth-century New England woman of Puritan ancestry who dared to write, who dared to not marry, who dared to live her life as individualistically as possible in a time and place in which women were expected to marry and bear children. Here we see that the dating and socio-geographic placement of the poem indicate the importance of particular language games whose investigations would help to clarify our perceptions and evaluations regarding the work. The 1863 dating and New England home of Dickinson indicate a time and place of turbulent societal change—a turbulence evident throughout the poem.

"My Life had stood—a Loaded Gun—." This first line immediately brings to mind the respective language games of a pre-Civil War United States, the reality of an Emily Dickinson, and the condition of women in nineteenth century America: a country fraught with the stress of divided cultures and goals, many of which were often in direct conflict with each other; a woman poet capable of revolutionizing the ways in which we write and read poetry, but caught in a no-win struggle with the literary powers that be, and whose only choice was to recoil from the battle and the world; and women, only fifteen years after the momentous feminist gathering at Seneca Falls, still denied the possibilities of fulfilling their lives beyond the reach of home and family. In one short line, Dickinson portrays the tension and stress involved in the dichotomy between lived realities and latent hopes and capabilities. And yet, the line offers a vision of change—perhaps through violence, but not necessarily. The past tense of "had stood" clearly indicates that the period of stagnancy is of the past, and the "Loaded Gun—" points forward to possible future change and eruption.

The second line emphasizes those held back from achieving their potentialities, as in the case of a gun (designed to be unloaded by means of shooting) which lies loaded and unused. "My Life had stood—a Loaded Gun— / In Corners—till a Day / The Owner passed—identified— / And carried Me away—." Wittgenstein stresses the importance of investigating the use of a word, object, or fact. A sign dissociated from its use is seen as lifeless, meaningless. "Every sign *by itself* seems dead. *What* gives it life?—In use it is *alive*. Is life breathed into it there?—Or is the *use* its life?" (PI, I, 432). In Dickinson's poem, we see a useless gun (a lifeless/meaningless sign waiting to be used) which has been put to the side to stand in corners. Dickinson emphasizes the word "Corners—" by capitalization and by the fact that the word is not followed immediately by another word but by a dash. A loaded gun in corners, a sense of entrapment, of enslavement, of second-class citizenship, of denied suffrage, of an unknown and hidden poet, of being cornered like the female deer/dear/"Doe" of the second stanza. The poem vividly portrays the awful reality of lives denied their meaning, of unfulfilled and unlived lives forced into misuse, abuse, and disuse. And yet, as in the case of the first line, the remaining lines of this first stanza offer hope and life.

The gun is left unused (but ready for use) in corners "till a Day." This "Day" signifies the transition—the end of disuse, the beginning of a new day. The importance of this "Day" is underscored by its capitalization and the end stop after the word (specifically, the fact that the word ends the line), which forces a brief pause separating the word from the succeeding words. Dickinson makes it very clear that this "Day" of change is of particular importance, for this is the day on which the one forgotten, ignored, denied, unknown, is recognized and brought out of the corner, out of obscurity, out of slavery, out of the home, and into the important world of [the][12] Sovreign Woods, the Mountains, and the Vesuvian Valley. "In Corners—till a Day / The Owner passed—identified— / And carried Me away—." The lack of any punctuation between "Day" and "The Owner" strongly indicates that the passing of the owner occurred on that day of liberation and that, perhaps, that passing served as the catalyst for change. The dashes on either side of "—identified—" separate the word from those preceding and following. This separation presents an ambiguity regarding exactly who is identified. Is it the owner who is identified, and, if so, by whom? Or is it rather the forgotten one who becomes identified, recognized, remembered?

At this point in the poem, the forgotten object gains its subjectivity. Subject and object merge as the subject "Owner" acts only with verbs in the past tense ("passed—identified— / And carried") indicating past but not present activity, and the passive object has its/her subjectivity emphasized in the strongly asserted and capitalized "Me." Both the grammatically past activity of the subject (as manifested in the three verbs listed in succession, which serve to further separate subject from object) and the isolation of the unused object are finally reconciled in their union in the final line of the stanza ("And carried Me away—"). We see the fruitfulness of the union as the next stanza begins with subject and object, Owner and Gun, master and slave, Union and Confederate, male and female, poetry and silence, joined in activity, in a strongly emphasized present tense ("And now We roam . . . / And now We hunt"), and in the use of the first person plural pronoun "We." Strength and activity lie in the dissolution of the grammatical and actual dichotomies. All involved benefit from the joining. The paralyzing contradictions emphasized in the previous deconstructive reading are seen to be the products of the past, only meaningful prior to the "Day" of reunification, and anachronistic for an organic world of united diversity. The disunified subject "He" is seen in his actual weakness. He dies sooner, for die he necessarily will, even though he longs for and insists ("must") on his unrealizable longevity—the poem serving to undercut and, perhaps, deny "His" dichotomized independence.

At this point, we see the striking difference between the two resulting readings of Dickinson's poem.[13] In the deconstructive interpretation, the dichotomies and fissures are made manifest in an assertion of their inevitability. But as Susan Howe, language poet and critic, asks, "Does a woman's mind move in time with a man's? What is the end of Logic?" (17). In the Wittgensteinian reading, the crevice separating woman from man, wife and mother from poet, logic from life, is dissolved. The distinctions become moot/mute when we look "descriptively" in order to see the poem and its world by means of a range of possible critical entryways. The poem's linguistic fragmenting, noted in both of the above readings, proves to be the means of resolution and unification, rather than merely the demonstration of an inevitable conflict. By virtue of a Wittgensteinian approach, we, as critics, are permitted a more complete entry into the poem and are enabled to see the longed for liberation as a realized fact. The poet writes, the woman empowers herself, the slave is freed, and the nation regains its lost sense of unity. As Dickinson writes in one of her letters, "Life is death we're lengthy at, death the hinge to life" (1986, 425). While "He—may longer live . . . —than I—," for Dickinson his longer life may, in fact, represent less his triumph and rather his loss, with death being the "hinge to life" and the woman-poet possessing the "power to kill" (his enemies, perhaps Him, perhaps even a phallogocentric world and literature), but she does not possess the "power [art] to die—" with the continuing life of the poem.

A deconstructive response would undercut this hopeful reading by pointing out the ever-present ruptures which decenter any sort of certainty. Dickinson did write but in obscurity; her poems were scarcely published in her day. And, yes, women have become more empowered, but suffrage for women did not come for almost another sixty years after the writing of the poem, and women, even today, are still the disenfranchised and colonialized objects of a phallocentric world. Slavery was made illegal, but the history of slavery and an enduring capitalistic objectification of people of color still informs the reality of race relations in this country, and racial equality is still only a dream. And perhaps the nation did regain its unity, but this unity carries with it the burden of its ruptured past. While these imperfect conditions are the case, they do not discount the profound significance of the actual voice of an Emily Dickinson as heard within the (con)text of her poem. As Wittgenstein stresses in the *Investigations,* every line is not a circle. There are those lines (texts) which do not have centers and therefore cannot be usefully decentered (deconstructed)—as in the case of some of the writings of Gertrude Stein or some contemporary language poets. And the lines which are circles, the texts which have centers, might not always be meaningfully decentered. It is essential that we differentiate among texts in order to ascertain which are and are not centered, and of those which are centered, which might be usefully decentered/doubted/ deconstructed.

Emily Dickinson's work is acknowledged, along with that of Stein and others, as an important precursor to language poetry. This fact alone indicates that readings of Dickinson's work should take note of what Marjorie Perloff has termed the "antisymbolist tradition" among poets of the last century or two. In other words, we should expect the poetry of Dickinson to resist the unyielding limits imposed by various critical approaches like deconstruction. "My Life had stood—a Loaded Gun—" resists its deconstructive reading throughout. Dickinson's variant readings, often listed at the end of her poems in the manuscript editions, strongly indicate her desire for the poem's center to be multifluous—changing with each divergent word. The variant reading for the twenty-third line (from "For I have but the power to kill," to "For I have but the art to kill,") shifts the poem's center and demands a radically different reading. Such a shifting of centers indicates a refusal to present a traditionally reified set of categories upon which theoretical approaches such as deconstruction depend.

A significant question is whether a deconstructive reading can adequately address a work of literature bereft of a center or with multiple centers. But in its playful dissolution of literary categories, deconstruction rejects the sort of limits which a Wittgensteinian would accept as meaningful demarcations between and within the diverse language games of texts, contexts, and criticisms. Rather, as a theoretical approach useful for literary criticism, deconstruction has been used as a means of critiquing many works of writing without asking the question of whether that particular approach is, in fact, more or less helpful in regards to certain texts. Shusterman notes "deconstruction's monotonous readings of the self-reflexive, aporetic, unreadable nature of all texts" (32-33).[14] And Susan Howe poignantly notes the potential problems associated with any sort of indiscriminate criticism: "The future will forget, erase, or recollect and deconstruct every poem" (13).

The deconstructive project directs its attention to a wide range of texts, often regardless of the viability or usefulness of the endeavor. When the deconstructor chooses to misapply a deconstructive reading to a text, a Wittgensteinian response might be to "simply say 'O, rubbish!' . . . That is, not reply to him but admonish him" for objecting to "propositions that are beyond doubt" (OC, 495). Our job as literary critics and theorists is not to doubt or deconstruct texts indiscriminately, but to discover which propositions can be profitably doubted and which not. What Quigley refers to as a Wittgensteinian-influenced "literary theorizing" may very well help to provide our method of "travel" or approach to literary texts. The Wittgensteinian critic will remember that doubting is not sensible in every case, that doubting comes to an end when we reach bedrock (the grounds of everyday life, the rules of our various language games), and that certainty can be ascertained by means of investigating language in use. A deconstructive refusal to consider the possibility of such certainty can lead to serious misreadings when the text is forced to fit the theoretical approach.

When we read "My Life had stood—a Loaded Gun—" as a manifestation of an irreconcilable dialectical aporia as seen in the tension between action and inaction, life and death, and power and powerlessness, we overlook that Dickinson very skillfully emphasizes the immortal and invincible power of the poem's speaker. Every reference that involves the persona is capitalized (My, Me, We, I), and the persona's power is demonstrated in each stanza ("—a Loaded Gun—," "I speak for Him— / The Mountains straight reply," "I smile . . . as a Vesuvian face," "I guard," "I'm deadly foe— . . . emphatic Thumb—" "power to kill, / Without—the power to die—"). Close textual investigations that place the work within its larger context are essential for any interpretive analysis. Such investigations could discover the poetical mastery and confidence of an Emily Dickinson—a discovery which might indicate the inadequacy of a strict deconstructive approach to her work. As noted earlier, when "we confuse prototype and object we find ourselves dogmatically conferring on the object [text] properties which only the prototype necessarily possesses. . . . [The] prototype ought to be clearly presented for what it is; so that it characterizes the whole discussion and determines its form" (CV, 14e). Descriptive investigations must be preliminary to any critical or evaluative stance; in fact, the results of the examination would determine the suitability of particular approaches. An investigation into the life and writings of Emily Dickinson demonstrates a strong feminist awareness and a conscious emphasis on alternative grammatical structures.

Referring to the poetry of another female poet, Dickinson writes "did you ever read one of her Poems backward, because the plunge from the front overturned you? I sometimes (often have, many times) have—A something overtakes the Mind" (1986, 916). Dickinson's acute awareness of her place in the world as a woman and as a poet indicates that, rather than approaching her poems with a deconstructive skepticism, the more efficacious reading would be by means of the language games in which Dickinson and her poetry, in fact, do participate. Such a Wittgensteinian approach permits a work to open itself to multiple critical pathways, rather than forcing it to fit into a particular theoretical mold. Rather than reading "My Life had stood—a Loaded Gun—" as a reflection of the aporetic tension inevitably demonstrated by any deconstructive reading, the poem is freed to be a powerful manifestation of the voice/ art of a poet who sees/presents the world in a radically new form, which is beyond the bounds of theoretical approaches constrained by prior notions of traditional logocentrism. Dickinson's alternative language games present a different sort of centering (or centerings), and therefore necessitate an alternative approach (or approaches) as indicated by Wittgensteinian investigations.

As is evident, the usefulness of the deconstructive methodology is contingent upon its being used appropriately (e.g., towards those texts with identifiable, and problematic, centers). As Wittgenstein reminds us, "each morning you have to break through the dead rubble afresh so as to reach the living warm seed" (CV, 2e). In the domain of literary criticism, we often need to break though the lifeless (useless) rubble of our critical theories (PI, I, 118) in order to more clearly discern the language games of a text and the suitability (usefulness) of particular critical approaches. An investigation into an especially resistant text's language games might very well indicate the necessity of "turning our whole examination round" and rejecting the use of a particular theory we may have erroneously considered to have had global applications. As Wittgenstein writes, "What we have rather to do is to *accept* the everyday language-game, and to note false accounts *as* false" (PI, 200e).

6

Moving beyond Postmodernism: Future Directions for Wittgensteinian Critical Analyses

AS WE CONTINUE to wend our way through the seemingly endless dialectics of competing postmodern critical theories, Wittgenstein's philosophical approach to the world proves to be a refreshingly new method for critical entries in/to texts (literary and critical, written, oral, and lived). Insofar as contemporary criticism and theory are concerned, only two critical options present themselves: to either participate and perpetuate the oppositionality of a modern/postmodern, structural/ poststructural existential angst, or simply to not engage in these debates, thereby choosing to play an entirely different critical language game. Applications of Wittgenstein's heuristic of the language game, his categoric rejection of theory, his concept of family resemblance, and his methodology of descriptive investigations can facilitate this shift to critical deliberations that escape both the absolutism of a problematic logocentrism and the decentered critical solipsism of poststructural theories. From issues of canonicity to questions concerning the appropriateness and accuracy of textual readings, a Wittgensteinian approach enables the critic to read and enter texts through a categorically new method distinct from the more common imposition of preconceived critical theories upon those texts.

At this point, several related topics present themselves as areas for future investigations regarding the interrelations between Wittgensteinian philosophy and literary criticism and theory. Those I introduce in this conclusion rely upon the crucial Wittgensteinian concern for recognizing and establishing limits to both critical endeavors and the objects of those endeavors. Initial investigations will discuss (1) the effects of Wittgenstein's discussions about certainty and skepticism insofar as they might affect critical determinations of textual axiology, (2) the divergent grammars surrounding the use of the term "theory" and their implications for definitional and evaluative stances regarding various critical theories (particularly those of women and writers of color), and (3) Wittgenstein's descriptive methodology as it relates to general determinations of canonicity. These concerns will be discussed in relation to textual language-game entry, specifically as it bears on the postmodern critical methods of New Historicism and cultural criticism. Here a discussion of the mestiza language game is broadened into more general investigations of intertextual and intercritical cultural diversity. I end with a brief consideration of contemporary language poetry as one type of literature ostensibly influenced by Wittgenstein's writings.

The establishment of clear limits surrounding our investigations (which, for our purposes, includes delineating the language games in which the critical object or text and the critical discourse participate) is crucial as a means of reducing those impediments to our investigations which adversely affect our perceptions. The importance given to the delineation of limits, specifically in relation to the fact that certainty does exist in the world, is evident throughout much of Wittgenstein's work, from his earlier stance of the *Tractatus* to his later work, which argues against the rigidity of theoretical positions while holding, nevertheless, that culturally accepted notions reflect the basic grammar of our language games.[1] It is this belief in a foundational level of certainty, coupled with the concept of an organic diversity on the level of applications, that has direct implications for axiological evaluations on the literary front. Wittgenstein writes that "the application of a word is not everywhere bounded by rules" (PI, I, 84). In other words, within the bounds of a particular language game, only the foundational defining rules of the game (its essential grammar) are immutable. (Of course, those rules may change, but then we would have a different game.) However, the way in which those rules are applied is not completely restricted or predetermined (as in the case of chess moves).

The condition of absolute rigidity, where no doubt is possible at all, is one problem evidenced in logocentric approaches to the world and to texts. Wittgenstein describes this situation as a game which "is everywhere bounded by rules, . . . [which] never lets a doubt creep in, but stops up all the cracks" (PI, I, 84). This possibility he rejects, while also rejecting the opposite extreme of skepticism. The problem with logocentric critical stances is that they present artificially abstracted representations of the world such that there is not only no room for doubt, but further, no room for any flexibility or life whatsoever. While such approaches may have their limited uses, it is crucial that we understand their limitations and the fact that logocentric representations, as such, do not portray the world or a text in its organic reality, but merely portray a frozen slice of that world/text in terms of the respective critical orientations taken. The rejection of this extreme position does not necessarily lead us to the opposing extreme of skepticism; Wittgenstein sees the alternative of a categoric skepticism as comparably problematic. Even though there is room for doubt in the world, this is not to say that certainty and belief are impossible. Wittgenstein clarifies this by means of an everyday example noted in the discussion (in chapter 2) of a descriptive psychological approach to texts. Wittgenstein writes, "I can easily imagine someone always doubting before he opened his front door whether an abyss did not yawn behind it, and making sure about it before he went through the door (and he might on some occasion prove to be right)—but that does not make me doubt in the same case" (PI, I, 84). The grounds upon which Wittgenstein bases his arguments against skepticism or relativism are the many manifestations of certainty displayed in our everyday lives. When we go through our front doors, we do so with the certainty that we are not stepping into an abyss, but rather stepping onto our front stoop. This reliance on everyday life is fundamental to all of Wittgenstein's later work where meaning is determined by its uses in the world.

Such culturally accepted and delineated certainty on the foundational level, and organicism, flexibility, and diversity on the level of application present provocative implications for literary axiology. Chapter 4 discusses the implications of Wittgensteinian philosophy for a culturally-based critical method—particularly in relation to Native American Indian literatures. The determining rules of cultural and aesthetic language games provide a means by which works of literature (and criticism) can be confidently evaluated, and in new ways. Within the language game of Western literature, Shakespeare's plays are widely considered to be supremely successful works of literature. However, other language games, such as those of feminist and Caribbean criticisms, might point out particular problems with the plays (solipsistically indicating that the plays do not adequately portray their respective language games—namely, postmodern feminism and third world analysis). A Wittgensteinian analysis of these critiques would point out that they cannot successfully evaluate the plays where their engagement with those Shakespearean language games evidenced in the plays is limited by the imposition of their own critical language games upon the alien text. The point here is that the narrowing focus of such preconceived critical approaches serves to limit the resulting interpretations of the plays. A reverse corollary to this might be the inadequacy of a Shakespearean representation of Caribbean language games (as in the case of *The Tempest*) where an analogously skewed reading is imposed on the foreign text of Caribbean native and slave worlds. From a Wittgensteinian perspective, one would expect to find more thorough and accurate depictions of the world (and other texts) where the writer/critic /interpreter has a sufficient familiarity with the language game(s) of his object of investigation.

Wittgenstein addresses the lack of such language game familiarity regarding appropriate and inappropriate evaluations in relation to British critiques of African art. He argues that one cannot automatically assume that a British art critic would necessarily be more able to evaluate an African work of art than would an educated African (L&C, 8–9). "What belongs to a language game is a whole culture" (L&C, 8), and language games differ according to each culture. In other words, just as cultures change and evolve over time, their language games reflect analogous shifts across time and place. Accordingly, axiological valuations of art or literature must be based upon the fundamental grammar of the actual works. Thereby, works of literature would be evaluated in light of how well or poorly they play the language games in which they participate. The charge for the literary critic is to discern those language games and their respective limits. For example, an evaluation of a sonnet by Sir Philip Sidney would usefully investigate the poem in relation to the foundational rules of the sonnet language game. An evaluation of the sonnet which would, however, gauge the poem against contemporary standards of feminism might very well be less useful—and would be primarily informative regarding the feminist standard rather than about the poem. Where family resemblance might be concerned, however, a feminist approach might prove informative as a means of noting contemporary literary threads of phallocentric language games evidenced in their similarities to non-feminist Renaissance verse. Regarding diverse orientations to the world, Wittgenstein asserts that "we predicate of the thing what lies in the method of representing it" (PI, I, 104).

Insofar as literary criticism is concerned, works tend to be valued or devalued according to how well they measure up to the particular critical standards against which they are evaluated. Where predication is overly strained or impossible, the work is accordingly devalued (as in the case of the New Critical devaluation of the Romantics). The reverse is also true—where works are overly valued by virtue of their fitting well with a critical method (perhaps the New Critical valuation of Metaphysical poetry). However, a move away from such skewed valuations does not mean that purely objective evaluations are possible or desirable. Wittgenstein does acknowledge that our own language games and cultures are inextricably implicated in our judgments of works of art (regardless of the time and place of their origin). In other words, a refined postmodern evaluative judgment would differ significantly from a refined judgment of an earlier time. "The words we call expressions of aesthetic judgements play a very complicated role, but a very definite role, in what we call a culture of a period. To describe their use or to describe what you mean by a cultured taste, you have to describe a culture. What we now call a cultured taste perhaps didn't exist in the Middle Ages. An entirely different game is played in different ages" (L&C, 8). And the terms we use to critique and evaluate texts (e.g., beautiful, tasteful, sublime, natural, ambiguous, aporetic, dialogic, heterogeneous, or hegemonic) establish constraints which determine to a significant extent our perspective on those texts. Hence Wittgenstein's charge that we investigate the limits of our words as a means for clarifying, and adjusting where necessary, our views. As Wittgenstein recommends: "Seek your reasons for calling something good or beautiful and then the peculiar grammar of the word 'good' in this instance will be evident" (CV, 24e). Regarding linguistic adjustments, he notes that "sometimes an expression has to be withdrawn from language and sent for cleaning,—then it can be put back into circulation" (CV, 39e). For example, poststructural criticisms and theories have caused terms such as "center" or "foundation" to seem anachronistic, at best. Perhaps a Wittgensteinian laundering which places such terms within an organic language-game framework would provide the means for returning them to critical use.

Implications for New Historicism

HERE WE SEE a definite parallel between the Wittgensteinian emphasis on descriptively investigating a work in relation to its language games and the New Historicist emphasis on a critical application of what Clifford Geertz refers to as "thick description."[2] Of course, a significant difference is that Geertz's analysis of culture is "essentially a semiotic one" with "human behavior seen as symbolic" (5, 10). Towards the beginning of the *Investigations*, Wittgenstein clearly differentiates a symbolic interpretation of the world (or a text) from his focus on "use": "There are *countless* kinds [of sentences]: countless different kinds of use of what we call 'symbols', 'words', 'sentences'. And this multiplicity is not something fixed, given once for all; but new types of language, new language-games, as we may say, come into existence, and others become obsolete and get forgotten" (PI, I, 23). For Wittgenstein, any symbolic interpretation is simply an alternative sign system (as in the relationship between algebra and arithmetic), neither an explanation of a reality or text, nor necessarily a useful description. While some language games (or texts) may be ripe for a semiotic interpretation or description, it is also the case that there might be other language games which would not be usefully looked at on the symbolic level (perhaps, e.g., texts influenced by turn-of-the-century Naturalism, scientific texts, or the oral literatures of Native American Indian peoples)—games about which all we can say is that this is how they are played.

The confusions which arise when we rely upon some external context as a means of defining or otherwise illuminating a text are analogous to the condition of ostensive definitions in logic (where the object to be defined is pointed out and then characterized, often by its particular actual cases). An example Wittgenstein uses is that of telling someone the name of another person and following that with an ostensive definition. The potential problem he notes is that the listener/interpreter might "take the name of a person . . . as that of a colour, of a race, or even of a point of the compass" (PI, I, 28). For clarification, perhaps I might say to Wittgenstein's listener, "Nordstrum is over there," and then I point north. Wittgenstein's point is that the listener might take "Nordstrum" not for a person, but as a foreign word for "north." Wittgenstein states that "an ostensive definition can be variously interpreted in *every* case" (PI, I, 28). And these interpretations are skewed according to our own biases, which determine the questions we are asking and the cases we choose to examine (PI, I, 30). If we approach an eighteenth-century text in light of the demise of the masquerade,[3] a Wittgensteinian response might be that such an orientation and relationship to a text could be interpreted in many different ways. If we assume the demise of the masquerade (interpreted as a meaningfully subversive activity on behalf of its participants), then perhaps, by virtue of our interpretive constraints, we might miss its possible continuations in the potentially subversive elements of the theatre or contemporary film, or the perceived necessity for television and other forms of media to be so tightly controlled throughout the world.

While New Historicist readings do bring aspects of texts which might otherwise be missed to critical attention, a Wittgensteinian approach would add to such readings a realization of the diversity of language games and family resemblances, which could indicate the importance of investigating further textual distinctions and connections. Whether literary critics interpret the demise of the carnivalesque to have been a disappearance or merely a shift in forms (with the underlying reality of the carnivalesque continuing, albeit differentially) indicates the divergences which arise when critical readings vary in the degree in which they are rooted in the actual language games of a text. From a Wittgensteinian orientation, our critical readings would tend to diverge most seriously from the text when our interpretive discourses radically diverge from the text's language games. This is the situation where "language goes on holiday" as we separate it from its "use" or everyday life and give it our own interpreted "use." As Wittgenstein notes, "interpretation may also consist in how [we] make use of the word" (PI, I, 34). These sorts of difficulties, which arise when a text is divorced from its use, are what Wittgenstein wants us to avoid. We will see that the absence of clearly defined limits differentiating more and less useful investigations is a primary cause for many of our "forced" critical interpretations—a difficulty which even the New Historicism (with its emphasis on interrelationships between text and culture) does not completely avoid.

New Historicist investigations, according to H. Aram Veeser, focus on a cultural analysis which is seen as inextricably connected to its material practices as a means "to expose the manifold ways culture and society affect each other" (xii). History, or the external or surrounding context, is brought to bear on a reading of a text. Such a focus parallels the Wittgensteinian thrust towards investigating a text (or any element of the world) in "use." Where the New Historicist project and a Wittgensteinian approach diverge, however, is in the postmodern distinction between a text and its larger context. Veeser draws a hard line between the "empty formalism" combatted by New Historicists and the more meaningful object of their attention—namely, the larger "culture in action" (xi). The text as isolated by formalist criticism is perceived as an abstraction because it obscures the text's participation in the discursive structures of the culture. The importance of situating texts in their historical moments is evident in the New Historicist revisionism of the prior privileging of the text by New Critics, structuralists, and deconstructionists—what Jane Marcus refers to as "the return of the repressed desire for history, for knowing what happened" (1989, 132). Elizabeth Fox-Genovese explicitly notes the text/context dichotomy as it relates to the New Historicist enterprise. She writes that "the center of attention can be seen to be shifting from text to context, with a healthy emphasis on the concept of hegemony and the notion of struggle within and between discourses" (217). And Hayden White points out that "it is the 'text' [or context] of 'a cultural system' that is to be substituted for the 'text' of 'an autonomous literary history'" (294).

Whereas both Wittgensteinian and New Historicist approaches emphasize the problems of separating a text from its culture or use, Wittgenstein's philosophy offers a clearer language for looking at those elements of a literary work which reflect that work's place in the world. Since, as has been noted, our language does influence our views of the world (or a text), the effects of our investigating "language games" and "family resemblances" (rather than "hegemonic repression" or "aporetic fissures") could be far reaching. While a developed investigation into the advantages of such new terminology is beyond the bounds of this discussion, I would like to note that Wittgenstein's terms are generally value-free in the sense that neither do they automatically point towards views of the world which mainly indicate the depressed condition of today (e.g., fissures, ruptures, aporias, oppression, repression, privilege, alienation, absence), nor do they nostalgically point back to an unrealistic and overly optimistic view of the world (e.g., homogeneity, presence, centers, absolutism, universalism, subjectivity). Rather, a Wittgensteinian approach provides a terminology for clearer descriptions by permitting the text (and its language games) to determine the critical terminology appropriate for the text's description.

For Wittgenstein, works of art or literature represent "forms of life" no less than do other elements (such as behaviors, institutions, or artifacts). Language games often cut across such artificially contrived boundaries as distinctions between text and context; investigations on the level of language games prove to be more informative, useful, and meaningful. Accordingly, such investigations might indicate that a formalist or structuralist approach to a Navajo chant (noting significant elements of circularity, repetition, references to four or seven directions, specific emphatic markers, or the absence of a sharp grammatical separation between subject and object) might be more useful in opening up the chant, than would the introduction of extraneous information (perhaps useful, but not necessarily so). Fox-Genovese notes that "the new historicism [tends] to restore context without exploring the boundaries between text and context. In this respect, it is modifying, but not seriously questioning, the premises that have informed poststructuralist textual analysis" (222). According to Fox-Genovese, New Historicists strive to remove the distinctions between text and context without first investigating those boundaries. Such investigations might show those boundaries to be other than assumed (perhaps placed differently, perhaps with different forms or uses). Instead of perpetuating certain fixed premises, the Wittgensteinian response is to investigate the language games surrounding each work of art or literature as a guide for our critical endeavors.

In some cases, it might be appropriate and useful to draw a distinction between the text qua text and some sort of external context beyond the text (perhaps in the cases of some contemporary language poetry).[4] However, it is more likely that those language games in which a literary text participates cut across any such boundaries delineating the text from the world—especially in light of the Wittgensteinian assertion that any language use (written or otherwise) is a "form of life." These differentiations separate the text from its actual "use" or life in the world and further complicate descriptive investigations. As Wittgenstein points out: "Our forms of expression prevent us in all sorts of ways from seeing that nothing out of the ordinary is involved, by sending us in pursuit of chimeras" (PI, I, 94). Our charge from Wittgenstein is not to struggle in order to work around the various boundaries we erect in our way, but rather to circumvent those which impede our view in the first place. Such a clarified view of texts does not necessarily lead to a total lack of positionality. For example, where a critic's aim might be to foreground the subjectivity (or lack thereof) of women characters in a novel, a feminist approach would be useful. Those interpretive biases which would impede such a feminist approach would be those it would be necessary to remove. Investigations into the text's language games, the critic's interpretive biases, and her chosen critical approach to that text are essential in the determinations regarding which biases, if any, serve as impediments.

In a discussion of problematic terminology regarding the material conditions of society, Stephen Greenblatt calls for "a search for a new set of terms to understand . . . [each] cultural phenomenon" (12). Perhaps a stronger and clearer reliance upon the literary texts as "forms of life" (which would directly include investigations into their respective language games) might prevent many of the linguistic confusions and limitations we run up against, such that a "new set of terms" would no longer be necessary. An important area in which Wittgensteinian philosophy and New Historicist concerns about revisioning history clearly converge is in Wittgenstein's emphasis on the importance of seeing the world (or a text) from different angles: "One of the most important methods I use is to imagine a historical development for our ideas different from what actually occurred. If we do this we see the problem from a completely new angle" (CV, 37e). Wittgenstein is not asserting the possibility of ascertaining what actually happened as a correction to history books, but rather a significantly divergent alternative as a means of generating a significantly divergent reading. Insofar as literary history might be concerned, such an approach would provide an organic responsiveness to a divergent and evolving set of language games which would necessitate continual revisionings.

This is not to say that every revisioning will lead to a significantly new view of literary history, but rather that our perspectives would be kept continually open to the possibilities of meaningful or useful change. And determining the usefulness of such revisionings would also be organically responsive and circumstantial. Regarding such alternative views of the world or texts, Wittgenstein writes, "We ought to think: it may have happened *like that*—and also in many other ways" (CV, 37e). Hence Wittgenstein's repeated assertion that "a multitude of familiar paths lead off from these words in every direction" (PI, I, 525, 534). Even here, where we see a similar concern with looking at the world as a means of describing it, the Wittgensteinian focus includes history as it might and might not have occurred, whereas the New Historicist thrust is towards a view of history as it did occur (according to a New Historicist). It is possible that there might be situations in which a mythical representation of the world (or a literary text) might supercede a less useful but more realistic representation. For example, the historical errors in Judy Grahn's *Another Mother Tongue* might be less significant than the actual usefulness of the text as a groundbreaking affirmation of gay culture. The Wittgensteinian emphasis, however, focuses on language games as the starting point for the descriptive analytics of a text.

Wittgenstein stresses the importance of first educating ourselves about the language games of various works of literature in order to approach those works more closely and thereby effect a "change in [our] style of thinking" (L&C, 28). We would then be able to provide more accurate and useful descriptive analyses of those works and to evaluate them more effectively by means of our improved (or "refined") judgment. As Wittgenstein explains: "In learning the rules you get a more and more refined judgement. Learning the rules actually changes your judgement" (L&C, 5). Therefore, in becoming more familiar with a text's language games (and their rules), the literary critic can achieve two direct results. One is that we can determine the usefulness of particular facts (in relation to the text) by discerning whether or not those facts are indeed relevant to our reading of the text; in other words, the relevancy of specific facts is determined by the limiting rules of the language games in which the text is a participant. For example, a bilingual Navajo/English text might indicate the importance of investigating the "mestiza consciousness" language game played and delineated by Gloria Anzaldúa; however, investigations into the Navajo language game might indicate that bilingualism in one case (e.g., Navajo) does not necessarily involve the bilingual language games of a completely different case (e.g., mestiza consciousness), even though their respective playing moves (bilingualism) might be strikingly similar. In Nia Francisco's bilingual poem, "Male and Female" (discussed in chapter 4), she keeps the two languages separate and uses English as a means of presenting Navajo ways to her readers. There is little, if any, sense of being torn between worlds. Francisco is Navajo, and that identity comes through strongly whether she is using English or Navajo in the poem. The bilingualism in the poem does not represent the mestiza problematic as discussed by Anzaldúa.

Here we see a clear example regarding the limitations of a misdirected focus on culture or context or history which is bereft of the guidance given by the rules of the games. Similar cultural behaviors or artifacts (playing moves or positions in their respective language games [e.g., bilingualism]) do not necessarily indicate the same or even analogous situations. This is one of the reasons why Wittgenstein strongly argues against looking for explanations, causal relationships, and fixed symbolic meanings in nonscientific realities (texts), for all of these shift as we shift our stances on the objects of our observation. Description of language games can help critics avoid the various confusions and misreadings which might arise when we take an awkward (or less useful) position towards a text—be it demanding a semiotic symbolism from a text which may resist such a linguistic dualism of language and meaning (perhaps in the case of a Navajo chant), or insisting on a New Historicist or other reading of a text that emphasizes cultural elements of language games in which the text does not participate.

This is not to say that semiotic, New Historicist, or other cultural critiques might not be useful in opening up particular texts, but that a Wittgensteinian descriptive analysis, which emphasizes the discernment of language games as a means of determining the essential grammar of those games and of the text, must come first. The grammatical rules of the text then assist critics in determining which critical biases might be useful and which need to be removed (by virtue of their serving as impediments to our view of the object/text). Our goal is not that such views need be comprehensive, but that we have a clear view of our work. Wittgenstein stresses the importance of our *"commanding a clear view* of the use of our words" (PI, I, 122)—of obtaining a level of "perspicuity" in our grammar. However, Wittgenstein does point out that our depictions of the world (or texts) need not always be "clear" or absolutely free of bias: "Is it even always an advantage to replace an indistinct picture by a sharp one? Isn't the indistinct one often exactly what we need?" (PI, I, 71). Our clear view of our critical work is essential in helping us to discern where more and less clear descriptions are useful.

Expanding the Boundaries of Cultural Criticism

EMBLEMATIC OF POSTMODERN criticism are those debates concerning issues of race, ethnicity, and culture. Critical deliberations of gender issues (nonetheless crucial and timely as long as phallogocentric discourse constitutes one of the rules of the language game of gender relations), however, have begun to appear relatively anachronistic and inconsequential in light of the newer and louder voices of cultural criticism—many of which voices hail from the camps of feminist critics. In fact, the discursive concerns regarding cultural diversity found their critical beginnings in the seventies and early eighties as women of color critiqued the ethnocentrism, classism, and heterosexism of feminist scholarship. Lesbians, women of color, and working-class women argued for their inclusion within the power structures of the predominant feminist discourse. And now, in the early nineties, the era of Madonna and Camille Paglia, of queer theory and men's studies, we see the ultimate implosive force of the hypostatization of human desires for a subjectivity that must necessarily remain, by definition, on the level of narrative myth.

While the poststructural criticism of the 1970's and 1980's correctly noted the mythical dimensions of those historical constructs previously given an essentialist validation, cultural criticism nevertheless argued that the displacement and disenfranchisement of people of color was not merely on the level of a discursive narrative struggle, but that the struggle for subjectivity reflects the real and lived struggles of those peoples whose histories have been the reality of violent diasporizations. Through a Wittgensteinian orientation to the world and to literary texts, literary criticism can achieve a means of escape from the dialectical struggles of a postmodern skepticism, a skepticism that discursively dismantles the past and opens up the present and future to new discursive structures, but that is incapable of effecting change beyond the superficial level of discourse. John Edgar Wideman has pointed out that "history is a cage" and that only through the process of rehistoricization can those on the margins assert their own lived realities (vi, ix)—realities whose (dis)placement has traditionally been that of a devalued subalterity and a marginalized otherness. And in an essay focusing on literary depictions of Native American Indian peoples, Ward Churchill writes: "Literature in America is and always has been part and parcel of the colonial process" (39). Cultural critics work to give voice to those who have been silenced as a means of moving literary criticism and literature beyond the colonial reality of their origins. Celeste Olalquiaga, however, suggests that such discursive shifts, less radical than might be hoped by cultural critics, are emblematic of the very essence of a postmodern fragmentation.

Olalquiaga notes that "one of the most conspicuous features of postmodernity is its ability to entertain conflicting discourses simultaneously"(42)—a fact which has served to enable the awkward process of broadening the literary canon and critical discourse. However, as she further notes, postmodernity's all-too-ready acceptance of diversity is dangerously deceptive in its inclusive superficiality: "Rather than erasing previous practices, [postmodernity] enables and even seeks their subsistence. This peculiar coexistence of divergent visions is made possible by the space left in the vertical displacement of depth by surface, which implies a gathering on the horizontal level" (42). But such inclusivity and acceptance is primarily cosmetic, whether it is played out in the literary, critical, or even political domain. Real change must occur deep down on what Wittgenstein refers to as the underlying grammatical level of language games. Only once the fundamental grammar of the societal language game of racism is changed will that game evolve into one whose essential rules embody concepts and practices of inclusion rather than exclusion.

Cultural critics point out that the United States is a nation of many divergent cultures conjoined through a historicized erasure of difference. Those cultures and peoples who accepted this melting-pot process of assimilation did so out of a desire for acceptance into the dominant culture. Those cultures and peoples, however, who either rejected the promises of admission (admission at the expense of their cultural identity) or who were never offered such "hope" were enabled to perpetuate their own cultures, somewhat autonomously, on a subaltern level. Such cultural fragmentation has kept the United States from developing a national culture other than the hegemonically imposed, dominant, white, middle-class reality that never has cohesively existed other than in the realm of B movies and TV soap operas.

Wittgenstein asserts that contemporary civilization will never produce a culture until it achieves some degree of coherence on the grammatical level. While superficial diversity is and always will be the rule (contrary to the hopes of those who call for getting "back to the basics" of the "Great Books"), what holds such diversity together are those underlying grammatical rules which serve to define a national, cultural, or subcultural discourse. Wittenstein suggests that the sort of fragmentation emblematic of contemporary postmodernity reflects the lack of a cohesive culture.

> In an age without culture . . . forces become fragmented and the power of an individual man is used up in overcoming opposing forces and frictional resistances; it does not show in the distance he travels but perhaps only in the heat he generates in overcoming frictions. . . . The disappearance of a culture does not signify the disappearance of human value, but simply of certain means of expressing this value. (CV, 6e)

From a Wittgensteinian perspective, it is not diversity that is emblematic of postmodernity. Cultural diversity is emblematic of life. Such diversity is merely manifested differently in a postmodern era that is striving to deconstruct modernity's presumed lack of diversity. The fragmentation of postmodernity reflects our inability to recognize the fact that difference does not signify any sort of hierarchized valuation, but merely represents a perceived difference on the superficial level. The dialectical juxtaposition of a dominant subjectivity (generally white, male, and affluent) over an oppressed objectivity (generally non-white, female, and working-class or poor) reflects a mythical hierarchy that has been realized in a nation that has yet to learn how to achieve a meaningful unity with diversity. Regarding her recent anthology of African-American literature, Terry McMillan comments that she "wish[es] there hadn't been a need to *separate* our work from others, and perhaps, as Dr. Martin Luther King expressed, one day this dream may come true, where all of our work is considered equal, and not measured by its color content, but its literary merit" (xxiv). Dr. King's vision as interpreted by McMillan in a literary context is what Wittgenstein would explain as a national or perhaps global culture. A Wittgensteinian critical strategy that emphasizes "family resemblance" can provide literary critics with a powerful methodology to begin a shift away from the competing voices of a postmodern *dys*cursive oppositionality to a more conversive strategy comfortable with both differences and resemblances.

One feminist critic, Gloria Anzaldúa, sees the problems which arise when particular aspects of a text are ignored or overlooked. In the introduction to her anthology of literature by women of color, she calls for a categoric inclusion of particular sociohistorical categories, such as race, class, and gender, as a means of eliminating otherwise skewed readings. Rather than rejecting the value of theory, as other feminist critics have done (seeing it as elitist and hegemonic), Anzaldúa urges non-white women and men to "occupy theorizing space . . . [and] not allow white men and women solely to occupy it" in order to "transform" that space (xxv). This "occupation" suggests an image of the marginalized and colonialized usurping the former hegemonic role of their oppressors by means of a sort of reverse "occupation" of territory (or "space") reminscent of Wittgenstein's recognition of the superficiality of our seemingly endless dialectical battles (textual and societal).[5] While a Wittgensteinian response would value Anzaldúa's addition of the new theoretical file drawers of race and class, which provide a more complete view of texts and the world, a cautionary note would be added to the effect that arguments regarding any existential preference of one drawer over another are not as useful to a critic as is the placement of a text within the scope of its practice (language games). In other words, the value of any particular drawer (theory or critical approach) is dependent upon its usefulness with regard to actual textual entry.

Nevertheless, even a cursory view of literary theory and criticism does indicate that serious critical imbalances have occurred which need to be redressed. As Anzaldúa correctly points out, theory must be "de-academized": "*Necesitamos teorías* that will rewrite history using race, class, gender and ethnicity as categories of analysis, theories that cross borders, that blur borders—new kinds of theories with new theorizing methods" (xxv). Rather than continuing to rely exclusively upon theoretical frameworks that continue to exclude and marginalize diverse peoples and ways of looking and being in the world, Wittgenstein repeatedly emphasizes the importance of discovering, investigating, and describing language games and their family resemblances—a process much more potentially fruitful than that of attempting to fit a changing and diverse world into the static mold of pseudo-scientific theories that claim to be global and/or absolute.

Since meaningfulness, for Wittgenstein, is contingent upon actual use, it is only when things are seen in context (or in use) that their meanings can be ascertained. What this means for critical evaluations of diverse literatures is a categorically new approach towards these literatures which de-emphasizes preconceived theoretical orientations to texts and stresses the primacy of textual/contextual investigations before theoretical concerns are even considered. Since the primary emphasis is on a familiarity both with texts and their respective contexts, the responsibility of the critic lies in two related areas. The first is in developing a sufficient familiarity with the text (which includes familiarity with the language games in which the text participates and the manner by which the text participates in those games). This is the process whereby the critic approaches the text, may actually enter some of the language games in which the text participates, and discovers pathways into the text other readers might be able to traverse as well. This uncovering of previously undiscovered textual/contextual entries leads to the critic's second domain of critical responsibility. The first is towards the text; the second is in relation to other readers, for whom the critic serves as a guide. In this role, the critic delineates entries into particular literary works as a means of guiding readers in their own literary experiences with the texts.

From such a Wittgensteinian view, the cultural critic's responsibilities involve, first, a familiarity with the text (a familiarity which does not necessitate that the critic's own ethnicity be that of the text's author, though language game familiarity based in part on coincident ethnicity would certainly enable effective textual entry), and second, a commitment to facilitating entry into the text for other readers of diverse backgrounds. Wittgenstein points out that an inadequate knowledge of any object in use (e.g., a text within its context) leads to serious problems of devaluation and misconstrual. For example, what might be a poorly constructed narrative within one literary framework might be a particularly well crafted work in terms of another. As Wittgenstein notes, "I think it might be regarded as a basic law of natural history that wherever something in nature 'has a function,' 'serves a pupose,' the same thing can also be found in circumstances where it serves no purpose and is even 'dysfunctional'" (CV, 72).

Wittgenstein specifically notes the example of European antisemitism as a function of inadequate knowledge of something (in this case, a group of people) which has led to its devaluation.[6] Within the language game of European antisemitism, the Jews "are experienced as a sort of disease" ("Krankheit"). He states that this condition of illness (referred to as a tumor ["Beule"] on a body) could be changed by a revisioning of the entire body—in other words, by redefining what constitutes health and disease. "People only regard this tumour as a natural part of the body if their whole feeling for the body changes (if the whole national feeling for the body changes)" (CV, 20e). Where health is desired for a society riddled with an endemic ethnocentric bias, the Wittgensteinian response would be to clearly discern the language games of the society in order to determine which preconceived biases are harmful or beneficial to societal functioning.

Such discernments and determinations are necessary in order to perceive the problems at the foundational level of language game grammar. The difficulties have "to be pulled out by the roots; and that involves our beginning to think about these things [those which led to "conceptual confusions"] in a new way" (CV, 48e). The shift from a confused way of thinking (such as a problematically ethnocentric or phallocentric orientation towards the world) to a more realistic one is compared to the change "from the alchemical to the chemical way of thinking" (CV, 48e) with the prior view being less grounded in the actual world and more a product of "preconceived notions" and the latter view being more rooted in the world rather than in our own particular biases. For Wittgenstein, correcting our imbalanced views of the world (or a text) is seen as a powerful means of eradicating problematic (and destructive) prejudices (personal and societal).

Anzaldúa echoes Wittgenstein's call for a new way of thinking in her discussion of mestiza (hybrid or mixed) consciousness: "The future depends on the breaking down of paradigms, it depends on the straddling of two or more cultures" (379). As she correctly notes, monocultural paradigms are often adversely constrictive in their inability to respond to change and diversity. The concept of a language game prevents the static nature of paradigmatic designs on/in the world. The organicity of the language game provides a more useful model for approaching a living and changing world than do the static and unresponsive paradigms of a homogeneous and logocentric absolutism. We can certainly see significant parallels between Anzaldúa's analysis of the mestiza consciousness and Wittgenstein's discussion of diverse language games and their respective resemblances. The reality of the Chicana/o speaks most profoundly of the crossing or "straddling" of borders, cultures, language games. The Chicana/o reality straddles languages (Spanish and English), nation-states (Mexico and the United States), ethnicities and cultures (Indian and Hispano/European), and a very real geographical border (the Rio Grande).

Mae Gwendolyn Henderson echoes Anzaldúa's awareness of the problems inherent in static and absolutist paradigms. She writes that a "dialogic of difference and dialectic of identity characterize both black women's subjectivity and black women's discourse" (121). Whereas in the case of the Chicana/o, we can readily discern the primary distinctions noted above, for the black woman or man such divisions are less clear-cut or at least less evident—hence Henderson's emphasis on the dialogical and dialectical shifts in subjectivity and discourse. Anzaldúa points out that the reality of the mestiza, whether dual or multiple, is that of borderlands (377-89). Here we see in the concept of borders the usefulness of Wittgenstein's discussions of the language game and family resemblance. There are two significant aspects to Anzaldúa's mestiza concept which are particularly germane to a Wittgensteinian investigation. The first is that the mestiza reality straddles diverse language games within its own language game (say the Chicana/o language game); the second is that the concept of the mestiza cuts across the diverse language games of ethnicity, culture, gender, and class in representing any individual whose subjectivity and discursive reality are not homogeneous. As we shall see, Anzaldúa's concept of the mestiza clearly exemplifies Wittgenstein's idea of family resemblance.

When we, as literary critics, note family resemblances in the connections within and between diverse literary texts, we enable ourselves to see aspects of those texts not perceptible beyond the limits of particular theoretical and critical constraints. A language game and family re-semblance focus can assist us in moving beyond the discursive limits of our theoretical boundaries as we learn not only to cross those bound-aries but to question them in relation to each case. As Wittgenstein emphasizes, the boundaries we set around those perceived language games, while useful and informative, often prevent our noting other significant relationships about the objects of our inquiry. For example, while the struggles of a Chicana poet do, indeed, reflect the larger struggles of race and gender as particularly noted by cultural critics, they may also indicate other related struggles as well. And while there are very real parallels between the games of checkers and chess, when we limit our focus to those parallels we miss their important similari-ties to other games, such as football or war.

Wittgenstein urges us to always investigate further, continually-questioning our limits and constraints, as we look for both differences and similarities in the world and in and between texts. And for a Witt-gensteinian critic, both similarities and differences are meaningful, even those which might not be so obvious to us as we peer through the boundaries of our respective theoretical and critical networks. Wittgen-stein stresses that we investigate and reinvestigate the world in order to see more clearly the relationships between various phenomena:

> Consider for example the proceedings that we call "games". I mean board-games, card-games, ball-games, Olympic-games, and so on. What is common to them all?—Don't say: "There *must* be something common, or they would not be called 'games' "—but *look and see* whether there is anything common to all.—For if you look at them you will not see something that is common to *all*, but similarities, relationships, and whole series of them at that. To repeat: don't think, but look! (PI, 66)

According to Wittgenstein, our focus must be on investigating our texts, even beyond the limits of our preconceived critical methodolo-gies and theories. A critical approach that privileges those elements of a text that are culturally specific to a particular group can serve to facili-tate readers' familiarity with those language games involved in the text. The telescoping advantages of cultural criticism's orientations to di-verse peoples and literatures brings to light both family resemblances within cultural groups and family differences between those groups. However, a critical assumption of homogeneity within groups and heterogeneity between groups leaves unaddressed both the actual and diversity that exists within cultural groups and the very real and mean-ingful similarities across diverse groups. What a Wittgensteinian ap-proach offers is the means and the incentive to investigate beyond the bounds of our established critical language games in order to discern further relationships within and between diverse texts and objects/subjects in the world.

Sherley Anne Williams argues strongly for the importance of our maintaining (developing?) a breadth to our critical inquiries that is not unnecessarily limited by particular critical or political agendas, which lead to a separatism that prevents the critic from seeing relationships outside certain prescribed bounds. She argues that, "like the black aesthetics that arose as a response to black arts poetry, black feminist criticism runs the risk of being narrowly proscriptive rather than broadly analytic" (74). While the concept of breadth linked with the limiting criterion of analysis poses additional problems of constraint, Williams's concern regarding the limiting difficulties imposed by particular critical approaches is valid. However, even our respective critical boundaries, while constraining, are often useful as a means of providing a specific focus towards aspects of texts that might otherwise be overlooked. Were it not for the feminist agenda towards the world and towards literary texts (as reflections of the world), we would still be overlooking aspects of texts not readily discernible without the telescoping vision of feminism.

African-American feminist critics, such as Valerie Smith, have pointed out the importance of feminism as a response to the limitations of patriarchal discursive structures. And yet, Smith stresses the necessity of calling into question those discursive boundaries of all our theories, be they patriarchal or feminist: "To fail to confront the contingencies that both enable and impede our theoretical work, is to risk replicating the exclusionary self-mystification, the pretense to objectivity, that characterizes phallocentric humanism" (57). As Smith notes, the shift from one set of discursive structures to another (or from one language game to another) does not eradicate the problem of boundaries and their inherent limitations—limitations that "both enable and impede our theoretical work."

While it is the case that different works produced within divergent cultures and times vary from one another in significant ways, nevertheless we can identify sufficient pathways into texts such that a contemporary American female critic of Jewish descent can confidently approach a wide range of literary works in English from the Navajo poetry of Luci Tapahonso to Shakespearean sonnets and the postcolonial novels of Nigerian writer Buchi Emecheta. Here we see the especial strength of a Wittgensteinian methodology for any type of literary criticism (cultural or otherwise). Tony Bennett is correct in his assertion that literary criticism historically "has often played an important role in the symbolic processes through which social strata are culturally differentiated" (193). A Wittgensteinian critical method shifts the role of criticism away from that of a superimposition of critical frameworks onto literary texts—a superimposition that inevitably replicates, rather than alters, the underlying assumptions upon which those criticisms are based.

Cultural criticism does point out the cultural distinctions evident in literary texts, but it does not and cannot eradicate the stratifying hierarchy it critiques. Feminist criticism is contingent upon the phallogocentric discourse it struggles against; cultural criticism is analogously tied up with the very axiological determinations of alterity it rejects. Edward Said accurately notes the problematic limitations of theory. He boldly asserts that "it is the critic's job to provide resistances to theory, to open it up toward historical reality, toward society, toward human needs and interests, to point up those concrete instances drawn from everyday reality that lie outside or just beyond the interpretive area necessarily designated in advance and thereafter circumscribed by every theory" (241–42). Like Wittgenstein, Said is wary of theory—however his criticism smacks of the same sort of constraints Wittgenstein rejects for theory. Wittgenstein writes that his "aim in philosophy . . . [is] to shew the fly the way out of the fly-bottle" (PI, 309). Said looks at particular critical fly-bottles and strives to release literary texts from those bonds: but in his dialectical resistance to particular theories, he perpetuates their hegemonic hold and, in fact, ends up creating new fly-bottles in his prescriptions for acceptable criticism.

Largely the result of cultural and feminist criticism, the range of the English literary canon has been expanding at a tremendous rate as it becomes much more open and inclusive (incorporating the works of female, minority, gay and lesbian, working-class, colonial, and postcolonial writers). A Wittgensteinian-based criticism can enable the critic to approach these diverse texts through pathways previously impassable by virtue of their being beyond the bounds of particular critical and theoretical frameworks. By means of a Wittgensteinian methodology, critics can begin to enter texts through a broader range of entryways more representative of the diversity of language games in which those texts actually participate. If cultural critics desire to bring marginalized texts and literatures up from the subaltern of critical displacement, then this emergent body of literatures needs to be accessible to a wide range of readers and critics. A Wittgensteinian approach will further this process through a descriptive methodology aimed at opening texts through critical entry into the world of the text, rather than through the more standard approach of fitting the text into our preconceived critical frameworks. Accordingly, a Wittgensteinian-influenced criticism responds to the text (rather than the reverse, as in the case of reader response criticisms) and provides accessibility and entry in/to works by writers of color and others whose works as yet are unfairly devalued and marginalized due to their perceived inaccessibility to diverse criticisms.

Axiology and Canonicity

A DIRECT EFFECT of discerning textual language games returns us to our earlier discussion of axiology in that such investigations put us in a stronger position to evaluate the text in relation to those games (or rules), since our judgments would be "more refined." For Wittgenstein, a "refined judgement" is preferable by virtue of its being more informed and more capable of ascertaining the value of a work of art or literature by engaging more fully with the work and its respective language games (and culture). Such "refined" axiological determinations are rooted in the essential grammar of a culture's language games as reflected in its productions of art and literature. For example, a contemporary Navajo reared traditionally on the reservation might very well have a more "refined judgement" with regard to any evaluation or appreciation of a sand painting or a Navajo chant than would a non-Navajo critic. A contemporary avant-garde woman poet from New England (such as Susan Howe) might have a more "refined judgement" regarding the poetry of Emily Dickinson than would an academically trained Dickinson scholar, and a medieval resident of England might in all likelihood be more "refined" in her appreciation of Chaucerian poetry than would a later scholar such as Sidney.

We can never fully escape the limitations of our own culture and time ("One age misunderstands another" [CV, 86e]), but through educating ourselves in the language games of a particular work, we can achieve what Wittgenstein terms a more "refined judgement" than we would have otherwise achieved. Here we see that a reliance on Wittgensteinian philosophy strives to situate the work within its historical moment, and yet does not leave us with the sort of axiological relativism propounded by Barbara Herrnstein Smith, who asserts that "all value [is] radically contingent, being neither a fixed attribute, an inherent quality, or an objective property of things but, rather, an effect of multiple, continuously changing, and continuously interacting variables" (30). While a Wittgensteinian approach towards literary texts emphasizes the importance of historically situating a work by delineating and describing the particular language games in which the text participates, such an approach nevertheless recognizes that elements of language games (e.g., rules) are not restricted to particular cultures and times, but in fact can and do cut across such boundaries. Even though the games of chess and checkers are completely different games, such that a proficiency in one would not necessarily lead to a proficiency in the other, there are foundational rules which overlap between the two games (for example, both are played on the same sort of board).

For Wittgenstein, rules and their attendant games are organic and living and subject to change, but this change does not necessarily deny the possibility of constancy. There could be games that have a rule which determines that the game be continuously changing and a product of "multiple, continuously changing, and continuously interacting variables" (such as the game of "beerball" described in chapter 5); however, from a Wittgensteinian perspective, it is not the case that every game must be so designed. Hence the greater likelihood of a postmodern feminist critic, for example, gaining a clear access to works of an earlier time by virtue of those language games (or elements thereof) which cut across time and place. It is not surprising that a contemporary feminist critic might have a more "refined judgement" regarding the writings of Gertrude Stein than even many of Stein's contemporaries might have had. While this is not the place for an extended discussion of language game heuristics as they apply to literary axiology, suffice it to say that, as we have seen in the preceding chapters, a Wittgensteinian approach is not restricted to either the problematics of the extreme cases of logocentric absolutism and skeptical relativism (historicized or not) or the difficulties presented by firm adherence to any particular critical stance, but rather provides us with an alternative means of evaluating literary texts. What this means for literary critics is an unwavering openness towards divergent texts. Even though it is more likely the case that we will still maintain particular critical stances (generally reflecting our respective strengths and expertise), a reliance upon Wittgensteinian directives would lead us to a more informed criticism—either by a clearer determination of the texts we choose to critique or by our "more refined" choices concerning suitable critical approaches towards those texts.

Such evaluations have been especially crucial insofar as decisions of canonicity are concerned. Phallogocentric evaluations of literature routinely reject inclusion of the vast majority of women's literature. Not until the establishment of feminist criticism in the 1970's were the fairly established canonical choices of literature departments questioned at all. Further poststructural developments in literary theory and criticism continued the process of unsettling the canon by denying any possibility of certainty—thereby seriously undermining the foundations upon which a supposed objectivity rested. What was believed to be an objectively absolute and homogeneous approach to the world and to texts was demonstrated to be little more than a hegemonic repression of heterogeneity by a privileged minority defined according to class (affluent), race (white), and gender (male). The responses of a variety of postmodern critics have been to question seriously the limitations of prior determinations. This questioning has generally taken the form of a fairly radical skepticism (most evident in much of the work of deconstructive critics and theorists) or a strong insistence that any determinations of meaning or value are historically contingent and thereby relative (as manifested in the work of many New Historicist and cultural critics).

As discussed in chapter 4, a Wittgensteinian view of canonicity differs from both traditionalist and postmodernist approaches to the literary canon in several important ways. Perhaps most important is the Wittgensteinian rejection of theory and the related emphasis on the value of descriptive analyses. Wittgenstein asserts that, in the arena of philosophy, mathematics, and aesthetics (and here we include both the literary and fine arts), our investigations must be descriptive rather than explanatory. Wittgenstein states: "We may not advance any kind of theory. There must not be anything hypothetical in our considerations. We must do away with all *explanation,* and description alone must take its place" (PI, I, 109). How these concepts would affect determinations of canonicity is profound. As we have seen in the earlier chapters, rather than imposing our expectations upon texts (thereby resulting in a canon which fits into our preconceived theoretical mold— be it a product of views believed to be ostensibly objective or historically political), by relying exclusively upon our descriptions of diverse literary language games, we as critics may become more responsive to the texts by permitting them (and their respective language games) to define the literary canon itself as an organically evolving entity. As Wittgenstein notes, "description gets its light, that is to say its purpose, from the philosophical problems" (PI, I, 109). In other words, whether our investigations be philosophical or literary, by means of a descriptive analysis, the object of the investigations (whether a philosophical problem or a literary text) is permitted to speak more strongly for itself. Or, in fact, rather than the text speaking more strongly, the Wittgensteinian critical response is for critics to position themselves more efficaciously such that their perceptions of the text become more acute.

The discussion of the Native American literature canon in chapter 4 is a useful case in point. The traditional literary canon completely ignores Native American Indian literatures. A revisionist canon which incorporates the contemporary responses of feminist and cultural critics has come to include the works of a number of important Native American writers, but (as we saw in chapter 4) the majority of these inclusions tend to privilege the works of mixed-blood writers rather than those full-blood, perhaps more traditional, Indian writers. A Wittgensteinian analysis might point out the fact that, by and large, our critical and evaluative decisions reflect the biases and interpretive bases of our own language games, with the resulting hegemonic effect often being exclusionary. Wittgenstein points out that "we remain unconscious of the prodigious diversity of all the everyday language-games because the clothing of our language makes everything alike" (PI, 224). This is to say that actual diversity is obscured by externally imposed standards of sameness—in this case, imposed by linguistic uniformity, which produces what Wittgenstein terms "a false appearance" (PI, I, 112). Wittgenstein stresses that our language affects our perceptions of the world. Within a literary framework, we can see the result on judgments of canonicity, for even when we attempt to ameliorate the problematic exclusions of the past, our remedies often fall prey to our own exclusionary tendencies (intentional or not)—often the result of linguistic barriers.

As we have seen in the limited and skewed canon of Native American literature, critical confusions arise when the same descriptive phrase is given for both the literatures of mestiza Indian writers and full-blood Indian writers. These sorts of difficulties, acknowledged by many postmodern cultural critics, can be if not entirely surmounted, certainly sufficiently so for our critical and canonical determinations to be "more refined," and perhaps more useful, than they might be otherwise. Insofar as the literary canon is concerned, such a Wittgensteinian approach would lead us towards not one literary canon universally applied, but rather a diversity of canonical determinations which would vary according to their use. For example, the usefulness of a course in contemporary American literature might demand different textual choices based on the instructor's strengths and interests, the nature and locale of the school, and the demographic makeup of the students in the class. Within the organic framework of a Wittgensteinian critical responsiveness, it would seem that there would be cases in which a syllabus would need to be altered in mid-semester—with texts added, deleted, or substituted by virtue of a change in the grammar of the language game of the class. Such grammatical shifts reflect alterations in the elements listed above. Further work utilizing Wittgenstein's language game heuristic as a tool for descriptive analyses will help to demonstrate additional possibilities involved in a more organic and progressive means of textual evaluations and discriminations.

Theory, Criticism, and Language Poetry

DESCRIPTIVE INVESTIGATIONS are not to be limited to critical analyses or literature, but extended to the more esoteric work generally grouped under "theory." As chapter 1 briefly mentions, the term "theory" has been used in a variety of ways across a variety of disciplines. In his discussion regarding the "theoretical" work of the mathematician David Hilbert, Wittgenstein states that Hilbert's theories should be more appropriately understood as "meta-mathematics" rather than "theory." The importance of such investigations is particularly significant in light of the contemporary privileging of theory in literature departments (as evident in the selection of papers presented at conferences and published in academic journals). While many of the recent "theoretical" developments in the field have been useful, especially in light of the greater diversity of critical methodologies available for textual access, a serious problem is the privileging and devaluing of certain types of theory. More often than not, the theoretical work of white males who come out of the Eurocentric tradition of Western philosophy (theorists such as Northrop Frye, R. S. Crane, Roland Barthes, Jacques Lacan, Jacques Derrida, Michel Foucault, and Stanley Fish) is privileged and accordingly used as the rule against which other forms of theory are measured. As Barbara Christian notes: "The new emphasis on literary theory is as hegemonic as the world which it attacks. . . . There has been a takeover in the literary world by Western philosophers from the old literary elite, the neutral humanists. . . . The New Philosophers have changed literary critical language to suit their own purposes as philosophers, and they have reinvented the meaning of theory" (338, 335). Christian argues that the current usage of the term "theory" devalues any sort of theory which cannot be subsumed within the dominant language game of literary theory. She further states that "people of color have always theorized—but in forms quite different from the Western form of abstract logic" (336). Christian and other literary theorists attempting to work outside the dominant critical language game find themselves constrained by limits not of their own choosing. From a Wittgensteinian framework, we would readily understand the confusions which occur when the rules of one language game are imposed upon a language game if not entirely different then certainly sufficiently different to cause significant language-game translation problems (as in the case of the application of Western philosophical language-game rules to the literary theory of non-Western theorists).

Again, it is important to note that such critical and theoretical difficulties do not necessarily indicate the inherent uselessness of any literary theories. The Wittgensteinian focus is on their uses in actual cases. Rather than choosing to silence or dismantle any theoretical or critical approach, we determine its usefulness (or lack thereof) in each situation. In other words, while the poststructural rejection of subjectivity may be useful and informative (perhaps in bringing to light aspects of a text other than subjectivity), there may be cases in which such a categoric rejection of subjectivity may not be the most useful (perhaps in the case of feminist assertions of subjectivity as a means of adjusting [correcting?] phallocentric views). Within a Wittgensteinian framework, the "conceptual confusions" involved in the privileging of theory are clearly resolved when we understand the forced nature of such theoretical impositions. Wittgenstein came to the realization that the tradition of Western philosophy was merely one language game among many— not the only or primary philosophical approach to the world. When feminist literary theory or the theoretical work of cultural critics is disparaged as inadequately theoretical or unsophisticated, a Wittgensteinian response would be to investigate the underlying terms of the debate in order to clarify and dispel the problem resulting from an overly narrow and rigid use of the term "theory." The problems which we are noting are the result of our lack of clearly delineated discursive boundaries. First of all, the vast majority of what is referred to as literary or critical theory could be more precisely termed metacriticism—being alternative discourses which describe our critical work by means of a different terminology (as algebra presents arithmetic in different terms).

With theory no longer understood as foundational or privileged, but as an alternative discourse only describing certain language games with different terms and focuses, the definitional debates regarding who is really doing theory and who is not should become less important and certainly less useful to the field. However, such an open stance toward "theory" is not a tacit avowal that all such metacritical work is to be equally valued. Some of our metacriticism (a term useful in differentiating critical theory from "theory" as rejected by Wittgenstein)[7] is more useful and more appropriate than other such work. As is noted in chapters 3 and 4, one kind of feminist analysis (as reaction to phallogocentric discursive structures) of Navajo literature might not be the most useful approach in opening up a Navajo text. However, feminist metacriticism might, in fact, be an essential element for contemporary literary criticism as a means of helping to clarify how much of this criticism is seriously constrained by its phallogocentric biases. Here again we see the crucial need for the limiting precision advocated by Wittgenstein. While we will never remove all of our biases and preconceived theoretical notions, we can note and avoid those which seriously impede our work.

One final and important area in which Wittgensteinian philosophy can prove useful to literary criticism is in relation to our discussions (critical, metacritical, and evaluative) concerning contemporary language poetry. A number of language poets have referred directly to Wittgenstein as a philosopher influential to their work, and he is widely quoted by language poets as diverse as Ron Silliman, Joan Retallack, and Rosmarie Waldrop. In fact, a recent collection of prose poems by Waldrop, *The Reproduction of Profiles,* relies heavily on Wittgenstein. Waldrop explains that she "used Wittgenstein's phrases in a free, unsystematic way, sometimes quoting, sometimes letting them spark what they would, sometimes substituting different nouns within a phrase (e.g., his famous anti-metaphysical statement that 'the deepest questions are no questions at all' becomes 'You could prove to me that the deepest rivers are, in fact, no rivers at all')" (back cover notes, n.p.). Perhaps as we (literary critics) develop a fuller understanding of the usefulness of Wittgenstein's philosophy for our work, we will be enabled to approach language poetry with greater ease as we gain access to the Wittgensteinian language game in which language poetry participates. Marjorie Perloff notes the importance of Wittgenstein for a wide range of "poems and fictions [that] have declared themselves as manifestly Wittgensteinian" (193). Perloff writes that "Waldrop is especially interested in the way *meanings* are created in everyday language use," exploring such meaning creation in her poetry and prose

(202). As Wittgenstein pushed the limits of philosophy (for all intents and purposes redefining the essential grammar of philosophy such that in his hands it is an entirely new philosophical language game), contemporary language poets (and others ostensibly influenced by Wittgenstein) push the limits of poetic language to the point of poetic language game redefinition. As Wittgenstein notes, "A *picture* held us captive. And we could not get outside it, for it lay in our language and language seemed to repeat it to us inexorably" (PI, I, 115). Insofar as contemporary poetry is concerned, language poets are those who grapple and play with this issue most profoundly and successfully. As Perloff demonstrates, one effective means of critical entry into language poetry is through the language game of Wittgensteinian philosophy.

Perhaps the most striking element of Wittgenstein's work is what can best be described as a profound sense of faith or trust. For Wittgenstein, a clarity *and* accuracy of thought and perception are possible. From his early Tractarian belief that whatever we might think can be thought clearly[8] to his later stress on the clear delineation of language-game boundaries, Wittgenstein emphasizes the importance of avoiding misconstruals—particularly those that confuse a useful condition with one that is "dysfunctional." As Wittgenstein notes, "wherever something in nature 'has a function', 'serves a purpose', the same thing can also be found in circumstances where it serves no purpose and is even 'dysfunctional'" (CV, 72e). By means of a clear delineation of textual language games (literary and critical) and their boundaries, critics can shift towards descriptive investigations, analyses, and evaluations more propitiously situated for better (clearer, more efficacious, more precise, and more accurate) entry into the discursive structures of those texts. For Wittgenstein, such clarity and access is not only possible, it is crucial to our engagements with/in the world. As Wittgenstein reminds us, "don't think, but look!" (PI, I, 66).

If, in fact, we generally do go out our front doors without suspecting that instead of our front stoops we will find an abyss, then it seems paramount that we seriously question critical and metacritical work, which seems to continually doubt or flatly reject the existence of our front stoops. As Clement Rousset points out, "what makes reality confused is neither the multiplicity nor the divergence of our points of view on it, but rather the absence of any *useful* point of view" (83). Such a "useful point of view" is exactly what criticism needs today as we look beyond postmodernism and the end of this century. A reliance on the philosophy of Ludwig Wittgenstein will prove to be enormously useful to the future development of literary criticism and theory (metacriticism): from issues of axiological debate (on critical and metacritical fronts), to investigations into the foundational grammars of critical and literary language games; from a realization of the possibility of organic certainties which need not be hegemonic nor adversely limiting in their effects, to an acceptance of the importance of useful critical discriminations. As Wittgenstein asserts: "Different interpretations must correspond to different applications" (CV, 40e). The question which we must continually remember to ask ourselves in relation to any aspect of our work is this: "Can this [critical] game be played at all now and what would be the right game to play?" (CV, 27e). Only by ascertaining the parameters of the various language games of our critical debates will we be enabled to make the necessary adjustments requisite for more useful and directed textual, critical, and metacritical analyses and evaluations. Descriptive criticism is the "right game to play," and Wittgenstein points us in that direction.

NOTES

Chapter One

1.   Here we see the difference between a Wittgensteinian sense of the concept "unity with diversity" and the analogous view as represented by the Romantic poets with their valuation of "oneness with multeity." The difference here is the awareness of the process of historicization. Diversity occurs not only in a synchronic sense, but also cuts across time, and, perhaps more importantly, diversity does not consist in the static grouping of difference but in the recognition that difference as manifested in the world is continually changing and evolving.

2.   René Girard presents an insightful discussion of the problems connected with an acceptance of all possible readings of texts—a situation he refers to as "bleak nihilism" (225-254).

3.   Wittgenstein clearly differentiates natural science from other areas of scholarship which he understands as human constructs. "Logic does not treat of language—or of thought—in the sense in which a natural science treats of a natural phenomenon, and the most that can be said is that we *construct* ideal language" (PI, 81). Nature is not a human creation, as is language (and its various manifestations as mathematics, philosophy, or aesthetics, for example), so Wittgenstein sees natural science as more independent or scientifically verifiable than the humanities or social sciences. Regarding social science, Wittgenstein commented extensively on the burgeoning field of psychology. See the two volume set of his *Remarks on the Philosophy of Psychology,* and his *Lectures and Conversations on Aesthetics, Psychology, and Religious Belief,* as well as the discussion on psychological approaches to literature in Chapter 2 of this volume.

4.   For a more complete reference to this discussion between Wittgenstein and Waisman, see LWVC, 133.

5.   Regarding misunderstandings caused by our skewed orientations, see Malcolm Budd, "Wittgenstein on Seeing Aspects." Budd asserts that Wittgenstein's "primary concern in the case of every kind of aspect perception . . . was to combat various misconceptions that the phenomenon of noticing an aspect is liable to generate," such that our resulting descriptions of the phenomenon would end up being "misdescriptions" (1987, 5).

6.   For Fish's discussion on the demise of theory, see "Consequences."

7.   For a helpful discussion of Wittgenstein's conception of "objective certainty," see Norman Malcolm's "Wittgenstein's 'Scepticism' in *On Certainty.*"

8.   At this point, it is important to clarify the fact that the focus of the *Tractatus* is that of logic. The work is Wittgenstein's attempt to resolve and prevent "the most fundamental confusions" of philosophy and language. At TLP 4.003, Wittgenstein writes: "Most of the propositions and questions to be found in philosophical works are not false but nonsensical." Through an understanding of the logic of language, these propositions and questions would be resolved, or no longer even raised.

9.   Wittgenstein explicitly asserts that skepticism is dependent upon the existence of certainty. "Doubting and non-doubting behavior. There is the first only if there is the second" (OC, 354).

10.   Piotr Giza offers an interesting discussion of the viability of theorizing. He argues that in light of the fact that theories are created rather than deduced from evidence, "their ontologies approach reality only approximately" (88).

11.   James Guetti discusses Wittgenstein's negative view towards theory throughout his article "Wittgenstein and Literary Theory." For Wittgenstein, " 'theory' is thus transformed from an attempt at the highest or deepest truth to an effort at some special, and temporary, ideological utility" (1985, 75).

12.   "What we are supplying are really remarks on the natural history of human beings; we are not contributing curiosities however, but observations which no one has doubted, but which have escaped remark only because they are always before our eyes" (PI, 415).

13.   Insofar as the *Investigations* is concerned, even the rules of mathematics or logic are seen to be no more objective or static than the rules of any language game. "The fundamental fact here is that we lay down rules, a technique, for a game, and that then when we follow the rules, things do not turn out as we had assumed. That we are therefore as it were entangled in our own rules."

"This entanglement in our rules is what we want to understand (i.e. get a clear view of" (PI, 125). This is by virtue of the fact that rules (of the game of logic or any other game) represent forms of life.

14.   Shusterman notes the general ineffectiveness of scientific theories and methodologies in criticism: "Wittgenstein's doctrines have freed criticism from the need to seek justification and legitimacy by aping (inductive or deductive) science through the construction of such allegedly systematic frameworks as that suggested by Northrop Frye or through the proposed subsumption of criticism into an accepted science like linguistics" (1986c, 103). Even though Shusterman broadens the Wittgensteinian reference to science to include linguistics (a field that is not one of the natural sciences and one that Wittgenstein would have considered to be one among many language games), the criticism regarding the ineffective "aping" of science holds.

15.   Walter Glannon looks at Wittgenstein's strong rejection of theory and asserts that to apply his philosophy to literary or rhetorical purposes would result in "misleading analogies." His article appropriately ends with such an analogy; Glannon writes: "like a graft rejected by an incompatible host, Wittgenstein has little in common with literary theory" (270). While Glannon is correct in that much of contemporary literary theory would be rejected by Witt-

genstein for the same reasons that he rejects any theoretical approach outside of the realm of the sciences, this is not to say that Wittgenstein's admonitions could not be heeded to good effect even by those of us in the field of literary theory. As Austin Quigley explains, a Wittgensteinian perspective would "restore mobility and multiplicity to literary theory" once we realize that the "function [of interpretation] is to provide access to an experience that is always more than and other than the interpretation can incorporate" (232).

16.   For a detailed discussion on the topic of Wittgensteinian "aspects," see Malcolm Budd's "Wittgenstein on Seeing Aspects."

17.   For a discussion of the possibility of aberrant or "really unheard-of" (*wirklich Unerhortes*) situations, see OC, 512-519.

18.   "If we imagine the facts otherwise than as they are, certain language-games lose some of their importance, while others become important. And in this way there is an alteration—a gradual one—in the use of the vocabulary of a language" (OC, 63).

19.   "Words had to change their ordinary meaning and to take that which was now given them" (Thucydides, 189).

20.   In *The Order of Things*, Michel Foucault explains that modernity has asserted the death of metaphysics. "Modern thought, then, will contest even its own metaphysical impulses, and show that reflections upon life, labour, and language, in so far as they have value as analytics of finitude, express the end of metaphysics: the philosophy of life denounces metaphysics as a veil of illusion, that of labour denounces it as an alienated form of thought and an ideology, that of language as a cultural episode" (317).

21.   "The important fact was that I read [the poem] again and again. . . . But the important thing was that I read the poems entirely differently, more intensely" (L&C, 4-5). This emphasis on looking closely at the poem to arrive at a clearer and more complete description is discussed in G. E. Moore's notes from Wittgenstein's lectures in 1930-33. "What Aesthetics tries to do, he said, is to give *reasons*, e.g. for having this word rather than that in a particular place in a poem. . . . *Reasons*, he said, in Aesthetics, are 'of the nature of further descriptions' . . . and all that Aesthetics does is 'to draw your attention to a thing', to 'place things side by side'" (*Mind* 64 [1955]: 19). Analogous to the case of philosophy, aesthetics (or literary criticism) does not find reasons or explanations as the sciences do; rather, the realm of aesthetics is more suited to investigative discoveries that serve to describe and note comparisons and contrasts between works of art.

22.   Trevor Pateman suggests that members of a particular community and language game share certain "cognitive strategies" which inform any product of that community—be it artistic or otherwise. He questions whether artistic conventions are shared at all and argues that what appear to be artistic conventions might reflect what is more shareable—namely cognitive strategies (174). Joachim Schulte correctly asserts that there are artistic conventions or rules which artists and critics invoke in the process of determining aesthetic correctness (298-310).

23.   When asked about the problem of understanding or appreciating art from a culture that is very different from one's own, Wittgenstein acknowl-

edges that the appreciation will necessarily be different from that of someone native to that other culture. But this does not preclude the possibility of an American appreciating non-American art. "I don't know how Frank Dobson's appreciation of Negro [African] Art compares with an educated Negro's. . . . The Negro's and Frank Dobson's are different appreciations altogether. You do something different with them" (L&C, 9). It is significant to note here that Wittgenstein is not making an evaluative judgment at all. He emphasizes that the two appreciations are different, but this is not to say that one is necessarily better than the other.

24.   Much of Wittgenstein's later philosophy can be summed up by his repeated emphasis on learning to perceive language and reality differently. "How much we are doing is changing the style of thinking and how much I'm doing is changing the style of thinking and how much I'm doing is persuading people to change their style of thinking" (L&C, 28). Instead of approaching reality with certain preconceived perspectives (theories), we are to approach reality as openly and as closely as possible in order to perceive it more accurately and usefully.

25.   I use the term "multifluity" to signify the conjoined senses of fluidity and diversity, as well as its homophone "mellifluous."

26.   It is important to reiterate at this point that the language games of a text are not necessarily the same as those evidenced outside the text, and that the world of the text is necessarily other than the real world. For a more complete discussion of this distinction, see Chapter 2, which deals with textual psychology.

27.   Shusterman refers to Wittgenstein's work as "revolutionary" especially in relation to its effect on the field of aesthetics (1986c, 91).

Chapter Two

1.   Paul-Laurent Assoun notes this limiting aspect of theoretical constructs. In a discussion of Freudian and Lacanian theories, he agrees with Lacan's theory of the division of the subject ("Lacan a si bien pensée") but then qualifies his statement with an assertion of the larger difficulty with theory per se. "[Cette théorie] est à las fois importante mais un peu stérile, comme toutes les théories structurales" (in Gentis, 17).

2.   In Navajo, linguistic hierarchy does not follow a pattern of privileging a linguistic subject over a linguistic object in a sentence. For example, in Navajo one would not say that "a horse kicked me" even though that describes the event. The horse (subject) did the kicking—but this, to a Navajo, makes no sense, since actual subjectivity (in a Navajo worldview) involves control and responsibility. And this is not always reflected in the linguistic subject of the sentence. In Navajo, one would say "I was kicked by the horse" to communicate that the responsibility for the injury is the human's. Navajos know that horses do not go around willy-nilly kicking humans. The converse is also true: in Navajo, one can say "I kicked the horse," but not "the horse was kicked by me." In all cases, the subject is the kicker, but such subjectivity is merely linguistic and does not reflect the more important underlying grammar, which

points to the human as the actual subject in both cases—a distinction unaccounted for within the bounds of Lacanian discourse theory.

3. For a good introduction to Wittgenstein's distinction between seeing/perceiving and seeing as/perceiving aspects, see Malcom Budd's volume, *Wittgenstein's Philosophy of Psychology*, in which he devotes an entire chapter to this complex issue.

4. Here I want to note that the works of more marginalized mestizo/a Native American writers like Leslie Marmon Silko, Gerald Vizenor, Paula Gunn Allen, or Louise Erdrich, present themes similar to those in Tapahonso's work, though in a more postmodern frame of fragmentation and uncertainty. For a discussion of some of these differences, see chapter 4.

Chapter Three

1. Postmodernism has tended to be resistant to any clear front for actual social or political change. Not only have the grounds of oppressions been questioned, but so have the grounds upon which social change might be based. Feminist critics such as Linda Hutcheon and Nancy Hartsock question the validity of postmodernism as a useful strategy for feminists. However, a number of other feminists, such as Chris Weedon and Bell Hooks, hail postmodernism as an important tool for change. As Hooks points out: "Postmodern critiques of essentialism which challenge notions of universality and static over-determined identity within mass culture and mass consciousness can open up new possibilities for the construction of self and the assertion of agency" (28).

2. I strongly recommend Howe's volume, *My Emily Dickinson*. It is a superlative work of deep criticism—refreshingly divergent from what is generally produced within the halls of academe.

3. For a more complete discussion of the Navajo clan system, see Gary Witherspoon, *Language and Art in the Navajo Universe*.

4. Wittgenstein's statement discusses the problems that occur when language (texts) is taken out of context. "The confusions which occupy us arise when language is like an engine idling, not when it is doing work" (PI, I, 132).

Chapter Four

1. In this chapter, the descriptive appellations, Native American, American Indian, Indian, Native American Indian, Native peoples, and Indian peoples are used differentially. Among the majority of Native American Indian peoples in the United States today (as evidenced in the preferred appellations by tribal bodies), they refer to themselves by either their tribal names (e.g., Dine' or Navajo) or as Indian. This can be seen in the chosen titles of their newspapers: *The Navajo Times, Indian Country Today* ("American Indian Newspaper"), *The Lakota Times*. However, amongst academics, the politically correct term tends to be Native American. The appellations, Indian, Native American Indian, and Native or Indian peoples (terms commonly used among Indian peoples), are used interchangeably throughout the text. The one

exception is my use of Native American—all usages of this appellation designate the externally imposed objectification of Indian peoples—particularly regarding those Native literary works valorized and canonized by literary scholars. For example, the Native American literary canon refers to a select grouping of texts valorized today, as distant from the reality of Native American Indian literatures, which represents a categorically different depth and range of literature.

2. In regards to the issue of aesthetic evaluation, Wittgenstein acknowledges that various musicians, composers, artists, and writers achieve varying degrees of artistic success. This can be seen in his thoughts regarding different artists and their works, which appear throughout *Culture and Value*. However, Wittgenstein hesitates to impose any set interpretive theory against which such works must be evaluated. "I am not interested in constructing a building, so much as in having a perspicuous view of the foundations of possible buildings" (CV, 7e).

3. Kolodny has not been alone in noting the problematic of biased inquiry. In her controversial essay, "Archimedes and the Paradox of Feminist Criticism," Myra Jehlen points out that "in posing a question one already circumscribes the answer; [therefore] analytical neutrality is a phantom" (581). Wittgenstein refers to such neutrality or objectivity as a bewitchment, a phantasm, and an illusion.

4. For a more complete discussion of these terms, see Gary Witherspoon, *Language and Art in the Navajo Universe*.

5. It is important to note that, per the tradition of storytelling, each rendition will vary somewhat in the particulars, but less so in the essentials. The colors and genders associated with the directions accordingly vary on occasion, but the essential concepts regarding the balance of the genders, seasons, directions, as well as the importance of harmony between thought and speech/action are consistent.

6. See PI, I, 520 for a discussion of the arbitrariness of meanings extracted from/imposed upon a work taken out of context.

7. The particular usefulness of Nia Francisco's poetry in my Native American Indian literature classes is inextricably linked to my previous studies in New Mexico. My graduate work was completed at the University of New Mexico, where I studied Native American Indian literature with Navajo poet Luci Tapahonso, Navajo language and linguistics with Roseann Willink and Mary Ann Willie, and previously I lived in Gallup, New Mexico, a border town to the Navajo Reservation. My relative familiarity with Navajo language game play, in large part, determines my textual selections (privileging certain Native texts with which I am familiar and which might prove less accessible to other critics), enabling a deeper approach into those works and greater success with them in the classroom.

Chapter Five

1. Derrida explains: "There is no sense in doing without the concepts of metaphysics in order to shake metaphysics. We have no language—no syntax and no lexicon—which is foreign to this history" (1978, 280-281).

2.   "If something happened (such as someone telling me something) calcu-
lated to make me doubtful of my own name, there would certainly also be
something that made the grounds of these doubts themselves seem doubtful,
and I could therefore decide to retain my old belief" (OC, 516).

3.   Law explains that both Wittgenstein and Derrida extend "the definition
of language to include all sorts of gestural or game-playing activities" (150).

4.   Law echoes this view of Wittgenstein in asserting Wittgenstein's work
to be deconstructive: "Wittgenstein performs his deconstructions of binary oppositions . . ." (163).

5.   Here we have one of Wittgenstein's strongest arguments for acknowledging that certainty exists. Throughout *On Certainty*, Wittgenstein reiterates
the point regarding the grounds upon which the game of doubting is based:
"The game of doubting itself presupposes certainty" (115). For example, if we
doubt whether there is a door into the next room, this presupposes that there is
such a thing as a door whose immediate existence we are calling into question.
"Doubting and non-doubting behavior. There is the first only if there is the
second" (354).

6.   Abrams comments on the dual effects of this Derridean textual inclusivity. He explains that we are both trapped within the text ("it is a closure in
which both its seeming author and the people and objects to which the text
seems to refer are merely 'effects' engendered by the internal action of *différance*") and are refused the existence of anything "in the world that is not a text"
(279).

7.   "What I need to shew is that a doubt is not necessary even when it is
possible. That the possibility of the language-game doesn't depend on everything being doubted that can be doubted. (This is connected with the role of
contradiction in mathematics.)" (OC, 392). Wittgenstein further emphasizes
the fact that in certain circumstances negation is meaningless. He presents the
example of $\sqrt{1}$ in order to demonstrate that in this case, one *cannot* negate the
number $\sqrt{-1}$ and have a meaningful statement. The $\sqrt{-1}$ is meaningless.

8.   In a discussion regarding truth and falsity, Wittgenstein notes that language is a form of life. "So you are saying that human agreement decides what
is true and what is false; and they agree in the *language* they use. That is not
agreement in opinions but in form of life" (PI, I, 241).

9.   Wittgenstein notes the temptation to focus primarily on the sign per se,
rather than the sign in use. This was what lured him to his earlier Tractarian
views. In *On Certainty*, he writes: "There is always the danger of wanting to
find an expression's meaning by contemplating the expression itself, and the
frame of mind in which one uses it, instead of always thinking of the practice.
That is why one repeats the expression to oneself so often, because it is as if one
must see what one is looking for in the expression and in the feeling it gives
one" (601).

10.   M. H. Abrams points out that deconstructive readings are "single-goal-
oriented. The critic knows before he begins to read what, by deep linguistic
necessity, he is going to find—that is, an aporia." This "inevitable" interpretation leads Abrams to assert that deconstruction is, essentially, a conservative

practice that reduces "the variousness of literary works to allegorical narratives with an invariable plot" (331).

11.   Wittgenstein actually discusses the situation of exchanging the meaning of a term within a particular context (see PI, 176e). He explains that when the statement and context are constant, any exchange of meanings leads to a disintegration of its sense. The emphasis on use is significant here, for where there is a communicable meaning which is denied/refused/exchanged, what occurs is altogether different from what goes on during the ordinary use of language. While we do need to note errors as erroneous, we nevertheless must *"accept* the everyday language-game" (PI, 200e). And this acceptance precludes any simplistic exchange of meanings willy-nilly.

12.   In the edited version of Dickinson's poem, the fifth line reads "And now We roam in Sovreign Woods—." However, in the original manuscript version, Dickinson included a footnote to the word "in" with the alternate choice of "the—." This would give us the line as follows: "And now We roam the— Sovreign Woods—."

13.   While a complete reading of the poem would reach far beyond the limits of this chapter, an extensive reading by Susan Howe presents diverse means of critical entry via a number of the language games in which the poem participates. Howe's multiple points of entry might very well be a reflection of her own participation in several of those language games—a strong asset in descriptive criticism. Howe, as a New Englander and a woman and an experimental language poet, displays a familiarity with these language games, as well as others she has researched for her book (such as the Civil War and New England Protestantism language games).

14.   Also see Jonathan Culler on the "monotonous method" of the deconstructive textual approach (184).

Chapter Six

1.   Regarding the concept of cultural acceptance, Wittgenstein writes that "culture is an observance [*Ordensregel*]. Or at least it [*Kultur*] presupposes an observance" (CV, 83e). And the language games of that culture are demonstrated in cultural products—music, literature, art, etc.

2.   For a more complete discussion of Geertz on "thick description," see his volume *The Interpretation of Cultures,* a work which explicitly acknowledges his debt to Wittgenstein in a number of specific references. These passages unfortunately indicate a serious misreading of Wittgenstein, as in Geertz's erroneous conflation of the Wittgensteinian emphasis on the "use" of cultural behaviors and artifacts and Geertz's emphasis on a semiotic interpretation of their "roles." It is far from clear that the symbolism of "roles" is synonymous with "use."

3.   On this topic of the carnivalesque, a thorough New Historicist reading is provided in Terry Castle's *Masquerade and Civilization: The Carnivalesque in Eighteenth-Century English Culture and Fiction.*

4.   For an interesting discussion in regards to three contemporary avant-

garde writers (loosely grouped under the rubric of language poetry), see Marjorie Perloff's "Toward a Wittgensteinian Poetics." In this article, Perloff selects a range of passages from Wittgenstein and notes their applicability for recent work by Ron Silliman, Rosmarie Waldrop, and John Cage. While the extent to which Wittgenstein's philosophy is understood (or not) by the various writers is not discussed, the article is a strong introduction to the influence of Wittgenstein on contemporary writers and their poetics.

5.   For a more detailed discussion of the problems inherent in such dialectical repetitions of theses and antitheses, see Chapter 1 and CV, 30e.

6.   Here we note that it is not clear whether Wittgenstein perceived the condition of antisemitism as the disease or the situation of Jews living in Europe as the disease or imbalance. Nevertheless, we further note that Wittgenstein himself was ethnically Jewish (three of his four grandparents were Jews).

7.   Again, Wittgenstein does not reject theory per se, but rather theory used outside of the realm of the natural sciences. For a more extensive discussion of this topic, see chapter 1.

8.   "Everything that can be thought at all can be thought clearly. Everything that can be put into words can be put clearly" (TLP, 4.116).

WORKS CITED

Abrams, M. H. *Doing Things with Texts.* Edited by Michael Fischer. New York: Norton, 1989.

Altieri, Charles. "Life after Difference: The Positions of the Interpreter and the Positionings of the Interpreted." *Monist* 73 (1990): 269–295.

———. "Style as the Man: What Wittgenstein Offers for Speculating on Expressive Activity." *The Journal of Aesthetics and Art Criticism* 46 (1987): 177–192.

———. "Wittgenstein on Consciousness and Language: A Challenge to Derridean Literary Theory." *Modern Language Notes* 91 (1976): 1397–1423.

Anzaldúa, Gloria, ed. *Making Face, Making Soul = Haciendo Caras: Creative and Critical Perspectives by Women of Color.* San Francisco: Aunt Lute Foundation, 1990.

Arac, Jonathan, and Barbara Johnson, eds. *Consequences of Theory.* Baltimore: Johns Hopkins University Press, 1991.

Barrett, Cyril. "Wittgenstein, Leavis, and Literature." *New Literary History* 19 (1988): 385–401.

Benjamin, Jessica. "The Bonds of Love: Rational Violence and Erotic Domination." In *The Future of Difference,* edited by Hester Eisenstein and Alice Jardine, 41–66. New Brunswick: Rutgers University Press, 1988.

Bennett, Tony. *Outside Literature.* London: Routledge, 1990.

Bohman, James. "Critical Theory as Metaphilosophy." *Metaphilosophy* 21 (1990): 239–252.

Brooks, Peter. "The Idea of a Psychoanalytic Literary Criticism." *Critical Inquiry* 13.2 (1987): 334–348.

Brown, Terry. "Feminism and Psychoanalysis, a Family Affair." In *Discontented Discourses: Feminism/Textual Intervention/Psychoanalysis,* edited by Marleen S. Barr and Richard Feldstein, 29–40. Urbana: University of Illinois Press, 1989.

Budd, Malcolm. "Wittgenstein on Seeing Aspects." *Mind* 96 (1987): 1–17.

———. *Wittgenstein's Philosophy of Psychology.* London: Routledge, 1991.

Castle, Terry. *Masquerade and Civilization: The Carnivalesque in Eighteenth-Century English Culture and Fiction.* Stanford: Stanford University Press, 1986.

Christian, Barbara. "The Race for Theory." In *Making Face, Making Soul,* edited by Gloria Anzaldúa, 335–345. San Francisco: Aunt Lute Foundation, 1990.

Churchill, John. "Reading Wittgenstein: Romantic and Prosaic Appropriations." *Southwest Philosophy Review* 4 (1988): 71–83.

_____. "Wittgenstein and the End of Philosophy." *Metaphilosophy* 20 (1989): 103–113.

Churchill, Ward. *Fantasies of the Master Race: Literature, Cinema and the Colonization of American Indians,* edited by M. Annette Jaimes. Monroe, Maine: Common Courage, 1992.

Culler, Jonathan. *On Deconstruction: Theory and Criticism after Structuralism.* Ithaca, N.Y.: Cornell University Press, 1986.

Dasenbrock, Reed Way. "Accounting for the Changing Certainties of Interpretive Communities." *Modern Language Notes* 102 (1987a): 1022–1041.

_____. "Intelligibility and Meaningfulness in Multicultural Literature in English." *PMLA* 102 (1987b): 10–19.

_____, ed. *Redrawing the Lines: Analytic Philosophy, Deconstruction, and Literary Theory.* Minneapolis: University of Minnesota Press, 1989.

Davis, Keith E., and Mary K. Roberts. "Relationships in the Real World: The Descriptive Psychology Approach to Personal Relationships." In *The Social Construction of the Person,* edited by Kenneth J. Gergen and Keith E. Davis, 145–163. New York: Springer-Verlag, 1985.

de Man, Paul. *The Resistance to Theory.* Theory and History of Literature 33. Minneapolis: University of Minnesota Press, 1986.

Derrida, Jacques. *Of Grammatology.* Baltimore: Johns Hopkins University Press, 1976.

_____. *Positions.* Chicago: University of Chicago Press, 1981.

_____. *Writing and Difference.* Chicago: University of Chicago Press, 1978.

Diamond, Cora. "Throwing Away the Ladder." *Philosophy* 63 (1988): 5–27.

Dickinson, Emily. *The Letters of Emily Dickinson.* Edited by Thomas H. Johnson. Cambridge: Harvard University Press, 1986.

_____. *The Manuscript Books of Emily Dickinson.* Edited by R. W. Franklin. Cambridge: Harvard University Press, 1981.

DuPlessis, Rachel Blau. "For the Etruscans." In *The New Feminist Criticisms: Essays on Women, Literature and Theory,* edited by Elaine Showalter, 271–291. New York: Pantheon, 1985.

Eldridge, Richard. "Problems and Prospects of Wittgensteinian Aesthetics." *The Journal of Aesthetics and Art Criticism* 45 (1987): 251–261.

Ellis, John M. "Playing Games with Wittgenstein." *New Literary History* 19 (1988): 301–308.

Fischer, Michael. "A Critical Discussion on Henry Staten's *Wittgenstein and Derrida.*" *Philosophy and Literature* 10.1 (1986): 93–97.

_____. *Does Deconstruction Make Any Difference?* Bloomington: Indiana University Press, 1985.

Fish, Stanley. "Consequences." *Critical Inquiry* 11 (1985): 433–458.

Foucault, Michel. *The Order of Things*. New York: Vintage Books, 1973.

Fox-Genovese, Elizabeth. "Literary Criticism and the Politics of the New Historicism." In *The New Historicism*, edited by H. Aram Veeser, 213-224. New York: Routledge, 1989.

Francisco, Nia. *Blue Horses for Navajo Women*. Greenfield Center, NY: Greenfield Review Press, 1988.

Fuss, Diana. *Essentially Speaking: Feminism, Nature and Difference*. New York: Routledge, 1989.

Gallop, Jane. "Reading the Mother Tongue: Psychoanalytic Feminist Criticism." *Critical Inquiry* 13.2 (1987): 314-29.

Gates, Henry Louis, Jr., ed. *Reading Black, Reading Feminist: A Critical Anthology*. New York: Meridian, 1990.

Geertz, Clifford. *The Interpretation of Cultures*. New York: Basic Books, 1973.

Gentis, Roger. "Freud, la femme, Wittgenstein et quelques autres." *La Quinzaine Littéraire* 431 (1985): 16-17.

Girard, René. "Theory and Its Terrors." In *The Limits of Theory*, edited by Thomas M. Kavanagh, 225-254. Stanford: Stanford University Press, 1989.

Giza, Piotr. "On the Problem of Theoretical Entities." In his *The Tasks of Contemporary Philosophy*, 86-89. Vienna: Holder-Pichler-Tempsky, 1986.

Glannon, Walter. "What Literary Theory Misses in Wittgenstein." *Philosophy and Literature* 10 (1986): 263-72.

Glasgow, Joanne, and Karla Jay, eds. *Lesbian Texts and Contexts: Radical Revisions*. New York: New York University Press, 1990.

Godzich, Wlad. Introduction to *The Resistance to Theory*, by Paul de Man. Minneapolis: University of Minnesota Press, 1986.

Goldfarb, Warren. "Wittgenstein, Mind, and Scientism." *The Journal of Philosophy* 86 (1989): 635-42.

Greenblatt, Stephen. "Towards a Poetics of Culture." In *The New Historicism*, edited by H. Aram Veeser, 1-14. New York: Routledge, 1989.

Greene, Michael Kevin. "Response to Cynthia Willett-Shoptaw's 'A Deconstruction of Wittgenstein.'" *Auslegung* 10 (1983): 82-85.

Guetti, James. "Wittgenstein and Literary Theory." Parts 1-2. *Raritan* 4 (1984): 67-84; 4 (1985): 66-84.

Hartsock, Nancy. "Foucault on Power: A Theory for Women?" In *Feminism/Postmodernism*, edited by Linda J. Nicholson, 157-175. New York: Routledge, 1990.

Henderson, David. "Wittgenstein's Descriptivist Approach to Understanding: Is There a Place for Explanation in Interpretive Accounts?" *Dialectica* 42 (1988): 105-115.

Henderson, Mae Gwendolyn. "Speaking in Tongues: Dialogics, Dialectics, and the Black Woman Writer's Literary Tradition." In *Reading Black, Reading Feminist*, edited by Henry Louis Gates, 116-142. New York: Meridian, 1990.

Hogan, Patrick Colm, and Lalita Pandit, eds. *Criticism and Lacan:*

Essays and Dialogue on Language, Structure, and the Unconscious. Athens: University of Georgia Press, 1990.

Holmes, James R. "The Status of Persons, Or Who Was that Masked Metaphor?" *Advances in Descriptive Psychology* 6 (1991): 15-35.

Hooks, Bell. *Yearning: Race, Gender, and Cultural Politics.* Boston: South End Press, 1990.

Howe, Susan. *My Emily Dickinson.* Berkeley: North Atlantic, 1985.

Hughes, Peter. "Painting the Ghost: Wittgenstein, Shakespeare, and Textual Representation." *New Literary History* 19 (1988): 371-384.

Hunts, Carol. "Wittgenstein's Seeing-as and a Theory of Art." *Auslegung* 9 (1982): 157-172.

Hutcheon, Linda. *The Politics of Postmodernism.* New York: Routledge, 1989.

Jameson, Fredric. "Marxism and Historicism." *New Literary History* 11 (1979): 41-73.

Jardine, Alice. *Gynesis: Configurations of Woman and Modernity.* Ithaca, N.Y.: Cornell University Press, 1985.

Jehlen, Myra. "Archimedes and the Paradox of Feminist Criticism." *Signs* 6 (1981): 575-601.

Johnson, Barbara. *The Critical Difference: Essays in the Contemporary Rhetoric of Reading.* Baltimore: Johns Hopkins University Press, 1980.

Kauffman, Linda, ed. *Gender and Theory: Dialogues on Feminist Criticism.* Oxford: Basil Blackwell, 1989.

Kavanagh, Thomas M., ed. *The Limits of Theory.* Stanford: Stanford University Press, 1989.

Kawin, Bruce. "On Not Having the Last Word: Beckett, Wittgenstein, and the Limits of Language." In *Ineffability: Naming the Unnamable from Dante to Beckett,* edited by Peter S. Hawkins and Anne Howland Schotter, 189-202. New York: AMS Press, 1984.

Kolodny, Annette. "Some Notes on Defining a 'Feminist Literary Criticism.'" *Critical Inquiry* 2 (1975): 75-92.

Krieger, Murray. *Theory of Criticism: A Tradition and Its Systems.* Baltimore: Johns Hopkins University Press, 1976.

Krupat, Arnold. "Identity and Difference in the Criticism of Native American Literature." *Diacritics* 13 (1983): 2-13.

———. "Native American Literature and the Canon." In *Canons,* edited by Robert von Hallberg, 309-335. Chicago: University of Chicago Press, 1984.

Law, Jules David. "Reading with Wittgenstein and Derrida." In *Redrawing the Lines,* edited by Reed Way Dasenbrock, 140-168. Minneapolis: University of Minnesota Press, 1989.

Lugones, María. "Hablando cara a cara/Speaking Face to Face: An Exploration of Ethnocentric Racism." In *Making Face, Making Soul,* edited by Gloria Anzaldúa, 46-54. San Francisco: Aunt Lute Foundation, 1990.

Lurie, Yuval. "Wittgenstein on Culture and Civilization." *Inquiry* 32 (1989): 375-397.

Malcolm, Norman. "Wittgenstein's 'Scepticism' in *On Certainty*." *Inquiry* 31 (1988): 277–293.

Marcus, Jane. "The Asylums of Antaeus: Women, War, and Madness—Is There a Feminist Fetishism?" In *The New Historicism*, edited by H. Aram Veeser, 132–151. New York: Routledge, 1989.

———. "Daughters of Anger/Material Girls: Con/textualizing Feminist Criticism." *Women's Studies* 15 (1988): 281–308.

McMillan, Terry, ed. *Breaking Ice: An Anthology of Contemporary African-American Fiction*. New York: Penguin, 1990.

Messer-Davidow, Ellen. "The Philosophical Bases of Feminist Literary Criticism." In *Gender and Theory*, edited by Linda Kauffman, 63–106. Oxford: Basil Blackwell, 1989,

Mitchell, W. J. T. "Wittgenstein's Imagery and What It Tells Us." *New Literary History* 19 (1988): 361–370.

Montefiore, Alan. "Philosophy, Literature and the Restatement of a Few Banalities." *Monist* 69 (1986): 56–67.

Moore, A. W. "On Saying and Showing." *Philosophy* 62 (1987): 473–497.

———. "Transcendental Idealism in Wittgenstein, and Theories of Meaning." *The Philosophical Quarterly* 35 (1985): 134-155.

Mora, Pat. *Borders*. Houston: Arte Público, 1986.

Moraga, Cherríe. *Loving in the War Years: lo que nunca pasó por sus labios*. Boston: South End, 1983.

Motoyoshi, Michelle M. "The Experience of Mixed-Race People: Some Thoughts and Theories." *The Journal of Ethnic Studies* 18 (1990): 77–94.

Nicholson, Linda J., ed. *Feminism/Postmodernism*. New York: Routledge, 1990.

Niedecker, Lorine. *The Granite Pail*. Edited by Cid Corman. San Francisco: North Point, 1985.

Norris, Christopher. *Deconstruction: Theory and Practice*. New York: Methuen, 1982.

———. *The Deconstructive Turn*. New York: Methuen, 1984.

Olalquiaga, Celeste. *Megalopolis: Contemporary Cultural Sensibilities*. Minneapolis: University of Minnesota Press, 1992.

Ossorio, Peter G. "A Multicultural Psychology." *Advances in Descriptive Psychology* 3 (1983a): 13–44.

———. "An Overview of Descriptive Psychology." In *The Social Construction of the Person*, edited by Kenneth J. Gergen and Keith E. Davis, 19–40. New York: Springer-Verlag, 1985.

———. *"What Actually Happens": The Representation of Real-World Phenomena*. Columbia: University of South Carolina Press, 1978.

———. *Why Descriptive Psychology?* L. R. I. Report No. 35. Boulder, CO: Linguistic Research Institute, 1983b.

Pateman, Trevor. "Wittgensteinian Aesthetics." *British Journal of Aesthetics* 26 (1986): 172–175.

Perloff, Marjorie. "Toward a Wittgensteinian Poetics." *Contemporary Literature* 33 (1992): 191–213.

Quigley, Austin E. "Wittgenstein's Philosophizing and Literary Theorizing." *New Literary History* 19 (1988): 209-237.

Ragland-Sullivan, Ellie. "The Limits of Discourse Structure: The Hysteric and the Analyst." *Prose Studies* 11.3 (1988): 61-83.

Rebolledo, Tey Diana. "The Politics of Poetics: Or, What Am I, a Critic, Doing in This Text Anyhow?" In *Making Face, Making Soul*, edited by Gloria Anzaldúa, 346-355. San Francisco: Aunt Lute Foundation, 1990.

Roberts, Mary Kathleen. "Worlds and World Reconstruction." *Advances in Descriptive Psychology* 4 (1985): 17-53.

Rousset, Clement. "Reality and the Untheorizable." In *The Limits of Theory*, edited by Thomas M. Kavanagh, 76-118. Stanford: Stanford University Press, 1989.

Said, Edward. *The World, the Text and the Critic*. London: Faber and Faber, 1984.

Schulte, Joachim. "Aesthetic Correctness." *Revue Internationale de Philosophie* 43 (1989): 298-310.

Shideler, Mary McDermott. *Persons, Behavior, and the World: The Descriptive Psychology Approach*. Lanham, MD: University Press of America, 1988.

Showalter, Elaine, ed. *The New Feminist Criticism: Essays on Women, Literature and Theory*. New York: Pantheon, 1985.

————, ed. *Speaking of Gender*. New York: Routledge, 1989.

Shusterman, Richard. "Analytic Aesthetics, Literary Theory, and Deconstruction." *Monist* 69 (1986a): 22-38.

————. "Deconstruction and Analysis: Confrontation and Convergence." *British Journal of Aesthetics* 26 (1986b): 311-327.

————. "Wittgenstein and Critical Reasoning." *Philosophy and Phenomenological Research* 47 (1986c): 91-110.

Slater, Hartley. "Wittgenstein's Aesthetics." *British Journal of Aesthetics* 23 (1983): 34-37.

Smith, Barbara Herrnstein. *Contingencies of Value*. Cambridge: Harvard University Press, 1988.

Smith, Joseph H., and William Kerrigan, eds. *Taking Chances: Derrida, Psychoanalysis, and Literature*. Baltimore: Johns Hopkins University Press, 1985.

Smith, Valerie. "Gender and Afro-Americanist Literary Theory and Criticism." In *Speaking of Gender*, edited by Elaine Showalter, 56-70. New York: Routledge, 1989.

Spivak, Gayatri Chakravorty. Translator's Preface to *Of Grammatology*, by Jacques Derrida, ix-lxxxvii. Baltimore: Johns Hopkins University Press, 1976.

Staten, Henry. *Wittgenstein and Derrida*. Lincoln: University of Nebraska Press, 1986.

————. "Wittgenstein and the Intricate Evasions of 'Is.'" *New Literary History* 19 (1988): 281-300.

————. "Wittgenstein's Boundaries." *New Literary History* 19 (1988): 309-318.

Stenius, Eric. *Wittgenstein's Tractatus: A Critical Exposition of Its Main Lines of Thought.* Westport, CT: Greenwood, 1981.

Tapahonso, Luci. *A Breeze Swept Through.* Albuquerque, NM: West End Press, 1987.

————. *Sáanii Dahataal, The Women Are Singing: Poems and Stories.* Tucson: University of Arizona Press, 1993.

Thucydides. *The Peloponnesian War.* New York: Modern Library, 1951.

Todd, Janet. *Feminist Literary History.* New York: Routledge, 1988.

Veeser, H. Aram, ed. *The New Historicism.* New York: Routledge, 1989.

von Hallberg, Robert, ed. *Canons.* Chicago: University of Chicago Press, 1984.

Waldrop, Rosmarie. *The Reproduction of Profiles.* New York: New Directions, 1987.

Weedon, Chris. *Feminist Practice and Poststructuralist Theory.* Oxford: Blackwell, 1987.

West, Cornel. "Theory, Pragmatisms, and Politics." In *Consequences of Theory,* edited by Jonathan Arac and Barbara Johnson, 22–38. Baltimore: Johns Hopkins University Press, 1991.

Wheeler, Samuel C., III. "Wittgenstein as Conservative Deconstructor." *New Literary Theory* 19 (1988): 239–58.

White, Hayden. "New Historicism: A Comment." In *The New Historicism,* edited by H. Aram Veeser, 293–302. New York: Routledge, 1989.

Wideman, John Edgar. Preface to *Breaking Ice: An Anthology of African-American Fiction,* edited by Terry McMillan, v–x. New York: Penguin, 1990.

Willett-Shoptaw, Cynthia. "A Deconstruction of Wittgenstein." *Auslegung* 10 (1983): 75–81.

Williams, Sherley Anne. "Some Implications of Womanist Theory." *Reading Black, Reading Feminist: A Critical Anthology,* edited by Henry Louis Gates, 68–75. New York: Meridian, 1990.

Winch, Peter. "True or False?" *Inquiry* 31 (1988): 265–276.

Witherspoon, Gary. *Language and Art in the Navajo Universe.* Ann Arbor: University of Michigan Press, 1977.

Wittgenstein, Ludwig. *The Blue and Brown Books.* New York: Harper Torchbooks, 1965.

————. *Culture and Value.* Edited by G. H. von Wright with Heikki Nyman. Translated by Peter Winch. Chicago: University of Chicago Press, 1984.

————. *Lectures and Conversations on Aesthetics, Psychology and Religious Belief.* Edited by Cyril Barrett. Berkeley: University of California Press, 1967.

————. *Ludwig Wittgenstein and the Vienna Circle: Conversations Recorded by Friedrich Waismann.* Edited by B. F. McGuiness. Oxford: Blackwell, 1979.

————. *Notebooks 1914-16.* Edited by G. E. M. Anscombe and

G. H. von Wright. London: Blackwell, 1961.

————. *On Certainty.* Edited by G. E. M. Anscombe and G. H. von Wright. Translated by G. E. M. Anscombe and Denis Paul. New York: Harper Torchbooks, 1969.

————. *Philosophical Investigations.* 3d ed. Edited by G. E. M. Anscombe and R. Rhees. Translated by G. E. M. Anscombe. New York: Macmillan, 1968.

————. *Remarks on Color.* Edited by G. E. M. Anscombe. Translated by Linda L. McAlister and Margarete Schattle. Berkeley: University of California Press, 1977.

————. *Remarks on Frazer's "Golden Bough."* Edited by Rush Rhees. Translated by A. C. Miles. Doncaster, England: Brynmill Press, 1979.

————. *Remarks on the Philosophy of Psychology.* Vol. I. Edited by G. E. M. Anscombe and G. H. von Wright. Translated by G. E. M. Anscombe. Chicago: University of Chicago Press, 1988.

————. *Remarks on the Philosophy of Psychology.* Vol. II. Edited by G. H. von Wright and Heikki Nyman. Translated by C. G. Luckhardt and M. A. E. Aue. Chicago: University of Chicago Press, 1988.

————. *Tractatus Logico-Philosophicus.* Translated by D. F. Pears and B. F. McGuiness. Introduction by Bertrand Russell. London: Routledge, 1988.

————. *Zettel.* Edited by G. E. M. Anscombe and G. H. von Wright. Translated by G. E. M. Anscombe. Berkeley: University of California Press, 1970.

Zeiger, Carolyn Allen. "The Miss Marple Model of Psychological Assessment." *Advances in Descriptive Psychology* 6 (1991): 159–183.

INDEX

Abrams, M. H., 22, 24, 102
absolutism, 19, 20, 30, 55, 96–97,
    102
  in criticism, 31, 107, 132
  in theory, 11, 13, 44, 74, 117
aesthetics, 15, 89–90, 138
  culturally bound, 28, 29
African art, 120
Allen, Paula Gunn, 63, 75, 90
Altieri, Charles, 98, 99
American Indian, 72, 86, 139
  See also Native American In-
    dian literatures; Native
    American literature; Navajo
antitheses, 8
Anzaldúa, Gloria, 84, 126,
    129–30, 132
argument. *See* debate
aspects, 46–47, 103
  of texts, 16, 45–47, 58, 85, 108,
    122, 129, 134
Austen, Jane, 14–15
axiology, 30, 48, 73, 85, 117–20,
    136–39
  Wittgensteinian, 73, 89–90, 142
  See also evaluation

Bakhtin, Mikhail, 68
bilingualism, 84–85, 126
boundaries, 73–74, 87, 127–35,
    136, 142
  conceptual, 36, 42
  critical, 8, 17, 25, 47, 87, 93,
    110, 133–34
  crossed, 84, 132–33
  descriptive, 54–57
  feminist, 65–70
  interpretive, 16, 40, 88, 90

of language games, 3, 15
  perceptual, 57–60
  textual, 32, 74, 83, 94
  See also limits; theory, limits

canonicity, 25, 71–91, 118, 136–39
  exclusivity, 71, 73, 87–88,
    138–39
  inclusivity, 71, 73, 87, 128–29,
    135, 138
  organic, 138
  usefulness of, 73, 90–91
certainty, 17, 118–19, 142
  in criticism, 26, 57, 115, 117
  determined by language game
    rules, 23, 57, 93, 99, 105
  grounds, 99, 101, 104, 111, 113
circumstance, 1, 2, 15
coherence, 1
colonization, 128, 130
concepts, 12, 35, 90
  confused, 27, 53, 103–4, 131,
    140
  forced, 7, 21, 107
  preconceived, 36, 103, 106, 131
constructs. *See* critical constructs
contradiction, 104–5
critical constructs, 15, 26
  forced on texts, 4, 31, 115, 135
  preconceived, 4, 133
critical fit
  canonical effects, 25–26, 60,
    76–77
  between criticism and text, 4,
    25–26, 31, 48, 55, 78, 89, 135
  between theory and practice,
    60, 115
critical method

163

A NOTE ABOUT THE AUTHOR

Susan B. Brill is an Assistant Professor of English at Bradley University, where she teaches critical theory and Native American Indian literatures.